Group Purchasing Organizations

Group Purchasing Organizations

An Undisclosed Scandal in the U.S. Healthcare Industry

S. Prakash Sethi

palgrave
macmillan

GROUP PURCHASING ORGANIZATIONS

First published in 2009 by
PALGRAVE MACMILLAN®
in the United States—a division of St. Martin's Press LLC,
175 Fifth Avenue, New York, NY 10010.

Where this book is distributed in the UK, Europe and the rest of the world,
this is by Palgrave Macmillan, a division of Macmillan Publishers Limited,
registered in England, company number 785998, of Houndmills,
Basingstoke, Hampshire RG21 6XS.

Palgrave Macmillan is the global academic imprint of the above companies
and has companies and representatives throughout the world.

Palgrave® and Macmillan® are registered trademarks in the United States,
the United Kingdom, Europe and other countries.

ISBN: 978–0–230–60767–5

Library of Congress Cataloging-in-Publication Data

Sethi, S. Prakash.
    Group purchasing organizations : an undisclosed scandal in the U.S.
healthcare industry / S. Prakash Sethi.
        p. ; cm.
    Includes bibliographical references.
    ISBN-13: 978–0–230–60767–5
    ISBN-10: 0–230–60767–5
    1. Medical supplies—Purchasing—United States. I. Title.
[DNLM: 1. Group Purchasing—organization & administration—United
States. 2. Health Care Sector—organization & administration—United
States. WX 157 S495g 2009]
    RA971.33.S48 2009
    338.4'73621—dc22   2008043366

A catalogue record of the book is available from the British Library.

Design by Newgen Imaging Systems (P) Ltd., Chennai, India.

First edition: June 2009

10 9 8 7 6 5 4 3 2 1

Printed in the United States of America.

To my wife and best friend
Hillary

Contents

Exhibits and Tables

Exhibits

Tables

Preface

A large majority of U.S. hospitals procure their supplies through Group Purchasing Organizations (GPOs). Starting in 1910, these GPOs had made a modest beginning. Their avowed is to combine the purchasing power of hospitals, nursing homes, and other healthcare providers and thereby seek lower prices, which would help lower healthcare costs. Furthermore, to advance their mission, Congress provided them with a safe harbor from the Federal Anti-Kickback Act. Today's GPOs are radically different from their pioneering predecessors. Rather than being a mere extension of a hospital's purchasing function, they have become large corporate behemoths. They are estimated to account for more than $280 billion of contract purchases in 2009 and control contracted supplies of more than 90 percent of hospitals, nursing homes, and other healthcare providers in the United States. Furthermore, through consolidation, the industry has assumed an oligopolistic market structure where the top four GPOs account for more than 80 percent of the market share.

Today's GPOs are for the most part privately owned for-profit organizations who seem to put the financial interest of their owners and members ahead of their clients to whom they ought to hold a fiduciary duty, but do not. Furthermore, their private ownership allows them to withhold most financial information from public disclosure. Instead, they make claims of saving hundreds of millions of dollars through lower prices—claims for which they have failed to provide independently verifiable information.

By any measure, the GPO industry exercises tremendous influence on the financial health and operational policies of the hospitals and other healthcare providers. These organizations negotiate vendor contracts that are supposed to save money for hospitals and healthcare providers by using the combined purchasing power of member hospitals to negotiate significant discounts from manufacturers and distributors of medical supplies.

Unfortunately, the GPO performance under the umbrella of government protection has proven to be the worst case of unintended consequences of a regulatory munificence. The success of GPOs—in the face of rising public criticism—provide another example where an industry enjoying excessive profits, that is, nonmarket rent, under government's protective umbrella has converted its financial muscle into political clout. They have succeeded in fore-stalling most efforts toward reforming their conduct.

The futility of this effort can best be seen in the valiant efforts of some congressional leaders on the Subcommittee on Antitrust, Business Rights, and Competition of the Committee on the Judiciary United States Senate. This Subcommittee held an unprecedented series of four hearings during 2002–2006 but failed to develop any meaningful legislation that would move the GPO industry's conduct toward greater transparency and accountability.

The one modest success from the hearings—if indeed it could be called a success—came about from the industry's promise to institute a voluntary code of conduct or the Healthcare Group Purchasing Industry Initiative ("the Initiative"). However, as we shall demonstrate in the book, this code promised very little by way of measurable performance. It also strictly limited public access to information by making the governance structure of the code organization controlled by the CEOs of the same GPOs whose performance the code was intended to evaluate. And finally, to eliminate any possibility of undesirable public disclosure, the code did not allow for any third-party monitoring system that would independently verify the quality and veracity of information provided by the individual companies or that of the group as a whole.

The rationale for this study can be traced to an invitation to the author to testify before the Subcommittee on Antitrust, Business Rights, and Competition of the Committee on the Judiciary United States Senate with regard to industry's proposed code of conduct or the Initiative. As part of his testimony, this author prepared a report with the goal of subjecting the GPO industry to a careful analysis in terms of its oligopolistic structure that provided it with greater opportunity for earning excessive profits; and, the role of government protection from anti-kickbacks that enabled the GPO industry to exploit these opportunities for financial gains for their owners and managers, and at the expense of their beneficiary clients in the healthcare industry.

The core elements of this book are derived from the author's report to the Senate Subcommittee. However, the book covers a broader field of inquiry and provides additional information pertaining to GPOs' alleged fraudulent activities and potentially illegal conduct. It has been thoroughly revised, expanded, and updated to make it more relevant, comprehensive, and readable to health-care professionals, policymakers, and members of the public who are concerned about the quality and expense of healthcare in the United States and who seek to bring about necessary reform to minimize, if not completely eliminate, the abuse of market powers that is costing American taxpayers billions of dollars in unnecessary chargers. In the final analysis, political reforms in a democratic system rarely occur without heightened public concern about the unfairness of the current system and its institutions. It is hoped that this book will lead to a small step in this direction.

Acknowledgments

Most academic research is a collaborative effort and this one is no exception. The original GPO report, submitted to the Subcommittee on Antitrust, Business Rights, and Competition of the Committee on the Judiciary, United States Senate required extensive research effort and investigative inquiries, including data mining. These were admirably and unstintingly provided by a group of dedicated professionals at the International Center for Corporate Accountability, that is, Ms. Olga Emelianova, Director of Project Services; Mr. Gianmarco Torterolo, Senior Research Analyst; Mr. Sandeep Hajare, Senior Research Analyst; and Ms. Konstantina Kyrgidou, Research Analyst. The quality of this report owes a great deal to their thoroughness and energy in following multiple lines of inquiries that I have thrown at them, and finding factual evidence to support my theoretical postulations. They have been unrelenting in their efforts to confirm facts and figures and verify primary and secondary sources of quotes and citations.

In preparation of the revised and expanded manuscript of this book, four people played key role. These are Ms. Olga Emelianova; Ms. Olinda Anderson, Office Manager and Web site Administrator; Ms. Sridevi Chalasani, Research Analyst; and Mr. Jacqueline Stoute, Research Assistant.

In addition, I have immensely benefited from the insights, critical observations, and constructive comments from a number of distinguished scholars and experienced professionals. I have known them for a major part of my academic and professional career. I have been inspired by the commitment to independent inquiry, dispassionate analysis, and unbiased conclusions of the following individuals: Hon. Nathaniel J. Bickford, Retired, former Senior Partner, Windels, Marx, Lane & Mittendorf, New York, and Director of ICCA; Dr. William S. Laufer, Associate Professor of Legal Studies and Sociology, and, Director, The Carol and Lawrence Zicklin Center for Business Ethics Research, University of Pennsylvania; Dr. Sidney Lirtzman, Dean Emeritus, Zicklin School of Business, and Chairman of the Board of ICCA; Dr. Lee E. Preston, Professor Emeritus, University of Maryland; Professor Charles A. Riley II, The City University of New York; Professor Murray Weidenbaum, Mallinckrodt Distinguished University Professor, Washington University, St. Louis; and, Hon. J. Warren

Wood III, Attorney, Greenbaum, Rowe, Smith & Davis, Woodbridge, New Jersey.

Notwithstanding all the good advice and support that I have received from my friends, colleagues, and my associates at ICCA, I alone must bear total responsibility for the contents and conclusions of this book.

Prologue[*]: Hearing of the U.S. Senate Subcommittee on Antitrust, Competition Policy, and Consumer Rights

Venue: Hearing before the Subcommittee on Antitrust, Competition Policy and Consumer Rights of the Committee on the Judiciary United States Senate One Hundred Ninth Congress Second Session

The Play: Hospital Group Purchasing: Are the Industry's Reforms Sufficient to Ensure Competition?

Date: March 15, 2006

Subcommittee: Hon. Mike DeWine, Senator (R-Ohio)

Chairman:
Present: Hon. Herbert Kohl, Senator (D-Wisconsin)
Hon. Patrick Leahy, Senator (D-Vermont)
Hon. Charles E. Schumer (D-New York) (arrived late)

Other Assorted: Players

1. Richard J. Bednar, Coordinator, Healthcare Group Purchasing Industry Initiative
2. Mark B. Leahey, Executive Director, Medical Device Manufacturers Association
3. S. Prakash Sethi, Professor, Baruch College, The City University of New York
4. Mina Ubbing, President and CEO, Fairfield Medical Center

Audience: Hordes of lobbyists, members of the press, Subcommittee staff, and other persons interested in the Subcommittee's deliberations

Senator DeWine opened the meeting indicating that it was the fourth hearing in the last few years that the Subcommittee has held on the industry comprised of Group Purchasing Organizations (GPOs). This reflects the Subcommittee's assessment of the importance of this industry to the "health of our economy and, of course, to the health of our citizens" (p. 1).

> The purpose of this hearing this afternoon is to evaluate where we stand today. Is this industry competitive or is legislation required to inject competition into the industry? As we have discussed before, GPOs are simply organizations that manage purchasing of medical equipment and supplies for most of our Nation's hospitals. Their ability to combine the purchasing power of the hospitals makes them an important part of the health care market. Today, we will be evaluating current industry practices, as well as considering a number of legislative proposals for other ways that the industry could operate. I think a brief review of this Subcommittee's activity in this area will help to explain the various proposals. (p. 1)

> We held our first hearing on GPOs in April 2002. We did it because of complaints of ethical violations in the industry and also a more general complaint that the GPO system sometimes decreased the flexibility of hospital purchasing and made it difficult for doctors and nurses to get the best medical equipment. (p. 1)

> We found, unfortunately, that both of these allegations had some merit. During the course of our ongoing investigation, we also assessed a number of contracting practices, such as sole-source contracts, discounts based on high commitment levels, and bundling of clinical preference products with commodity products. All of these practices have positive aspects, but also may cause competitive difficulties. (pp. 1–2)

> Our analysis of the industry has been complicated further by the so-called safe harbor that underlies this industry. GPOs have an unusual business model. They are funded not by their member hospitals, but rather by their suppliers. In other words, GPOs agree to purchase equipment and supplies from certain companies and as part of those contracts, the suppliers pay an administrative fee based on the size of the contract which is used to fund the existence of the GPOs. (p. 2)

> Under normal circumstances, this would be considered a kickback, and so the GPOs require an exemption from the anti-kickback laws. We have been told this safe harbor is what allows the GPO industry to exist in its current form. However, this relationship between the GPOs and the manufacturers have led many to distrust the purchasing decisions that GPOs make because, in effect, they benefit from larger contracts which are easier to sign with larger suppliers. (p. 2)

> Despite the complexity of these issues, our efforts have paid off. Senator Kohl and I worked with the industry to resolve the ethical violations we uncovered (p. 2)

> Smaller manufacturers seem to have greater access to the market, and the industry generally is more aware of the potential problems and has been taking steps to avoid additional problems. Under these circumstances, the Subcommittee has turned its focus to ensuring the permanence of the industry's reforms, and Senator Kohl and I introduced Senate bill 2880 last term as an effort to do that. (p. 2)

> Senate bill 2880 would have given oversight of this industry to the Department of Health and Human Services, charging it with drafting rules for this industry to ensure that each GPO conformed with principles of competition, ethical standards and the goal of maintaining access to products necessary for proper patient care. If a GPO failed to follow these rules, it could lose its exemption from the safe harbor under that proposed legislation. (p. 2)

The GPO industry objected to this approach [emphasis added], and to address its concerns we agreed to hold off on introducing this legislation and allow them the opportunity to develop a method for ensuring their changes would be implemented effectively in a permanent way. The industry response is the so-called, quote, "Hospital Group Purchasing Industry Initiative," end of quote. This measure has been in place since July 2005, and it won't surprise our witnesses to hear some like it and some don't. (p. 2)

Our goal has been and will continue to be to promote vigorous competition which will ensure that GPOs both save money and allow new and improved technologies to get to the market to help medical professionals better care for all of us. We must strike the right balance and we are committed to do just that. (p. 3)

The Subcommittee's hearings were conspicuous in one respect in that not a single CEO, or for that matter, any executive representing any of the GPOs was present at the meeting. This fact was also noted by Senator DeWine who commented, "I am sorry that we don't have any of the GPOs here today" (p. 4). A similar sentiment was echoed by Senator Kohl, who stated, "I must express my disappointment that no representatives of the GPO industry accepted our invitation to testify here today. GPOs' willingness to provide us with candid answers is a factor we will evaluate in determining whether self-regulation will suffice" (p. 4). The only person representing the industry was Mr. Richard J. Bednar, a Washington, DC-based lobbyist, who was the coordinator of the Healthcare Group Purchasing Industry Initiative.

Excerpts from the Statement of
Senator Herbert Kohl (D—Wisconsin)

Senator Kohl commended the industry leadership for voluntarily creating this new initiative[1] and "to set standards and monitor the purchasing activities of hospital group purchasing organizations. The purpose of this new industry initiative is to ensure that GPOs do not engage in anticompetitive or unethical practices that freeze out new and innovative medical device manufacturers from the hospital market" (p. 3).

The important issue, from Senator Kohl's perspective was to consider whether this new "organization is strong enough to do the job. The founders of the industry initiative now argue that the creation of this organization means that we need to do nothing more, that we can rely entirely on the initiative to guarantee an open and honest marketplace. They argue that any further legislation is not necessary" (p. 4).

In order to assess this claim, at least two vital questions must be answered. First, is this organization really up to monitoring what is taking place in this enormous multi-billion-dollar industry? And, second, does this voluntary industry initiative contain sufficient sanctions to prevent wrongdoing and to penalize those GPOs that violate its founding principles? (p. 4)

Any industry plan must include real and meaningful sanctions if any GPO violates ethical principles or the rules of free competition. In an industry as important to health and safety as the purchasing of medical equipment for critically ill patients, half-measures which do not assure that the best medical devices are available for patients are simply not acceptable. (p. 4)

We have legislative tools available should we conclude that the industry initiative falls short. In the last Congress, Senator DeWine and I introduced the Medical Device Competition Act. This legislation will give the Department of Health and Human Services the authority to forbid GPO business practices which are anticompetitive or unethical. (p. 4)

Other commentators have suggested an alternative approach, namely to forbid GPOs from receiving payments from hospital suppliers. Advocates of this approach argue that such a prohibition would remove an inherent conflict of interest in the present system. No longer would hospital vendors pay the very organizations that are supposed to negotiate with these vendors to get the best deal for their hospitals. We will therefore need to pay close attention to the testimony of our witnesses today as we evaluate whether we need to take any further steps. (p. 4)

These two statements by Senators DeWine and Senator Kohl succinctly sum up the crux of the issue. To wit:

1. GPO industry plays a critical role in the provision of healthcare services to American citizens. The industry receives special dispensation from the application of antitrust laws and anti-kickback statues, which are justified on the basis of its success in providing efficient services and in the process save money to the hospitals and other healthcare providers. Although, it must be noted that these claims have not been definitely proven, since the industry has been extremely reluctant to provide such data and be more transparent about its financial affairs.
2. It is a very large industry and has in the past been accused of unethical conduct and anticompetitive behavior.
3. The industry has hitherto successfully resisted all attempts toward government oversight and monitoring to ensure that its conduct is ethical and procompetition. The latest effort in this regard has been the industry's creation of a voluntary code of conduct called the "Healthcare Group Purchasing Initiative" that would monitor industry performance and ensure its compliance with the industry's own standards of ethical conduct and avoidance of anticompetitive behavior. The important challenge in this regard is twofold:
   a. To what extent are the scope, implementation, governance, monitoring, and compliance verification robust enough to engender trust in the industry intended and proclaimed performance resulting from the implementation of the HGPI Initiative?
   b. How much public trust can be placed on the Initiative and its implementation when the Initiative does not provide for any independent external oversight and when there are no regulatory requirements to ensure that the industry delivers on its promises?

The testimony of the three principal witnesses at the Subcommittee's hearings highlights the challenges that would be confronted by the government and the industry in divining the future conduct of the industry under the auspices of the GPO Initiative. These are: Mr. Richard J. Bednar, Coordinator, Healthcare Group Purchasing Industry Initiative; Mr. Mark B. Leahey, Executive Director, Medical Device Manufacturers Association, and Dr. S. Prakash Sethi, University Distinguished Professor and Professor of Management, Baruch College, The City University of New York.

Mr. Bednar is an attorney with a Washington, DC-based law firm. He has had well more than 30 years of experience in working with other organizations in helping to develop organizational compliance and ethics programs. At the time of his testimony, he had been the coordinator of the GPO Initiative for three months. He indicated that the GPO Initiative, which was launched in 2005, "is a permanent, all-voluntary, self-governing organization committed to the highest level of ethical conduct and providing the best and safest products to patients, doctors, and health care workers at competitive prices."

According to Mr. Bednar, the GPO initiative has three main purposes. "First, it is intended to nurture and promote an ethical culture of compliance within every organization in the GPO industry. Second, the initiative promotes self-governance as the means by which each GPO's top-level commitment to abide by ethical standards is controlled. Third, the initiative enforces a requirement that each member of the organization share best practices in dealing with ethics and business conduct issues. This sharing of practices is done both informally by regular communication among the compliance officers as issues arise and by participating in an annual best practicesforum" (p. 5).

> To achieve these purposes, each GPO has pledged, first, to follow six core ethical principles; second, to report annually on adherence to these principles by responding to a public accountability questionnaire; and, third, to participate with other GPO representatives and interested parties in an annual best practices forum. (pp. 5–6)

> Each signatory is required to follow six principles: (1) to have and adhere to a written code of business conduct which establishes high ethical values and sound business practices; (2) to conduct learning within the organization as to personal responsibilities under the code; (3) to work toward the goals of high-quality health care and cost-effectiveness; (4) to work toward an open and competitive purchasing process, free of conflicts of interest and undue influence; (5) be responsible to each other to share best practices in implementing the principles; and (6) be accountable to the public. The public accountability process requires that each member organization annually respond to a detailed questionnaire, which responses are displayed publicly on our website. (p. 6)

What Mr. Bednar, however, did not say was the fact that all information generated by the GPOs was monitored internally by them. The coordinator did not have any independent staff to verify the quality or accuracy of this information.

Another highly unusual feature of the Initiative is the fact that "the initiative is governed by a steering committee of the nine founding GPOs, who are, in effect, our board of directors" (p. 6). Under most circumstances, this would be considered as significant conflict of interest, since those who monitor are the same individuals whose performance is being monitored by the Steering Committee's board of directors. Mr. Bednar defended this practice by asserting that this self-governance process will work because the CEOs believe in ethical leadership as the best way to introduce ethical business conduct within their organizations, and they do not believe in outsourcing this responsibility.

Mr. Mark B. Leahey is the Executive Director of Medical Device Manufacturers Association, Washington, DC. His testimony focused on the problems confronted by his industry members in gaining access to the healthcare industry. He blamed GPOs and their anticompetitive conduct for creating this problem which, in his opinion, resulted in higher prices for the hospitals and healthcare providers, and also impacted the quality of services provided to the patients. He challenged the industry's assertion and also comments made by Senators DeWine and Senator Kohl that GPOs have reformed and improved their conduct since the issue was raised in the Subcommittee's hearings in 2002. He asserted that GPOs have continued with their anticompetitive conduct through bundling of unrelated products and companies, executing long-term sole-source contracts, awarding no-bid contracts, collecting excessive fees, and policing the markets for the dominant suppliers in a way that excludes innovative, cost-effective technologies (p. 7). As further evidence of the significance of his complaints, he stated that in 2005, the Health and Human Services Inspector General looked at this very issue and the results were staggering. The IG found that six GPOs collected $2.3 billion in administrative fees from the vendors, and their operating expenses were a whopping $725 million. Mr. Leahey stated the obvious by pointing out that GPOs manufacture no product, nor do they distribute any product and promise to return all the savings back to the hospitals and other healthcare providers. The same IG report, however, indicated that GPOs siphoned off nearly $500 million for their own purposes, including for-profit business ventures.

Mr. Leahey pointed out that one of the principal culprits in this equation was the current fee structure and the safe harbor provisions that leave little incentive for the GPOs to either become more efficient or encourage competition in seeking best products and services for their clients at the lowest possible cost. In Mr. Leahey's opinion, the only solution and the best solution to this problem is to repeal the GPO safe harbor that Congress created nearly 20 years ago under much different circumstances, the repeal of these provisions would restore competition back in the marketplace. It would ensure that the GPOs would work for the best interests of their member hospitals and not the dominant suppliers who fund their activities. It would also ensure that patients, caregivers, and the American taxpayer receive the benefits of our healthcare system in the best manner possible (p. 8).

Dr. Sethi is the University Distinguished Professor at Baruch College at the City University of New York. He has spent a large part of his 30+ year academic career on this work. He is internationally recognized for his research and expertise in creating, implementing, and monitoring voluntary codes of conduct by individual companies and industries. He has written a book and numerous articles on this topic in scholarly and professional journals.

Dr. Sethi testified at the invitation of the Subcommittee. His testimony focused primarily on the viability of the GPO Initiative in providing a meaningful and effective means of addressing the problems that have become apparent in the GPO business model and operational conduct. He also examined the underlying flaws in the GPO business model that make it all but impossible for a voluntary initiative to deliver measurable and transparent improvement in performance.

In his statement he indicated that the success or failure of a voluntary code of conduct depends on two factors: (a) the character of underlying issues and problems that the code is intended to address and (b) the pertinence of various code attributes in addressing and resolving those issues. He states:

> Before addressing the GPO initiative, it is necessary to examine briefly the current GPO business model. My colleagues and I at ICCA have recently completed a thorough study of the GPO industry *"Group Purchasing Organizations: An Evaluation of Their Effectiveness in Providing Services to Hospitals and Their Patients"*. We examined virtually all of the public records on the GPO issue and have evaluated the GPO initiative against the principles referenced above. This is the customary process and a necessary pre-condition for drawing objective and unbiased conclusions. (p. 9)

> Based on our own analysis, it is evident that the current GPO model has built-in structural flaws and its financial incentives are so perverse that the GPO initiative cannot possibly remedy them even if it were a well designed and effectively implemented and governed code of conduct, which it is not. (p. 9)

> We cannot talk seriously about a meaningful GPO initiative until Congress realigns the financial incentives so that the hospitals and not the vendors are once again the GPOs' only clients. As long as vendors continue to pay fees to the GPOs, any attempt to create, implement and enforce a voluntary code is doomed to failure. It would not improve the situation, but would actually worsen it. (p. 9)

He went on to state that extensive research and field experience in monitoring code compliance has identified eight conditions that must be met for an industry-made code to demonstrate measurable and credible compliance. These include, among others, the code must be substantive in addressing broad areas of public concern pertaining to the industry's conduct: code standards must be specific in addressing issues embodied in those principles; the industry must create an independent governance structure that is not controlled by the executives of the member companies; and, there must be an independent external monitoring and compliance verification system, which is absolutely necessary to engender public trust and credibility in the industry's claims for performance.

In addressing the specific issues pertaining to the GPO Initiative, he states:

> In my professional opinion, the six principles of the GPO initiative fail to measure up even at the very minimal level to any of the eight criteria that we have

indicated. There is total lack of independence in the initiative's governance structure, which is entirely controlled by the top executives of the member companies. Although the initiative includes a coordinator, the coordinator has no real authority. (p. 9)

The principles are essentially a statement of intent. All measures of substance are left entirely to the member companies. Industry members also set their own criteria with regard to compliance, performance evaluation, implementation assurance and public disclosure. Reduced to its bare essentials, the final product of this process becomes nothing more than a compilation of the reports provided by the member companies based on their own self-evaluation. (p. 9)

The governance structure of the GPO initiative does not provide any mechanism for independent external monitoring and verification of member companies' self-reported performance. Instead, it expects the public to accept this self-reported performance at face value. Such an assertion would be a dubious proposition under the best of circumstances. It would be untenable, given the industry's current record. (pp. 9–10)

In summary, the GPO initiative is encumbered with a lack of specificity, nonexistent performance standards and an internally controlled and self-serving governance structure, and an absence of genuine independent external monitoring. (p. 10)

CHAPTER 1

Healthcare Industry in the United States

Healthcare industry in the United States is in a state of crisis. Healthcare spending in both absolute terms and as a percent of gross domestic product (GDP) is among the highest in the world. Furthermore, these costs are rising faster than GDP growth. It has been rising faster than the rate of the economy and workers' wages.[1] United States currently spends more than $1.8 trillion on healthcare. This is more than what Americans spend on housing, food, national defense, or automobiles.[2] Healthcare spending in the United States as a percentage of GDP increased from 15.8 percent in 2003 to 16 percent in 2006 and if left unchecked is projected to grow to approximately 19.5 percent by 2017.[3] The national health expenditure per capita increased from $6,649 in 2005 to $ 7,026 in 2006. It is estimated that healthcare spending in the United States would average 6.7 percent between 2006 and 2017.[4] Through 2017, growth in healthcare spending is expected to outpace that of GDP by an annual average rate of 1.9 percentage points.

This book has somewhat limited focus. It does not aim at analyzing all the issues and challenges that confront the U.S. healthcare system. Instead, it examines the role of one group, that is, the Group Purchasing Organizations (GPOs), which is a critical link in the healthcare delivery system. In many ways, it is also a microcosm of what afflicts the U.S. healthcare industry, where misguided government benevolence has protected important segments of the healthcare industry from the discipline of competitive markets. To this, we must also add a distorted and ineffective system of regulatory oversight that protects the industry at the expense of the public. And finally, it reflects the hypocrisy of the market-based institutions that loudly espouse the virtues of market-based competition while doing everything possible to subvert the efficient working of free and competitive markets.

In the sections that follow, we present a brief picture of the U.S. healthcare industry as it currently exists and also an analysis of how it compares with the healthcare systems prevailing in some of the other industrialized countries.

Our intent is to layout a framework that would help us in evaluating the multifaceted nature of the U.S. healthcare system and its ability to deliver the desired level of benefits to all its citizens.

The Overall Quality of the U.S. Healthcare System

Until recently, it was a matter of faith and conventional wisdom that the U.S. healthcare system is the best in the world. Industry advocates are never tired of touting the system's strengths. It is claimed to be among the most technologically advanced in the world. The U.S. healthcare industry has made tremendous advances containing and eliminating diseases that were considered incurable only a few years ago. The United States is considered the world's leading country in new drug discoveries and is the home of some of the world's largest pharmaceuticals and biotech companies.

The test of the system, however, cannot be judged solely on the basis of technological advances and medical miracles. Provision of adequate healthcare is one of the most fundamental human rights that a society must afford to all its citizens. Notwithstanding, the enormous amounts of money spent on healthcare, and its cost to individual patients and healthcare providers, it is not clear that the system has delivered the most efficient healthcare to most of its citizens in manner that is affordable, equitable, and responsive to the needs of the community-at-large and also individual patients.

The U.S. healthcare system is designed to be a combination of private and state-supported funding where market-based healthcare services are secured either through one's place of employment or paid by individuals. Public funding at the local and national levels is provided to guarantee adequate healthcare to those who cannot afford to pay for it. Unfortunately, the system has evolved into a web of vested interests, each seeking to maximize its own gains at the expense of other groups. In the process, it has failed to meet its obligations to provide all Americans— and not just the wealthy or the influential and well-connected—with an adequate level of healthcare that the society deems appropriate.

The complexity of the current healthcare system and its enormous cost have become a major political issue in the national and state politics leading to a profusion of new and repackaged proposals. Any significant reform effort must inevitably redistribute costs and benefits among current players. Unfortunately, to date, all efforts at major healthcare reform have failed to gain ground. For reasons that are all too apparent, our democratic system has been so subverted by the vested interests and their lobbying power that it is unable to deliver larger public good. Their combined lobbying power and political campaign contributions have hitherto largely succeeded in derailing all such efforts.

Characteristics of a Good Healthcare System

In a report published in 2000, the World Health Organization (WHO) outlined three principles for determining a good healthcare system. These are good health, responsiveness, and fairness in Financing.[5] Good health is intended to ensure that the health of the entire population is as good as possible through a person's entire life cycle. Good health includes not only delivery of medicines to cure diseases but also preventive healthcare that minimizes and eliminates the occurrence of disease. Responsiveness implies that healthcare providers treat all of their patients with compassion and respect within the framework of established societal expectations. Fairness in financing implies financial protection for everyone with costs distributed according to one's ability to pay. According to the WHO report, a healthcare system which is both good and fair would have

1. overall good health (e.g., low infant mortality rates and high disability-adjusted life expectancy;
2. a fair distribution of good health (low infant mortality and long life expectancy evenly distributed across population groups);
3. a high level of overall responsiveness;
4. a fair distribution of responsiveness across population groups; and
5. a fair distribution of financing healthcare (whether the burden of healthcare is fairly distributed, based on ability to pay, so that everyone is equally protected from the financial risks of illness).[6]

Comparative Analysis of Healthcare Expenditures

Healthcare spending in the United States is higher than most other industrially advanced countries. A comparison of healthcare expenditure between the United States and 30 of the world's most developed countries in the Organization for Economic Cooperation and Development (OECD) indicates that United States has been the highest healthcare spender for the past decade (table 1.1).

In 2006, healthcare expenditure in the United States accounted for 15.3 percent of the GDP. This is almost double the average healthcare expenditure of all OECD countries together at 8.9 percent. Even when compared to Switzerland, the next highest healthcare spender at 11.3 percent, United States is 4 percentage points higher. The figures get more troubling if we look at the per capita expenditure; United States spent $6,714 per capita on healthcare. This is more than double the OECD median of $2,824.

Analysts and policymakers have cited a variety of reasons to explain the disparity in spending patterns between United States and other countries. These include, among others, high administrative and overhead costs, investments in medical technology, high prices of prescription drugs, and differences in healthcare financing.[7] Of all the reasons enumerated above, the complexity of the U.S. healthcare system significantly impacts administrative expenses and healthcare financing. The multipayer system creates redundant layers and poses logistical challenges increasing the administrative and operational costs. It comes as no surprise that countries with a single-payer system or a combination of private-public insurance systems have low administrative costs. Recent data from the National Scorecard on U.S. Health System Performance, 2008,

Table 1.1 Expenditure on healthcare: Selected countries OECD health data, 2006

Country	Total expenditure on health, % GDP	Total expenditure on health, Per capita U.S. $ Purchasing Power Parity (PPP)
Austria	10.1	3606*
Belgium	10.4	3488
Canada	10.0	3678
Denmark	9.5	3349
France	11.1	3449
Germany	10.6	3371
Netherlands	9.3	3391
Portugal	10.2	2120
Switzerland	11.3	4311
United States	15.3	6714

Source: Data extracted on July 21, 2008, 18:14 from OECD.Stat

*Data are expressed in U.S. dollars adjusted for purchasing power parities (PPPs), which provide a means of comparing spending between countries on a common base. PPPs are the rates of currency conversion that equalize the cost of a given "basket" of goods and services in different countries.

states that United States could achieve cost savings of $51 billion by controlling the health insurance administrative costs to reflect averages in multipayer countries.[8] Healthcare financing in United States is split between business, households, and the government. The presence of multiple players and different cost-sharing agreements in addition to the changing economic conditions increase costs. While United States fascination for possessing the latest medical equipment and advanced technology naturally increases costs, it is but the tip of the iceberg. Costs increase while diffusing new technology and greater accessibility to new equipment means higher usage and additional maintenance expenses. Furthermore, to offset or recover the investments in technology, hospitals and doctors are pressured to recommend that patients undergo the latest diagnostic testing or procedures.[9] Patients in the United States also pay higher costs for prescription drugs because unlike many other countries, for example, Canada, the U.S. governmental agencies are barred from negotiating lower prices or seek volume discounts from the pharmaceutical companies. This is another instance of the lobbying power of the drug companies.[10]

Health Indicators by Country

Healthcare efficiency of a nation is measured by the quality of life led by its people and this in turn is determined by access to adequate and equitable healthcare. Life expectancy, under 5 mortality rate, and adult mortality rates are some of the important indicators used to measure the efficiency of a healthcare system. Table 1.2 summarizes these indicators for some of the OECD nations.

Table 1.2 shows that the United States falls short on all three counts. Its life expectancy is lower than Switzerland, the second most expensive healthcare system after the United States. The under 5 mortality rate in the United States is much higher compared to other OECD nations, and the recorded adult

Table 1.2 Indicators of quality healthcare

Country	Life expectancy at birth	Under 5 mortality rate (probability of dying by age 5 per 1000 live births) (2006)	Adult mortality rate (probability of dying between 15 to 60 years per 1000 population) (2006)
Austria	80	4	79
Belgium	79	5	86
Canada	81	6	72
Denmark	79	4	88
France	81	5	91
Germany	80	5	81
Netherlands	80	5	70
Portugal	79	4	93
Switzerland	82	5	63
United States	78	8	109

Source: World Health Organization statistics, 2008.

mortality rate of 109 per 1000 population ranks very high when compared to other countries.

Health Spending by Major Source of Funds

In 2006, the total spending on Medicare grew to $401.3 billion. It increased to 18.7 percent compared to 9.3 percent in 2005 due to the introduction of a new drug program for the elderly and the disabled.[11] As the expenditure on treating the uninsured rose, the costs were transferred to the average consumer, who experienced an increase in private health insurance premium that grew to 5.5 percent in 2006 (table 1.3).

It is interesting to note that even though from 2004 to 2006, Medicare and Medicaid expenditures rose and the private health insurance increased, the increase in Medicare and Medicaid expenditures did not offset the burden on out-of-pocket expenditures. Effectively, the healthcare spending increased by 12 percent between 2004 and 2006, but there was no relief to average person for his out-of-pocket expenditures that remained flat.[12] The rising costs of insurance adversely affect the potential of a consumer to purchase insurance, and they choose to be uninsured that further complicates the situation.

The Rising Cost of Insurance

According to the U.S. Census Bureau, the percentage of uninsured Americans rose from 15.3 percent in 2005 to 15.8 percent in 2006 and the number of uninsured rose from 44.8 million to 47.0 million.[13] The escalating cost of health insurance premium and lack of employer sponsored health coverage are some of the main reasons stated by people for remaining uninsured. Annual health premiums have been growing faster than workers earnings and faster than the rate of inflation.[14] For a majority of the Americans, health insurance is tied to their employment. Employment-based health insurance provides health benefits to approximately 158.5 million people or 54 percent of all

Table 1.3 Source of funding healthcare expenditures in the United States

Source	2004		2005		2006	
	USD in Billions	% Change	USD in Billions	% Change	USD in Billions	% Change
Medicare	309.3	9.9	338.0	9.3	401.3	18.7
Medicaid	170.9	6.7	177.6	3.9	174.3	-1.9
Private Health Insurance	645.8	7.1	685.6	6.2	723.4	5.5
Out-of-Pocket	234.9	4.5	247.1	5.2	256.5	3.8

Source: Centers for Medicare & Medicaid Services, Office of the Actuary, National Health Statistics Group.

Americans.[15] Research done by the Kaiser family foundation reveals that the average premium for employment-based family health insurance was $12,106 in 2007 of which the employee contributed an average of $3,281 and the annual total premium cost for single coverage was $4,479 of which workers paid an average of $694. Unable to control costs, employers were either seen shifting the burden of healthcare to their employees, or hiring more contract employees. Consequently, there has been a decline in the percentage of people covered by employment-based health insurance from 60.2 percent in 2005 to 59.7 percent in 2007.[16] Another component that adds to the rising health insurance premiums is the administrative costs. These costs have been on the increase in United States. Between 2000 and 2006, the per capita administrative costs increased by 68 percent from $289 to $485. The health insurance administrative costs are 3 times higher in the United States compared to countries like Finland, Japan, and Australia—the countries that have lowest insurance rates. Even when compared to countries like Germany, Switzerland, and Netherlands, where private insurance companies compete with public insurance, the administrative costs in the United States are 30 to 70 percent higher.[17] According to the testimony of Karen Davis, President of the Common wealth fund, before the Senate Appropriations Subcommittee on Labor, Health, and Human Services, "administrative expenses for private health insurance in U.S. are two-and-one-half times as high as those for public programs like Medicare."[18] Programs like Medicare are able to reduce their administrative costs by operating on minimal marketing, advertising and administrative overheads.[19]

Preventive Healthcare

Preventive healthcare is an important part of delivering effective healthcare to the population. Although billions of dollars are spent annually on treating illnesses and in acquiring the latest medical technology, less attention and resources are dedicated to preventive healthcare. Results from the National Scorecard on U.S. Health System Performance, 2008 data reveal that only 50 percent of adults received recommended preventive care such as immunizations, cancer screenings, and blood pressure and cholesterol tests.[20] Significant cost savings can be achieved by investing in preventive healthcare since early detection of chronic illnesses like diabetes, cancer, blood pressure, and so on could save precious resources used in treating them.

The Plight of the Uninsured

Financial constraints, affordability and rising costs of healthcare are the primary reasons for Americans to remain uninsured. National Scorecard on U.S. Health System Performance, 2008, data reports that more than one-third or 37 percent of all U.S. adults did not have healthcare, including prescription drugs in 2007 because of their inability to afford health insurance.[21] It is also important that we consider the fate of the "underinsured." The study reveals that the number of underinsured in 2007 was 25 million or 14 percent of the adult population.[22] It would not be long before the underinsured population[23]—unable to gain respite from the spiraling medical costs—will soon migrate to the uninsured category thus adding to the government's burden. Two of five adults or 41 percent of the adult population were grappling with medical debt and medical bill problems in 2005.[24]

Healthcare spending is further increased by costs incurred in treating the chronically ill patients. Unable to realize that delayed care is deferred expenditure, uninsured patients in an effort to cut costs postpone preventive healthcare only to be provided emergency care much later thus resulting in inadequate and slow healthcare or more medical errors during treatment. In 2006 medical errors, coordination problems and delayed care accounted for 22,000 uninsured deaths.[25] Kaiser family foundation study reports that approximately 45 percent of the uninsured nonelderly adults live with a chronic medical condition, the reason being that uninsured nonelderly adults are not covered by public programs such as Medicaid and cannot afford private health insurance.[26]

The present state of the U.S. healthcare industry illustrates a paradox, which suggests that the current model of public-private financing has not yielded desirable results. The effectiveness of the public financing has been considerably reduced by:

a. The public perception that greater public funding is needed to provide necessary healthcare for the U.S. citizens. In this equation, cost reductions are not associated with the efficiencies in the delivery of healthcare, but as an indirect method to deny healthcare benefits to those in greatest need; and

b. Unlike most other countries, where public funds are needed to provide healthcare, government agencies in the United States are not allowed to use their buying power to negotiate lower prices for pharmaceuticals and other services. As a result, the prices for the same set of drugs are 60 percent lower in Canada and France and 85 percent lower in Germany and United Kingdom than in the United States[27] In these countries, national governments are willing to negotiate prescription drugs are less expensive compared to their counterparts in United States.[28]

The role of competitive markets, envisaged in the insurance model has been considerably subverted due to consolidation in various industry segments, which has reduced competition. Increased healthcare spending in the United States should have benefited the two groups most in need for such help, that is, hospitals and their patients,[29] but this is not the case. Most hospitals are facing financial crises and some are struggling to survive.

Conversely, the two groups that appear to have benefited the most are the middlemen, that is, healthcare insurers[30] and GPOs whose primary role is to create economies and efficiencies in the purchase of hospital supplies—the second largest category of expenditure for the hospitals, nursing homes, and other healthcare providers.

There is ample literature discussing problems of competition and pricing associated with HMOs, private insurers, and even pharmaceuticals.[31] However, there is relatively little discussion relating to the impact of GPOs on the costs and efficiencies in the delivery of healthcare services. By any measure, the GPO industry exercises tremendous influence on the financial health and operational policies of the hospitals and other healthcare providers. According to the Modern Healthcare 2007 Annual GPO survey, GPO-contracted purchases are estimated to be approximately $125 billion dollars in 2007. Almost 90 percent of the hospitals, nursing homes, and other healthcare organizations procure a large part of their supplies through GPOs.

The activities of the GPOs, and the manner in which they are performed, have significant implications not only for the healthcare industry but also for the well-being of the U.S. healthcare system. And yet, the industry has largely escaped public scrutiny. In part, this is the outcome of the historical evolution and early beginnings of the GPOs when they were organized by the hospitals to combine their purchasing power in negotiation prices for hospital supplies and equipment.

Today's GPOs could not be more different than their predecessors. And yet, they have been able to sustain a public image as organizations that serve public interest and reduce healthcare costs by negotiating lower prices for hospitals, nursing homes, and other healthcare providers. Present day GPOs are mostly for-profit organizations. They are also for the large part privately owned. Through their iron control on both the suppliers and users of products and services, they have been able to subvert the discipline of the marketplace. This situation is further exacerbated by regulatory provisions that protect their anti-competition conduct. It is, therefore, important that the role of GPOs in the U.S. healthcare should be subjected to the harsh light of transparency and accountability.

CHAPTER 2

Industry Structure of Group Purchasing Organizations

A large majority of U.S. hospitals procure their supplies through Group Purchasing Organizations (GPOs). These organizations negotiate vendor contracts that are intended to save money for the hospitals and other healthcare providers, for example, nursing homes. The genesis of GPOs can be found in the common and quite essential activity where a number of small organizations combine their purchasing power to gain buying leverage on their suppliers to negotiate for lower prices and other discounts for related services. Buying cooperatives, or collective buying initiatives, of this type can be found in a number of industries especially when they are in the early stages of their growth.

The first known hospital GPO was the Hospital Bureau of New York, founded in 1910.[1] The proliferation of the GPO industry in the early nineties had a humble beginning. They were generally established by groups of small hospitals. Over the next half century, the GPO concept grew slowly. By the early 1970s, with the establishment of Medicaid and Medicare, there were 40 hospital GPOs in the United States.[2]

As companies in an industry grow, they become more complex and managing their supply-chain function may take different paths along a continuum. At one end, companies may create their own purchasing departments, which manage all aspects of purchasing and other elements of the supply-chain. At the other end, highly specialized middlemen may emerge to provide one or more of these services with greater efficiency in terms of product groups or concentrated geographical areas. Some hospital groups have chosen to locate these services within their own organizations or more recently through Integrated-Delivery Networks (IDNs).[3] However, a great many others have opted to work with independent middlemen, that is, GPOs. A large majority of the hospitals procure their supplies through GPO-negotiated vendor contracts.[4]

The modern-day GPOs could not be more different than their early predecessors. Rather than mere servants of their hospital masters, the new

GPOs are giant behemoths in a very large industry. The GPO industry is a classic example of a highly concentrated oligopolistic structure, where a handful of companies control more than 80 percent of the hospital supplies purchased through GPOs. This oligopolistic market structure has allowed these, mostly privately owned and controlled entities, to extract excessive rates of return for their own benefit and to the detriment of their member hospitals. In an economic situation that has been characterized by drastic increases in healthcare costs and inefficiency, the GPO oligopoly is a major factor of heretofore unrecognized significance.

GPOs as middlemen present a set of unique opportunities, which makes their role as agents to be highly lucrative. As agents, they operate with rather limited obligations of due diligence and fiduciary duty to their clients. They have also received special protection from antitrust laws. And lastly, while a very large part of their income is derived—directly or—indirectly from government programs such as Medicare and Medicaid, the responsible government agencies have been indifferent and inept in ensuring that government funds are prudently used.

An inevitable outcome of this state of affairs is that the system favors agency at the expense of stewardship. The GPOs' primary role is that of providing a service to their healthcare clients, for which they assess a service charge. However, as privately owned independent organizations, they also seek to maximize profits for their shareholders. Under normal conditions of competitive markets, these interests are balanced by market forces. This however, is not the case for the GPO industry. The enormous size of the industry, and the fact that it controls buying power of such magnitude, would raise anticompetitive concerns under the best of circumstances, that is, freely operating competitive markets. In the case of GPOs, the potential for abuse is even greater. As middlemen, they carry little risk or incur additional costs arising from normal business operations. The justification for their services—and the cost of these services, that is, GPO revenues—must rest on the criterion of efficiency, that is, low unit transaction costs arising from economies of scale, which would yield greater benefits to their clients and masters, that is, hospitals, nursing homes, and other healthcare organizations. However, these efficiencies and cost savings are unlikely to occur, if the agencies' costs, that is, opportunities and incentives toward self-enrichment on the part of GPOs, are not controlled.

Ownership Structure of GPOs

GPOs can be divided into three different categories based on their ownership structure. In the first category, each member is also an owner. An owner is involved in decision making and is represented by employees who have direct fiduciary responsibility to owner hospital and distribute excess supplier paid fees including but not limited to administrative fees. The management and employees of GPO are fully accountable to owners and owners are expected to provide necessary oversight. Consorta, Integrated Delivery networks (IDN) and growing number of purchasing cooperatives fall in this category. As number of members increase decision making becomes quite difficult.

The second category consists of membership-based GPOs. MedAssets is an example of a GPO that belongs to this category. Membership-based GPOs are owned by private third parties and operate as private, for-profit entities. Member hospitals have contractual relations with the GPOs and may have some input into the GPO decision making. However, the real impact of hospital members on GPO decision making is questionable given the very large number of hospital members and the difficulty in coordinating and developing a cohesive position on GPO strategy and decision-making process. In this category, GPOs may voluntarily distribute a portion of their surplus revenue, that is, revenue earned through administrative fee net of GPO expenses. However, they are not obliged to do so. Similarly, GPOs have no accountability to the member hospitals beyond the membership agreement.

The third category consists of hybrid GPOs. These GPOs are also privately owned, for-profit organizations and have participation from both the member hospitals and private owners as shareholders. Although member hospitals share in the surplus revenue, private owners have a determining role as to its distribution and receive a larger share. These organizations can be very large. For a majority of the hospital members, there is little or no real participation in decision making. Two largest GPOs, namely Novation and Premier, belong to this category.

Emergence and Growth of GPOs

Accurate data about the size and structure of GPOs is extremely hard to find. For reasons that would become apparent from the discussion in this and other chapters, GPOs have been adamant in controlling information on virtually every aspect of their operations. Whatever data are available, they are voluntarily provided by the GPOs to the industry's own association or GPO industry-supported data gathering organizations.[5] These data are not independently verified and their consistency and accuracy is subject to significant variability both across companies and over time.

The overall size of the GPO market has continued to grow in lock-step with the rise in healthcare expenditures. Estimates provided by GPO-financed studies indicate that GPO contract-covered purchases accounted for between $148 to $165 billion in 1999 and were expected to rise to $257 to $287 billion in 2009 (assuming a growth rate of 5.7 percent per year, which is well above the growth rate of the overall economy). Although more recent data are not available, projecting past trends would indicate that by 2005, GPO contract-covered purchases by the healthcare industry would be in the neighborhood of $218 billion.[6] We believe this to be a conservative estimate since it does not consider the higher growth rate of healthcare expenditures over the last five years, a trend that is likely to continue in the future.[7]

The late 1980s and the 1990s marked the highest growth rate in the number of GPOs. The impetus for this consolidation was provided by the enactment of the Medicare anti-kickback safe harbor.[8] This allowed the GPOs to charge an administrative fee of 3 percent from the suppliers on all purchases made by their member hospitals. However, various government investigations, private lawsuits, and reports in the news media indicated that in a significant number of instances, GPOs administrative fee had significantly exceeded the 3 percent level envisioned by Congress and ranged from 5 percent to as high as 18 percent.[9] During this time of consolidation, GPOs were able to create other contracting practices, which would further add to the fees and revenue-generating tactics. These included, among others, the landmark sole- and dual-source committed-volume deals.[10] GPOs had succeeded in broadening their "value added" services beyond of what they were intended to earn under the safe harbor provisions.

The GPO safe harbor and safety zone established by the federal government were followed by a massive consolidation of the GPO marketplace in the late 1990s and early 2000s. In 2003, a report by the GAO found that the seven largest GPOs controlled 85 percent of all hospital purchases nationwide that were purchased through GPOs.[11] In another, industry-reported study, GPOs indicated that the nine companies-signatories of the Healthcare Group Purchasing Industry Initiative (HGPII) represent 80 percent of the total GPO market.[12] By this time, GPO consolidation was almost complete. As we shall show in our analysis of intra-industry competition in the latter part of this book, any further consolidation would not be financially justifiable. In addition, consolidation would surely invite the unwanted attention of the antitrust division of the federal Justice Department.

Sources of Revenue

GPOs derive most of their revenue (more than 50 percent) from administrative fees paid by manufacturers and distributors, effectively capped at 3 percent of purchasing volume in tandem with Medicare Safety Harbor regulations. This was confirmed in the report prepared in May 2005 by the Office of Inspector General (OIG), U.S. Department of Health and Human Services. This report indicated that "three GPOs collected $513million in revenues for the period reviewed, mostly from administrative fees."[13]

Notwithstanding, GPOs also derive a handsome portion of their revenue from other "fees" paid by suppliers in excess of the 3 percent cap stipulated under Federal safe harbor regulations to attract GPO business. Estimates by various sources indicate that these fees can range anywhere from 6 percent to 18 percent of purchasing volume. In addition, another source of revenue is derived by GPOs from distribution fess levied on suppliers. Health Industry Distributors Association (HIDA) estimates that GPOs charge Medical Products Distributors, particularly those serving acute care facilities, distributor's fee in excess of 11 percent computed on a basis greater than the cost of the distribution service provided.[14] In some cases, GPOs may also receive a patronage fee or patronage dividend from a supplier as a reward for the successful negotiation of a contract with a GPO.[15]

Brief Descriptions of Major GPOs

Novation

Based on the number of covered hospitals, Novation is by far the largest national purchasing organization. It is also the largest GPO in the United States based on the volume of purchases. In the last several years, the company has been experiencing a stable annual purchasing growth of 13 percent. In 2007, Veterans Health Administration (VHA), University HealthSystem Consortium (UHC), and Provista members used Novation and alliance contracts to purchase $33.1 billion in supplies and services.[16]

Novation was established on January 1, 1998. It is an affiliate of healthcare alliances VHA and UHC and conducts supplies and services contract purchasing for VHA, UHC, and Provista. Novation currently is one of Cardinal Health's biggest GPO customers.

The company procures medical equipment and supplies, pharmaceuticals, laboratory equipment, food, and other products needed to run healthcare facilities. In addition to serving 2,500 members of UHC and VHA, Novation also provides supply contracting services to the 12,000 members of Provista (formerly HealthCare Purchasing Partners International LLC) a GPO owned by VHA and UHC that serves healthcare and education entities not belonging to the two alliance groups. Novation's combined membership was estimated to be 32,460 members in 2007, comprised of hospitals and other alternative sites.[17]

Many GPOs, including Novation are widely believed to demand excess fees from manufactures. Novation extracts fees from manufactures in a number of ways.[18] It requires suppliers to sell through a private label brand called NovaPlus, the largest comprehensive private label program in health care. The company also uses Marketplace@Novation and other incentive and performance-based programs such as OPPORTUNITY, the most active online exchange of its kind in the industry, to expand its presence in the market. In 2000, Novation got control over the electronic marketplace through the acquisition of e-commerce company Neoforma and partnering it with Premier's Global Healthcare Exchange (GHX), LLC.

Premier

Premier Inc. is one of the two largest GPO in the United States based on the annual purchasing volumes. Just like Novation, Premier's growth was relatively stable over the last few years, averaging 12 percent per year. Purchasing volumes for 2007 were estimated to be around $33 billion.[19]

Premier was founded in January 1996 through the merger of American Healthcare Systems (San Diego), Premier Health Alliance (Chicago), and the Sun Health Alliance (Charlotte, NC). The company offers a variety of healthcare services, including educational and consulting services. The purchasing body of the company is represented by Premier Purchasing Partners. The company has contracts with more than 200 medical products suppliers, including Aesculap, Kinetic Concepts, and the Nurture division of Steelcase.

Premier is a private company, owned by 203 not-for-profit hospitals and health systems composed of 892 hospitals plus 669 hospital purchasing affiliates. In addition, more than 900 hospitals and health facilities are Premier's nonowner members. Premier is the second largest GPO based on the number of member hospitals. However, the company's combined membership of hospitals and other alternative sites is estimated to be the largest in the industry—nearly 48,700 members.[20]

The similarities between the two largest GPOs continue in the way they control electronic purchasing and distribution market. In 2000 Premier cofounded GHX, LLC; an electronic online trading open to healthcare providers, suppliers, and manufacturers. The firm was initially founded by a group of five healthcare manufacturers: Abbott Labs, Baxter International, GE Medical Systems, Johnson & Johnson, and Medtronic. Other companies—including wholesalers, healthcare providers, and purchasing organizations—have since become equity owners.[21]

AmeriNet

AmeriNet Central was founded in 1986 as a purchasing cooperative by a consortium of regional purchasing organizations. It negotiates volume discount contracts with its suppliers, on behalf of its member facilities, providing members with very favorable pricing, terms and conditions, and other benefits. It operates as a healthcare group purchasing cooperative through its three participating shareholders: AmeriNet Central; Intermountain Health Care; and Vector.[22]

The company is located in Warrendale, PA and represents more than 700 hospitals in a 12-state region of the Midwest. AmeriNet is a "Pure" GPO with 1,817 hospital members. Just like the entire GPO industry, AmeriNet has experienced 11–12 percent growth since early 2000s. AmeriNet asserted that the company provided members with $335 million in contract portfolio savings on $6.5 billion in purchases resulting in $39 million returned to members.

AmeriNet Central recently partnered with four Ohio-based hospitals that are forming a new organization called the Ohio Valley Hospital Consortium. The Ohio Valley Hospital Consortium plans to serve as an independent organization with the goal of improving healthcare standards. AmeriNet Central assists members in reducing costs, enhancing revenue, and improving their operational performance. It has three divisions: Group Purchasing Education, Data Management, and Analysis.

MedAssets HSCA

MedAssets was established in 1999 through the acquisition of the GPOs, InSource Health Services, Axis Point Health services, and then Health Services Corporation of America (HSCA) in 2001. The acquisitions made MedAssets one of the largest GPOs in the country. The merged company is known as MedAssets HSCA. On April 11, 2003, MedAssets and Premier's GHX formed a strategic alliance with GHX set to be the integrated e-commerce solution for MedAssets' members.[23] The acquisition of OSI Systems put MedAssets Inc. into another category beyond just a "pure" GPO.[24] The addition of a revenue cycle management solution is aimed to enable members to correct billing errors and identify missed revenue.

MedAssets went public in 2007 and used part of the proceeds to pay down debt from earlier acquisitions. Acquisitions remain part of the company's growth strategy. MedAssets spent more than $227 million to acquire revenue management provider Accuro Healthcare Solutions in 2008.[25]

Broadlane

Broadlane was incorporated on December 9, 1999, as the corporate procurement division of Tenet Healthcare, one of the nation's largest hospital companies. The company is a spin-off of hospital operator Tenet Healthcare, which remains a client. Broadlane serves more than 900 hospitals and thousands of nonacute care facilities and physician practices representing more than $4.0 billion in annual purchase volume. According to Modern Healthcare's 2007 Group Purchasing Survey Report in 2006, Broadlane had 908 member hospitals, 23,733 alternate site, and 24,630 members.[26]

Broadlane is describing itself as a supply chain services company, which incorporates a whole series of services offerings to customers. While the primary focus of the company is to negotiate contracts on behalf of its clients, it also offers centralized materials management functions. Its proprietary OnRamp portal allows clients to order from an online catalog, view contracts, track pending transactions, and obtain reports. The company operates one of the largest B2B e-commerce exchanges in any industry.

MAGNET (Mid-Atlantic Group Network of Shared Services, Inc)

Created in 1979, Magnet develops contracts on behalf of its members in the niche market of capital equipment. According to Modern Healthcare's 2007 Group Purchasing Survey Report, in 2006 MAGNET had 750 member hospitals, 15,000 alternate sites.[27] MAGNET's major shareholders are Association Management Resources, Southwest Ohio Healthcare Associates, PRIME, MOHCC, HCSC, Diversified Network Services, JPC.[28]

CHAPTER 3

Market Dominance and Anticompetitive Conduct of GPOs

The group purchasing organization (GPO) industry is a classic example of highly concentrated oligopolistic structure, which is characteristic of an industry where the top 3–4 companies control more than 50 percent of the total market. In general, oligopolistic industry structure is symptomatic of mature industries where demand is relatively stable, the rate of innovation is minimal to moderate, and economies of scale—and therefore consolidation—offer the most promising source of increasing revenue and profits.

This is an important consideration because the oligopolistic structure of the GPO industry allows us to analyze the industry's conduct and that of its dominant members in the context of the established economic theory. It also makes it possible to predict the adverse consequences of industry conduct on other groups and individuals whose relative bargaining power is reduced because of lack of competition in the marketplace.

Companies in an industry are subject to two types of competitors: current competitors within an industry and potential competitors or future entrants into the industry. In an oligopolistic industry, market leaders can enjoy higher profit margins by avoiding price competition among themselves and also by controlling the conduct of small players. This stable market structure, however, would be threatened if the industry could not control entry by outsiders who would be attracted to enter the market because of higher profits. This stable environment can also be threatened by the relative buying power of the industry's consumers and suppliers.[1]

GPOs: Industry Size, Concentration, and Market Power

Reports of the number of current GPOs range all over the map. One GPO industry-financed study claims that there are between 600 and 900 GPOs, of which approximately 200 have direct contracts with suppliers.[2] In another study funded by the GPO industry, the author asserts that the market share of the top two GPOs was approximately 27 percent, and the top five GPOs had less than 40 percent of the total GPO market. Apparently, this is an attempt to suggest a heightened level of competition in the industry. In calculating lower market shares, the author had inflated the size of the total market by including hospital purchases that are not normally covered by GPOs.[3]

The GPO industry's own Web site, however, states that there are fewer than 30 GPOs that negotiate sizeable contracts for their members.[4] Information generated in various hearings of the Senate Judiciary Committee and other government-sponsored investigations also provide a consensus number in the range of 30 GPOs.[5]

Oligopolistic Structure and Diminution of Intra-Industry Competition

It is almost impossible to find independently collected or verified data on any aspect of GPO operations. All major GPOs are privately owned and are not obliged to make public any of their financial information. In its annual survey of GPOs, Cinda Becker of *Modern Healthcare* reported that judging from the responses to the survey, most GPOs are "disinclined to publicly disclose financial data as part of the voluntary ethics initiative."[6] The only exception to this rule was Consorta (one of the six largest GPOs) that reported earnings of $40.5 million in operating income on $58 million in revenue. Consorta also reported an operating margin of 70 percent and projected this margin to increase to 75.3 percent in 2005. Consorta also asserts that it returns 100 percent of its net income to members in cash.[7] It should be noted here that Consorta has since effectively merged with the HealthTrust Purchasing Group, the third largest GPO by market share. Henceforth, its financial data would no longer be publicly available.

Our estimates of market share and other related factors are based on the annual survey of GPOs conducted by *Modern Healthcare*. The survey report is based on unaudited information provided by the top GPO companies.[8] Self-reported data for the GPOs suggest that top GPOs have continued to increase their sales and revenue at an accelerated rate. The 16 companies reporting purchasing volume in 2004 collectively brokered $83 billion in supplies and services, a 17 percent increase from the $71 billion in purchasing volume in 2003.[9]

The total volume of negotiated purchases reported for the entire industry are in the broad range between $148 and $165 billion in 1999 and expected to rise from $257 to $287 billion in 2009. In 2006, *The Health Industry Distributors Association (HIDA)* in their "GPO Market Report" state that purchasing volume in the industry was as high as $125 billion and is projected to reach $220 billion by 2015.[10] These estimates are comparable to the self-reported GPOs' purchasing volumes presented in *Modern Healthcare* 2007 Annual GPO Survey.[11] The survey indicated that the industry's total purchasing volume in 2007 was estimated to be approximately $125 billion (exhibit 3.1).

Based on the purchasing volumes reported by the participating GPOs, the top three companies, namely Premier, Novation, and HealthTrust Purchasing

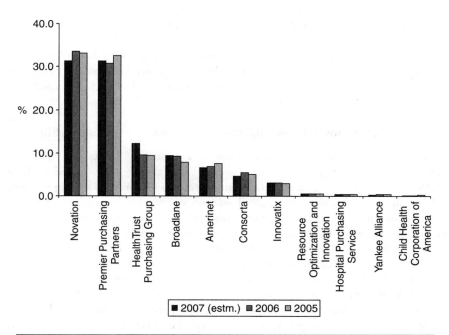

	2007 (estm.)		2006 (estm.)		2005 (estm.)	
		(%)		(%)		(%)
Novation	33,100	31.3	31,600	33.5	27,800	33.1
Premier Purchasing Partners	33,000	31.2	28,968	30.7	27,397	32.6
HealthTrust Purchasing Group	12,900	12.2	8,950	9.5	7,860	9.4
Broadlane	10,000	9.5	8,672	9.2	6,579	7.8
Amerinet	7,000	6.6	6,500	6.9	6,350	7.6
Consorta	4,950	4.7	5,159	5.5	4,240	5.0
Innovatix	3,200	3.0	2,900	3.1	2,500	3.0
Resource Optimization and Innovation	551	0.5	532	0.6	446	0.5
Hospital Purchasing Service	390	0.4	429	0.5	373	0.4
Yankee Alliance	347	0.3	342	0.4	305	0.4
Child Health Corporation of America	185	0.2	190	0.2	187	0.2
Total	105,623		94,242		84,037	

Exhibit 3.1 Market Share of the top 10 GPOs.

Group, represent on average 75 percent of the total healthcare group purchasing market. Although this self-reported statistics have not been verified and cannot be used as a reliable estimate for market share of individual companies, it provides an overall picture of the industry structure.

Notwithstanding the off-cited members of GPOs, all available evidence points to the GPO industry as a classic example of a highly concentrated oligopolistic structure, where a very small number of companies account for a very large part of the total market. Furthermore, the conduct of the industry members corresponds to behavior patterns that are characteristic of oligopolistic industries, for example, mature industry, enhanced profitability through consolidation, stable rankings, high entry barriers, and nonprice competition among the major competitors.

GPOs' Drive toward Consolidation and Elimination of Competition

The GPOs face a finite universe of hospitals and nursing homes and, with few exceptions, a vast majority of these hospitals had already been signed up by a GPO. Although there is a tendency among certain hospitals to belong to more than one group,[12] this is generally based on differences in product offerings and service packages and does not involve price competition. The large GPOs can capture extra profits through buying out the smaller ones, which either compete or have the potential of competing with the larger GPOs. Given market saturation, consolidation allows the acquiring companies to grow by capturing revenue streams of the acquired companies. Consolidation also creates enhanced profit opportunities through reduced competition. Smaller companies find it attractive to sell because of the premium price offered by the larger players, which can easily pass on the extra costs to the customers through increases in their operating costs. The only GPOs left out from these combinations are likely to be the ones that provide specialized services or serve remote areas that cannot be served more effectively by the larger GPOs.

The current larger GPOs have no incentive to compete with each other. They provide essentially similar services and draw from the same pool of suppliers. Profits would, therefore, come not from greater efficiencies but through the exploitation of their increased oligopolistic power. There is another equally important reason for the large GPOs not to compete with each other. Given the fact that their target competition is another equally large GPO, the potential competitor would offer strong resistance to losing market share. Survey findings by *Modern Healthcare* show that the composition of industry's top companies has remained relatively stable. When changes have occurred, they have resulted from consolidation from within the industry, which is also a typical characteristic of oligopolistic industries.[13] The end result of such competition would be increased costs for the two rivals. There is also the added risk of unintended disclosure of market practices of the GPOs, which may not be looked upon favorably by their customers, that is, hospitals or the regulators seeking lower costs and greater efficiencies from the GPOs.

GPO Defense of Market Domination and Large Size

GPOs have argued that their size is necessary to generate additional economies of scale and increased bargaining power with the suppliers. Thus, they may argue that large size translates into greater savings for their member hospitals.[14] Large size does not always yield economies of scale as alleged by the GPOs. If this were the case, large organizations would almost always be more efficient than small and medium size organizations. Arguably, one GPO could serve the entire industry. Experience in the competitive marketplace provides substantial evidence to indicate that small and medium size organizations often can be more effective and flexible in their operations and in their response to market conditions. Transaction cost economics theory suggests that all transactions have certain costs attached to them and that beyond a certain size these costs increase in larger organizations because of their increased complexity, bureaucratic controls, and multiple layers of management.

One way the GPOs can substantiate these claims would be to show that their operating expenses are declining with increase in the overall volume of contracting purchases. Total operating costs should also decline since a large number of suppliers, and a large volume of contracted purchases, remain the same over a number of years. Hence the cost of contract renewal negotiations and contract management should decline as percentage of operating costs. Unfortunately, GPOs have not made this type of information publicly available to permit such analysis.

Threat of Competition from New Entrants

For reasons described in the previous section, it should be clear that the current industry structure and concentrated market share by a small number of dominant players poses high barriers to entry by new companies from outside the industry. It is prohibitively expensive for a new entrant to gain significant market share because most current and potential customers are already locked into existing GPOs through various contractual arrangements. Evidence of this situation can be found in the fact that over the last five-plus years, industry dominance by the top GPOs has remained unchanged. There have been no new entrants of meaningful size from outside into the GPO industry to challenge the hegemony of current top players. Instead, there has been further consolidation among the current players through mergers and acquisitions. The most recent example of this conduct can be seen in the case of Consorta and HealthTrust Purchasing Group deal.[15] The combination of the two companies creates the nation's fourth largest GPO, with more than $13 billion in volume.[16] The espoused advantages of the merger were touted to be the economics of scale resulting in cost savings of $535 million over the next decade, which would benefit their shareholders and customers.[17] Industry critics, however, are not sanguine. According to Lynn Everard, a healthcare supply chain specialist, "it's impossible to predict savings with GPO pricing. Every contract has tiers and levels, so are they predicting on the highest or lower tier? What assumptions are they making about hospital buying patterns? And how can they be sure about the supplier's ability to get the price right? There are so many variables to it."[18]

Bargaining Power of Suppliers and Buyers

GPOs also face no threat from their current or future suppliers who might want to work directly with hospitals or promote competition among different

GPO	Member Hospitals				Alternate Sites				Total Members			
	2004	2005	2006	2007 (estm.)	2004	2005	2006	2007 (estm.)	2004	2005	2006	2007 (estm.)
Premier	1,433	1,478	1,494	1,555	30,731	33,952	41,246	47,137	32,164	35,430	42,740	48,692
Novation	1,545	1,671	2,379	2,433	12,925	15,090	34,904	30,028	14,470	16,761	37,283	32,461
Med Assets	2,200	2,400	N/A	N/A	18,000	21,028	N/A	N/A	20,200	23,428	N/A	N/A
Broadlane	856	935	908	1,086	13,169	20,935	23,733	27,999	14,025	21,870	24,630	29,085
Amerinet	1,856	1,890	2,315	2,168	18,703	22,227	33,374	41,873	20,559	24,117	35,689	44,041
Health Trust*	N/A	N/A	797	778	N/A	N/A	1,873	2,408	900	1,200	2,670	3,186
Consorta	338	363	367	4,950	1,171	1,550	2,305	3,032	1,509	1,913	2,240	7,358
GNYHA	110	132	N/A	N/A	N/A	N/A	N/A	N/A	110	132	N/A	N/A
CHCA	35	35	34	35	3,600	N/A	2,000	2,000	3,635	35	2,627	2,755
Total for surveyed GPOs	8,373	8,904	9,263	13,356	98,299	114,782	169,507	191,810	107,572	124,886	178,274	205,166

Source: Becker 2005; Rhea 2007.

*Information for Health Trust: 2004—"Group Purchasing Organizations," BusIntell Reports, May 2005; 2005—company's Web site.

Exhibit 3.2   GPOs' ranking by contract membership

GPOs. It is not financially attractive for the suppliers to compete because lower prices would become the prevailing prices. Instead, suppliers are happy to pay the higher fee and other charges to GPOs because (a) they benefit from larger production runs, (b) capital costs are amortized over larger volumes and thus reduce overall costs, (c) there is less pressure for product innovation that lowers their R&D expenses, and (d) all such fees are eventually passed on to the buyers in the prices they charge for their product.

GPOs have strong contractual lock-ins with both the suppliers and the hospitals (exhibit 3.2). The *Modern Healthcare* GPO annual surveys of the top 14–16 GPOs show that the number of contracted hospitals is increasing on average 5 percent per year with an estimated significant increase in 2007. The top three GPOs represent approximately 60 percent of the total number of hospitals and alternative sites covered by the surveyed GPOs' contracts. These contractual arrangements generally carry strong penalties and other disincentives to discourage both the suppliers and the hospital customers to change their relationship from their current GPO to another one.

Principal Agency Dilemma, Moral Hazard, and Unintended Consequences

GPOs as middlemen present a set of unique opportunities when operating under the anti-kickback safe harbor and antitrust safety zone. The system provides GPOs with a stable and predictable flow of revenue through administrative fees. It is also protected from certain antitrust laws and is not subjected to any meaningful regulatory oversight. This makes their agency role highly lucrative. The system favors agency (GPOs' self-interest) at the expense of stewardship and the best interest of their clients. Although their primary role is that of providing service to their healthcare clients, for which they collect a service charge, they are also for the most part independent privately owned organizations that seek to maximize profits for their shareholders.

Present day GPO organizations are radically different from their early predecessors. As a highly concentrated oligopoly, the industry members have the opportunity of earning large nonmarket rent, that is, above-average profits from their operations. At the same time, the structure of the industry is protected through the government exemptions and has provided the industry with virtually risk free incentive to exploit these oligopolistic conditions for realizing profits. The agency problem is further compounded by a relative lack of oversight on the part of regulators and little leverage by their clients. This condition has been widely studied in economics as a moral hazard. It arises whenever (1) a principal cannot perfectly monitor the actions of the agent and (2) the agent does not bear the total cost of its risk taking behavior.[19]

GPOs currently control the customer and the supplier through tied contracts, sole source buying, and customer use of bundled products and services. This makes it difficult for hospitals to exercise meaningful freedom of choice. Even where GPOs are member-owned, the very large number of member organizations makes effective governance all but impossible. The situation is quite well-known in economics where it is described as the "principal-agency" dilemma, where agents, that is, GPOs, are able to control and thereby render ineffective, the principal's role to monitor and govern the activities of the agent. The agent in return, exploits the situation for self-enrichment and to the detriment of the principal.

The justification for their service must rest on efficiency, that is, low unit transaction costs arising from economies of scale, which would yield greater benefits to their clients, that is, hospitals, nursing homes, and other healthcare organizations. However, these efficiencies and cost savings are unlikely to occur if the agency costs, that is, opportunities and incentives toward self-enrichment are poorly controlled.

The consequences of this structure should have been easily predicted and measures taken to minimize their occurrence. The negative consequences of this state of affairs have been revealed through various private lawsuits, investigations by regulatory agencies, and congressional hearings. The range of questionable activities is connected—in one way or another—with the GPOs exploitation of government exemptions. These include, among others, anticompetitive practices, conflict of interest, the discouragement of innovation, and improper use of tax-exempt funds. These issues have been discussed in the next chapter.

Not only do GPOs thrive in the marketplace through their oligopolistic industry structure, they also benefit immensely from the growth of healthcare industry. They have benefited handsomely through a combination of highly protected markets, a government guaranteed and predictable source of revenue, operating practices that give these GPOs significant control over both the suppliers and the buyers, and, finally little or no oversight on the part of the regulatory agencies or the GPOs' beneficiary clients. This combination of market control and resulting economic power, when combined with lack of oversight and accountability requirements, has led to the inevitable consequences, where GPOs have found ample opportunities for abuse of market power for their own benefit and at the expense of their principal clients, hospitals, nursing homes, and other healthcare organizations.

Perfect Paradise

In summary, the GPO industry in the United States enjoys the ultimate advantage of becoming a highly profitable and growth industry, where

a. the current players and market leaders can exercise their market dominance to maintain high profit margins;
b. GPOs operate in an environment of high growth in consumer expenditures while severely controlling access to markets from new competitors; and
c. The industry enjoys government mandated protection against anticompetitive behavior and anti-kickback revenue schemes.

These three conditions have created a "perfect paradise" for the GPOs to generate enormous profits. Moreover, by operating as privately owned, for-profit companies, they have succeeded in shielding their exorbitant profits from the scrutiny of the healthcare consumers who must pay higher costs and receive poor services, and the tax payers since the U.S. government has been ineffective in protecting its legitimate interests from the GPOs exploitation of their market power.

CHAPTER 4

Government Created Protections of the GPO Industry: Financial Burden of GPO Activities on the U.S. Healthcare Industry

A major culprit in the protection of the GPO industry and the resultant costs and economic inefficiencies can be found in the regulatory protections created by the federal government in the form of the GPO anti-kickback safe harbor and the joint purchasing antitrust safety zone. Notwithstanding their initial intent, the anti-kickback safe harbor and the antitrust safety zone have had significant unintended negative consequences. Rather than helping the hospitals in securing supplies at the least cost, they have created incentives for the GPOs to maximize their revenues without necessarily providing the hospitals with the most cost effective and least expensive products. Furthermore, by sheltering them from market competition, they have led to a massive consolidation of the GPO industry, a further weakening of the bargaining power of both their customers and suppliers, and, exploitation of the market power for the benefit of the GPOs.

The Safe Harbor and Safety Zone Exemptions

Historically, the purpose of GPOs was to use the combined purchasing power of their member hospitals to negotiate significant discounts from manufacturers and distributors of medical supplies. By using the system of bulk purchasing through GPO contracts, member hospitals are to save money by eliminating duplicative transaction costs.

GPOs operate under the benefit of multiple government-sanctioned exemptions that were intended to promote the growth of GPOs and assist hospitals in better negotiating with suppliers. The available evidence, however, suggests that these well-intended also created unintended negative consequences with regard to competition, innovation, and the cost and quality of healthcare.[1]

The GPOs' safe harbor from the Medicare anti-kickback statute allows them to collect an administrative fee of 3 percent from the suppliers on the value of the products sold to the GPOs' member hospitals. In negotiating these contracts, GPOs and suppliers must meet certain broad eligibility conditions as prescribed in the law.[2] The antitrust safety zone describes joint purchasing arrangements among healthcare providers that "will not be challenged, absent extraordinary circumstances, by the Agencies under the antitrust laws."[3] *Health Care Statement 7* and its antitrust safety zone aim to address monopsony and oligopoly concerns with the formation of a GPO.[4]

Safe Harbor in the GPO Industry

On August 17, 1987 the Social Security Act was amended by the Medicare and Medicaid Patient Program Protection Act. This Act specifically mandated the U.S. Department of Health and Human Services (HHS) to promulgate regulations specifying various payment and business practices that, although potentially capable of inducing referrals of business under federal and state healthcare programs, would not be treated as criminal offenses under the federal anti-kickback statute[5] (Pub.L. 100-93, section 14). One of the so-called safe harbor provisions protects healthcare GPOs from the anti-kickback statute by excluding:

> any payment by a vendor of goods or services to a group purchasing organization (GPO), as part of an agreement to furnish such goods or services to an individual or entity as long as both of the following two standards are met—

1. The GPO must have a written agreement with each individual or entity, for which items or services are furnished, that provides for either of the following:
   (i) The agreement states that participating vendors from which the individual or entity will purchase goods or services will pay a fee to the GPO of 3 percent or less of the purchase price of the goods or services provided by that vendor.
   (ii) In the event the fee paid to the GPO is not fixed at 3 percent or less of the purchase price of the goods or services, the agreement specifies the amount (or if not known, the maximum amount) the GPO will be paid by each vendor (where such amount may be a fixed sum or a fixed percentage of the value of purchases made from the vendor by the members of the group under the contract between the vendor and the GPO). (42 C.F.R. 1001.952(j))

On July 29, 1991, HHS and the Office of Inspector General (OIG) issued the final rule implementing section 14 of Public Law 100-93, the Medicare and Medicaid Patient and Program Protection Act of 1987, by specifying various payment practices that, although potentially capable of inducing referrals of business under Medicare or a state healthcare program, would be protected from criminal prosecution or civil sanctions under the anti-kickback provisions of the statute.

Specifically the Final Rule stated that the following payment practices would not be treated as a criminal offense under section 1128B of the Act and would not serve as the basis for exclusion:

(j) Group purchasing organizations. As used in section 1128B of the Act, "remuneration" does not include any payment by a vendor of goods or services to a group purchasing organization (GPO), as part of an agreement to furnish such goods or services to an individual or entity as long as both of the following two standards are met—

(1) The GPO must have a written agreement with each individual or entity, for which items or services are furnished, that provides for either of the following:
  (i) The agreement states that participating vendors from which the individual or entity will purchase goods or services will pay a fee to the GPO of 3 percent or less of the purchase price of the goods or services provided by that vendor.
  (ii) In the event the fee paid to the GPO is not fixed at 3 percent or less of the purchase price of the goods or services, the agreement specifies the amount (or if not known, the maximum amount) the GPO will be paid by each vendor (where such amount may be a fixed sum or a fixed percentage of the value of purchases made from the vendor by the members of the group under the contract between the vendor and the GPO).
(2) Where the entity which receives the goods or service from the vendor is a health care provider of services, the GPO must disclose in writing to the entity at least annually, and to the Secretary upon request, the amount received from each vendor with respect to purchases made by or on behalf of the entity. Note that for purposes of paragraph (j) of this section, the term group purchasing organization (GPO) means an entity authorized to act as a purchasing agent for a group of individuals or entities who are furnishing services for which payment may be made in whole or in part under Medicare, Medicaid or other Federal health care programs, and who are neither wholly-owned by the GPO nor subsidiaries of a parent corporation that wholly owns the GPO (either directly or through another wholly-owned entity).

Disclosure of Fees to Members and the Government

One of the most important principles of the safe harbor in ensuring hospitals' protection from possible abuse of power on the part of the distributor is the provision requiring GPOs to annually disclose fees received from vendors. Most of the GPOs specify this provision in their initial participant agreements and agree to disclose to their participants, and to the Secretary of the Department of HHS upon request, the amount received by them from each vendor relating to purchases made by or on behalf of each of the participant.

In its Annual Public Accountability Questionnaire, Healthcare Group Purchasing Industry Initiative (HGPII) asks all participating purchasing organizations several questions in regard to the fee disclosure.[6] HGPII's summary of findings for 2007 questionnaire states that all participating GPOs report to their members on the fees and benefits received and make all disclosures required by law or by agreement with government regulators.

This information, however, is not in the public domain and is only available to the GPO member companies. To ensure transparency in GPO reporting, OIG of the Department of HHS, reserves the right to periodically request a copy of the disclosure reports and review GPOs' statements. Two of such reviews have been conducted on six GPOs.[7] Both reviews found some deficiencies in GPOs' reporting systems especially as they pertain to Medicaid cost reports and recommended better guidance in preparation of the disclosure reports.

Antitrust Concerns

In addition to concerns with Medicare violations, the GPO system also raises antitrust concerns. In 1993 the Department of Justice (DOJ) and the Federal Trade Commission (FTC) issued joint "Statements of Antitrust Enforcement Policy in Health Care."[8] In 1996 the Statements were revised and included Statement 7, dealing with joint purchasing arrangements. Statement 7 specifies the agencies' enforcement policy on joint purchasing arrangements among healthcare providers, including the formation of GPOs. It states that "[m]ost joint purchasing arrangements among hospitals or other health care providers do not raise antitrust concerns. Such collaborative activities typically allow the participants to achieve efficiencies that will benefit consumers."[9] It outlines the following specific guidelines:

> Joint purchasing arrangements are unlikely to raise antitrust concerns unless (i) the arrangement accounts for so large a portion of the purchases of a product or service that it can effectively exercise market power in the purchase of the product or service, or (ii) the products or services being purchased jointly account for so large a proportion of the total cost of the services being sold by the participants that the joint purchasing arrangement may facilitate price fixing or otherwise reduce competition. If neither factor is present, the joint purchasing arrangement will not present competitive concerns.[10]

This statement sets forth an "antitrust safety zone" that describes joint purchasing arrangements among healthcare providers that "will not be challenged, absent extraordinary circumstances, by the Agencies under the antitrust laws."[11] The joint purchasing antitrust safety zone limits antitrust exposure for GPOs if two conditions are met: (i) membership purchases through the GPO must account for less than 35 percent of the total sales of the product or service; and (ii) the aggregate costs of the products and services each hospital purchases through a GPO must account for less than 20 percent of the hospital's total revenue.[12] In 2004, the FTC and DOJ released a report on healthcare competition and stated that Statement 7 is not a safe harbor for anticompetitive contracting practices and that such behavior is subject to antitrust scrutiny.[13]

Financial Burden of GPO Activities on the Healthcare Industry

In the previous chapter, we discussed the current GPO industry structure, operational policies, and their adverse impact on the GPOs' principal clients. The financial consequences of GPO market power on the healthcare industry can only be estimated indirectly. As privately owned, for-profit entities, most GPOs have strongly resisted disclosure of objective, verifiable information with regard to their sources of revenue, appropriateness of various categories of expenses, reasonableness of the top management compensation, and dividend returns to their shareholders. Instead, GPOs have made unsupportable assertions about the benefits of their operations to their member hospitals. They have also made specific but unsubstantiated claims that they save member hospitals billions of dollars through lower prices of goods purchased and improved efficiencies in the supply chain management.

This lack of information is contrary to the best interest of the hospitals, whose welfare is the *raison d'etre* for creating GPOs in the first place. This information should also be a mandatory requirement from the perspective of public interest because GPOs benefit from the government provided protection from antitrust laws and anti-kickback provisions. The GPOs' reluctance to provide factual information about their operations also raises questions about the credibility of their claimed contributions to the improved financial and operational performance of their principal clients, that is, hospitals, nursing homes, and other parts of the healthcare industry.

Our focus in this chapter is on the financial impact of GPO operations on their principal clients, that is, hospitals, nursing homes, and other healthcare providers. The full measure of the GPOs' financial activities can only be determined indirectly since GPOs have consistently resisted most attempts at voluntary disclosure. However, based on information generated in various governmental inquiries, and the sources of GPO revenue, some reasonable estimates are possible.

GPOs' financial operations have two important components. The first concerns the administrative fees collected by the GPOs from their contracted suppliers, and the extent to which the magnitude of these fees may have unintended and undesirable consequences. The second deals with the notion of appropriateness and reasonableness of various expense categories in which the GPOs apportion their fee-generated revenues. These include operating expenses, top management compensation, return to shareholders, and the allocation of retained earnings for future projects.

Administrative Fees

There are three problems with fixed fee arrangements that cause them to lose any direct and meaningful relationship to the cost of service that this fee is intended to cover:

1. Instead of creating incentives toward lower costs and better efficiencies, a constant fee rate creates incentives that do the opposite, that is, while the actual costs may be going down, the prices paid remain constant so as to protect GPO earnings from declining.
2. The fee structure generates rewards that further retard the process of innovation and cost efficiencies.
3. It is important to recognize that the administrative fee is not a "free good" delivered by the suppliers. For the seller, it is just another cost of doing business, which must be reflected either directly or indirectly in the price of the product.

In theory, GPOs can earn 3 percent of the value of supplies purchased by the hospitals through contracts negotiated by the GPOs. This is an "administrative fee" levied on the suppliers. However, in practice, GPOs' earnings have generally ranged well above the 3 percent threshold envisioned by Congress. A fixed fee structure based on the total revenue produced creates a strong disincentive for the GPOs to create cost efficiencies, which would reduce their income. Furthermore, the total fee, currently generated by the GPOs, far exceeds the GPO expenses and provides inducements for the GPOs to find ways to inflate their expenses and thus keep a larger part of the excess revenue for themselves. Finally, the supplier paid fee gives the false impression that it is a "free good" provided by the suppliers.

It is well highly impossible to find reliable financial data on any aspect of GPO operations. GPOs are privately owned for-profit organizations. They have no legal obligation to make public this data. GPOs have repeatedly made claims as to the benefits their operations generate for the healthcare industry. These claims, however, have not been supported by any verifiable data.[14] Nevertheless, an effort must be made to generate a reasonable projection of GPO revenues. This is needed for no other reason than to at least challenge the GPO industry into providing reliable financial and thereby become more transparent if they wish to garner public trust and retain regulatory protection.

An extensive inquiry into available information sources yielded only one study conducted by Dr. Hal J. Singer, president of Criterion Economics, LLC. The study entitled "The Budgetary Impact of Eliminating the GPO's Safe Harbor Exemption from the Anti-Kickback Statute of the Social Security Act," was published in June 2006.[15]

Dr. Singer's estimate assumes that 100 percent of the rebates (net of expenses) paid to GPOs by medical suppliers are passed on to member hospitals. He also provides GPOs with another amount in the form of "dividend" or return on investment to the GPOs' owners, that is, shareholders. This is calculated at the rate of 13.5 percent of a GPO's self-reported net expenses. For this exercise, he also assumes that there is no distortion effect of the current regime on the incentive of these GPOs to secure the best prices possible for hospitals.

Dr. Singer's estimate of the resultant savings to member hospitals ranges between $1.3 billion and $4.96 billion. These estimates consider that GPOs have created other ways to enhance their revenues from the suppliers that are in excess of the 3 percent administrative fee recognized under the safe harbor protection. These have been reported in the Government Accountability Office (GAO) findings and discussed in an earlier section of this report.[16] For example, the GAO report (2003) revealed that two out of seven GPOs admitted that the maximum contract administrative fee received from manufacturers in 2002 exceeded the three-percent threshold.[17] The GAO report also found that fee levels for private label products, that is, products sold under a GPO's brand name, were on average five percent higher.[18] For one of the GPOs in the GAO study, the administrative fee for private label products was nearly 18 percent.[19] GPOs are also known to have collected additional fees from suppliers.[20] These include marketing fees, licensing fees, stocking fees, switching fees, and growth fees. It should be noted that the original intent of the administrative fee was to cover the overhead of the GPO contracting functions. It was never intended for other business ventures or overages.[21] And as earlier stated, 2005 HHS OIG reported that six GPOs collected $1.6 billion in excess fees over a three to five-year period.[22]

There are two observations with regard to Dr. Singer's projections, which have the effect of underestimating the financial impact of GPOs' current business model. The first one deals with the operating expenses and the second one pertains to returns on shareholders' equity.

Deductibility of Operating Costs

Dr. Singer has accepted at face value the reasonableness of GPOs' claims of their operating costs. Since we do not have any comparable and verifiable data from various GPOs, there is no easy way to assess the reasonableness of these costs. Therefore, we have devised an alternative approach to measure these expenses.

Premier, the largest GPO in size and market share, has indicated on its Web site that in 2005 its operating expenses were 54.4 percent of its total revenue.[23] However, Premier did not provide any breakdown of these operating expenses. In our opinion, this amount is excessive and needs further justification when viewed in the context of GPOs' primary activities.

The main function for the GPOs is to negotiate and manage contracts with suppliers. GPOs do not undertake any activities that are normal for a business engaged in producing and delivering goods and services. They do not maintain inventories or engage in other aspects of supply chain management. Therefore, GPOs' operating costs are akin to general and administrative expenses in large corporations, where this category generally ranges between 15 and 20 percent. Even if we were to give GPOs extra credit for ancillary services, such as new product evaluation, information management systems, and so on, the total expenses should not exceed beyond 30 percent. One can only speculate on the reasons for such a high level of operating expenses, which may include high level of top management compensation, overstaffing, lobbying. One should also examine the character of ancillary activities, which are used to justify additional GPO expenses, but with no direct bearing on GPOs activities that should be covered by the 3 percent administrative fee. We therefore conclude that the gap between the current expense level of 54.4 percent and our projection of 30 percent legitimately belongs to the GPOs' client hospitals and should be returned to them.

Return on Shareholder Equity

Dr. Singer allows GPOs a rate of return of 13.5 percent of net operating costs. We have already argued these costs to be excessive. In the case of GPOs, the need for having shareholder equity is unnecessary and can only be explained as another way by the GPOs to keep a large portion of GPO income from its principal clients, that is, hospitals, nursing homes, and other healthcare providers, who are the true beneficiaries and entitled to these funds.

GPOs currently generate cash flows—through the levy of administrative fees and other charges on suppliers—that far exceed their operating costs. This fact has been recognized and admitted by the GPOs and well documented in the two HHS OIG audits published in 2005.[24] Furthermore, this revenue stream is predictable, stable, and totally risk free. The primary role of equity capital is to provide a company with "risk bearing" funds or operating funds when a company is unable to borrow short-term funds to cover operating expenses. The need for equity capital emanates from the nature of "risk" that is inherent to a business operation. It is the risk carrying capacity of the capital that determines shareholder expectations of commensurate return. Unlike other for-profit organizations, GPOs have no need to risk their capital and, therefore, do not need capital in the risk taking sense of the word. Given their strong financial position, the GPOs should have no problem in borrowing working capital from financial institutions at prime lending rates.

One possible explanation for GPOs seeking equity is that it allows private owners to earn above-market returns on their capital. The fact that GPOs managers may also be part of the "owner group," this private equity becomes another means for generating additional compensation for the GPO owner-managers.

For these reasons, we conclude that Dr. Singer's estimates are considerably below the level of reasonableness. Based on our analysis of the total revenue generated by the GPOs, their operating margins, and a careful assessment of their expenses, it is estimated that GPOs generate excess annual revenue in the range of $5 billion to $6 billion. These funds legitimately belong to their member hospitals since they are the ones who actually paid for it through higher costs of their supplies purchased under the GPO-negotiated contracts. To these estimates, we must also add further savings that would result from a more competitive environment of GPO operations. GPOs may wish to challenge these estimates with full disclosure and transparency with regard to their revenue and expenses. However, in the absence of such disclosure, our projections—based on sound economic principles are reasonable and defensible. GPOs may challenge the basis of our calculations and magnitude of our estimates.

GPOs have now enjoyed the protection from anti-kickback statute for nearly 20 years and antitrust safety zone for more than 10 years. During this time, GPOs have made strong claims regarding the savings generated by them in terms of lower prices and also by way of sharing their surplus with member hospitals.[25] They have also made dire predictions of financial hardships for the hospitals in the event of any constraints or oversight of their conduct.[26] However, to date GPOs have not provided any objective data to verify these claims. This issue lies at the heart of the controversy as to the proper role of GPOs and the extent to which they have performed this role in a responsible, objectively measurable, and demonstrably accountable manner.

The information provided by GPOs to date consists almost entirely of opinion surveys,[27] which cannot be a substitute for factual information. The only meaningful information about GPOs' financial operations to date was generated by the GAO reports in 2002 and 2003 as well as two HHS OIG audits that were published in 2005.[28] There have also been other investigative stories on other GPO operations that have been reported in the news media.[29] The GAO report found that GPOs' prices were not always lower and were often higher than those paid by hospitals negotiating with vendors directly.[30] The HHS OIG audits found that six GPOs collected $2.3 billion in fees from vendors over a three to five year period. This exceeded their operating expenses by $1.6 billion.[31]

We have already noted that as privately owned for-profit organizations, GPOs are not obligated to make public their financial data, and they have chosen to exercise their prerogative by not disclosing this information. It is, therefore, imperative that GPOs' activities be subjected to scrutiny to ensure that both their revenue generation and disposition functions are transparent and directly related to the interests of their clients, notably the hospitals and their patients. The situation in this context is best described by an industry analyst, Mr. L. J. Everard:

> The time has come to substantiate or refute GPO cost saving claims. If GPOs do produce valid and verifiable cost savings beyond what hospitals could do on their own . . . , then they should be given the full support of the government and the health care community. If, on the other hand, GPOs do not produce such cost savings or did once but not longer do so . . . then their future role in the health care supply chain must be questioned and the government protections afforded to them must be re-evaluated.[32]

CHAPTER 5

GPO Activities, Conflict of Interest, and Their Adverse Consequences for the Healthcare Providers

It should not come as a surprise to most knowledgeable observers that GPOs' operations have been rife with instances of self-enrichment and practices that are contrary to the best interest of their beneficial clients, that is, hospitals, nursing homes, and other healthcare providers. Our discussion in the previous two chapters suggests that market control, protection from antitrust conduct, and lax regulatory oversight have provided GPOs with an irresistible opportunity for self-enrichment with little downside risk. Under normal circumstances, even under oligopolistic conditions, dominant players would have reason to exercise self-restraint to minimize potential threat of prosecution for anticompetitive behavior. However, when oligopolistic market conditions are accompanied by high growth in revenue, and protection from anti-kickback penalties and anticompetitive behavior, the avarice becomes too hard to resist. The GPO industry is a prime example of this phenomenon.

Systemic misconduct on the part of major GPOs became more apparent as a consequence of several media investigations in the early 2000s. This was followed by the 2002 U.S. Senate Hearing before the Subcommittee on Antitrust, Business Rights, and Competition of the Committee on the Judiciary.[1] This period also coincided with the accelerated growth and consolidation in the GPO industry.[2]

In this chapter, we focus on various investigations by government agencies, news media, and private lawsuits that brought to light the nature and scope of GPOs practices that were considered questionable and contrary to the best interest of the GPOs primary beneficiaries, that is, hospitals, nursing homes, and other healthcare providers. It should be noted here that descriptive incidents covered in these reports are by no means exhaustive or all inclusive. As we have stated earlier, the industry's business model and operating practices impose strict control on information disclosure by the GPOs. Furthermore, their contracting partners are also dissuaded from information disclosure for a fear of

a. retaliation from GPOs and loss of future contracts; and,
b. public embarrassment and potential liability given the questionable nature of such transactions to those who were pressured to or willingly cooperated with GPOs.

It is, therefore, safe to assume that the magnitude of these transactions and their adverse financial impact on the healthcare industry would turn out to be quite large when this information becomes publicly available. An encapsulated summary of some of the major instances of GPO misconduct that have become public is provided in table 5.1. Most of these activities fall into two broad categories. These are

i. Anticompetitive Behavior, Discouraging Innovation, and Incurring Higher Cost for the Member Hospitals.

This category includes GPO business practices that negatively impact the efficiency and productivity of the entire healthcare industry. They also undermine the rationale by which GPOs justify their operations, and defend their government-sanctioned fee structure and protection from anticompetitive restraints.

ii. Conflicts of Interest, Nepotism, and Beneficial Business Practices.

This category includes various schemes by which GPOs and their top managers enrich themselves at the expense of their beneficiary clients, that is, hospitals, nursing homes, and other healthcare providers.

Anticompetitive Behavior, Discouraging Innovation, and Incurring Higher Cost for the Member Hospitals

A variety of questionable contracting practices that raise competitive concerns include exclusionary agreements, bundling of companies, bundling of unrelated products, inviting bundled bids, sole- and dual-source committed-volume deals, market share discounts, and tying.

Masimo Corporation

This case was brought to public attention in 2002 by the *New York Times* investigation of GPOs.[3] It dealt with an experimental monitor called "oximeter" that saved a 2-week-old baby's life. Seven years later, and after being recommended by many U.S. hospitals as a promising device for premature infants, the manufacturing company (Masimo Corporation) was unable to sell this device to hospitals because the GPOs had contracts with a competitor for an allegedly similar type of product.[4] The case uncovered a series of practices that

Table 5.1   Instances of GPOs questionable conduct

1. Anticompetitive behavior, discouraging innovation, and incurring higher costs for the member hospitals

Name of the GPO	Name of the Complainant	Details of Alleged Misconduct
Premier	ICU Medical Inc.	ICU Medical Inc. could not sell its Needleless Intravenous system to Premier supplied hospitals because Premier had already signed a $7 Billion seven-year contract with giant Baxter International Inc. for a similar although inferior product.
Premier and Novation	Retractable Technologies Inc. (RTI)	1996—RTI could not sell its products to Novation. The company's VanishPoint devices could not be sold to the hospitals that had a tie up with Premier. RTI sales people were not allowed to make presentations or sales calls to the hospitals affiliated with Premier. Further, doctors and nurses who requested RTI products were pressured to withdraw such requests. RTI filed a civil suit against Premier in 2003 and won $50 million damage award.
Premier	Remel Inc., a Lenexa (Kan.) unit of Sybron International	1997—Remel Inc., a Lenexa (Kan.) unit of Sybron International that makes culture mediums used for identifying various bacteria was dropped by 200 Premier supplied hospitals in favor of Becton Dickinson (BD) even though the food and drug administration admonished the BD's unit for poor quality control.
VHA	Shannon Medical Center	Reported on March 16, 1998—*BusinessWeek*— Shannon Medical Center in San Angelo, Texas stands to lose "incentive payments" of more than $100,000 a year if it fails to buy 95 percent of its products under 13 different VHA contracts.
Novation	Applied Medical Inc.	2000—Applied Medical's bid on a Novation contract for sutures, trocars, and other devices was rejected even though it offered the lowest quote of $150 against $250 offered by Johnson & Johnson. Applied's bid was rejected as it didn't have the rest of the products that Johnson & Johnson and Tyco bundled with the trocars.
Premier	St. Jude Medical	2000–2001—St. Jude Medical was not able to sell its pacemaker to Premier as Premier had contracts with Medtronic and Guidant, competitors of St. Jude Medical.
		Premier organized an expert panel of six cardiologists to evaluate the claim of St. Jude Medical that their pacemaker required less electricity. On September 19, 2000 the panel concluded that the pacemaker from St. Jude Medical indeed required less electricity and ease of use, but Premiers contracting committee, in March 2001, rejected St. Jude's request after concluding that the product's battery did not last significantly longer than the battery of the rivals.

Continued

Table 5.1 Continued

1. Anticompetitive behavior, discouraging innovation, and incurring higher costs for the member hospitals

Name of the GPO	Name of the Complainant	Details of Alleged Misconduct
Novation	Masimo	Masimo was unable to get a contract with Novation until congressional hearing of 2004. However, only few months after signing a contract with Masimo, Novation sent letters to its member hospitals to purchase 75–95 percent of their requirements from Nellcor and the remaining from Masimo.
GPOs in general	Biotronik Inc.	2002—Biotronik Inc. was prevented from fair competition in the U.S. market because of the overwhelming control of the market by the two largest GPOs.
Novation, Premier, VHA and Premier Purchasing Partners L.P.	Rochester Medical Corp. Inc.	2004—Rochester Medical Corp. Inc. sued C. R. Bard Inc, Tyco International Inc., Novation, Premier, VHA, and Premier Purchasing Partners L.P. charging them with anticompetitive practices related to the buying of catheter products that were inferior in quality to Rochester's patented silicone catheter products. Rochester Medical has reached an agreement to dismiss all except Tyco from litigation. Novation awarded Rochester a contract for its urological catheter products and related accessories. Tyco litigation is now scheduled for trial in February 2008.
Novation and BD	Retractable Technologies	2004—Retractable Technologies had filed an antitrust suit saying the BD had shut it out of the hospital market for its products due to illegal manipulation of the hospital-supply market for years. BD agreed to pay $100 million to Retractable Technologies to settle the accusations.
MedAssets— Aspen Healthcare Metrics	Guidant Corp.	2004—Cardiac manufacturer Guidant Corp. has brought legal action against Aspen Healthcare Metrics, a wholly owned subsidiary of MedAssets, a national GPO, for allegedly misusing proprietary pricing information in violation of confidentiality agreements.
Novation	U.S.A., State of Texas, Cynthia Fitzgerald vs. Novation and Affiliated Companies—a whistleblower lawsuit filed in Federal District Court, Dallas, TX on September 23, 2007	Pressing current contractors and potential bidders to make additional payments to Novation that were not specifically related to the contract. These payments were not reported by Novation to its member hospitals. Examples: Johnson & Johnson offer of additional payment to secure IV catheters contract with the GPO.

Table 5.1 Continued

1. Anticompetitive behavior, discouraging innovation, and incurring higher costs for the member hospitals

Name of the GPO	Name of the Complainant	Details of Alleged Misconduct
Novation	U.S.A., State of Texas, Cynthia Fitzgerald vs. Novation and Affiliated Companies—a whistleblower lawsuit filed in Federal District Court, Dallas, TX on September 23, 2007	Companies were given noncompetitive contract as authorized distributors in return for disguised fees and other forms of remunerations. Examples: distribution contracts with Cardinal Health, Inc., Allegiance Corporation, and Owens & Minor, Inc.
Novation	U.S.A., State of Texas, Cynthia Fitzgerald vs. Novation and Affiliated Companies—a whistleblower lawsuit filed in Federal District Court, Dallas, TX on September 23, 2007	Charging additional marketing fees in access to 3 percent on pharmaceutical contracts. Examples: Bedford Laboratories, Dupont Nuclear, Bristol-Myers, and Abbott Laboratories were paying 14–30 percent marketing fees for their contracts with Novation.
Novation	U.S.A., State of Texas, Cynthia Fitzgerald vs. Novation and Affiliated Companies—a whistleblower lawsuit filed in Federal District Court, Dallas, TX on September 23, 2007	Novation awarded Johnson & Johnson a contract for endo-mechanical products. This decision was based not on the quality, but on the higher prices for Johnson & Johnson products. Lower prices would have significantly reduced the marketing fee—calculated as a percentage of sale—that Novation would receive.
Novation	U.S.A., State of Texas, Cynthia Fitzgerald vs. Novation and Affiliated Companies—a whistleblower lawsuit filed in Federal District Court, Dallas, TX on September 23, 2007	Pressing companies to sell products through Novation's private label brand at inflated prices and thus bring more revenues to Novation at the expense of its member hospitals. Example: Novation proposed that RTI change the label to Novation's NOVAPLUS* and sell the tube holders for $1.0 per unit. Novation offered RTI to share the profit from the 270 percent mark-up.

2. Conflict of Interest, Nepotism, and Beneficial Business Relationships

Name of the GPO	Name of the Complainant	Details of Alleged Misconduct
Premier	Horizon Medical Products	1998—Horizon Medical Products offered 500,000 shares and positions on the board along with generous stock options packages to some of Premier's executives as a form of partial compensation for GPO services.

Continued

Table 5.1 Continued

2. Conflict of Interest, Nepotism, and Beneficial Business Relationships

Name of the GPO	Name of the Complainant	Details of Alleged Misconduct
Premier	Horizon Medical Products	1998—Horizon Medical Products offered 500,000 shares and positions on the board along with generous stock options packages to some of Premier's executives as a form of partial compensation for GPO services.
Premier	Norfolk Medical of Skokie, III	In 1996, a Premier official pressured Norfolk to provide company shares to the GPO to secure contracts.
Premier	Masimo	Reported on March 4, 2002—*NY Times*—Masimo could not compete with Mallinckrodt because this company had paid large fees to the Premier. It also helped to finance Premier's private venture-capital fund by contributing $1 million to a Premier research service.
Premier	Medibuy.com	2002—HCA and Premier own a substantial majority of Medibuy.com's stocks. They breached their fiduciary duties to common stock holders and other noncontrolling Medibuy shareholders by refusing to modify the outsourcing agreements for acquisition by Neoforma.
Premier	American Pharmaceutical Partners (APP)	Reported on March 4, 26, 2002—*NY Times*—APP received patronage from premier that helped the company to start and push hospital business with favorable contract agreement. Premier received APP's shares worth of $46 million. Some Premier's executives got APP's options worth millions of dollars.
Premier	Sicor Inc.	Reported on March 26, 2002—NY Times—Sicor Inc. paid American Pharmaceuticals as much as 10 percent of its net sales to Premier hospitals. That relationship ended in litigation that was settled out of court.
Novation	Novation's vendors	Reported on April 27, 2002—NY Times— Novation charges its vendors for required use of Neoforma, an e-commerce company whose largest shareholders are Novation's parent companies VHA and UHC.
VHA Health Foundation (VHAHF)	The Service Employees International Union	2004—VHAHF, a not-for-profit subsidiary of VHA Inc receives all of its support in the form of donations from the same manufacturers that have benefited from sole-source or bundled contracts with Novation. VHAHF spends a small portion of its annual donations on activities that are acceptable under 501 (c) (3) and spends substantial portions of annual contributions back to its owner VHA Inc in management fees, rent, and other miscellaneous and sometimes questionable payments.

Continued

Table 5.1 Continued

2. Conflict of Interest, Nepotism, and Beneficial Business Relationships

Name of the GPO	Name of the Complainant	Details of Alleged Misconduct
Novation	U.S.A., State of Texas, Cynthia Fitzgerald vs. Novation and Affiliated Companies—a whistle-blower lawsuit filed in Federal District Court, Dallas, TX on September 23, 2007	Senior executives from Novation and its affiliated companies owned beneficial interests, received company stocks, board seats, and other financial considerations from many vendor companies, including Johnson & Johnson, Tyco, Sherwood Medical, Kendell Sherwood-Davis & Geck, and Kendell Healthcare Products Company.
Novation	U.S.A., State of Texas, Cynthia Fitzgerald vs. Novation and Affiliated Companies—a whistle-blower lawsuit filed in Federal District Court, Dallas, TX on September 23, 2007	Contracts awarded at noncompetitive prices to Heritage Bag Company because Heritage Bag Company was represented by a former senior executive of one of Novation's affiliated companies.
Novation	U.S.A., State of Texas, Cynthia Fitzgerald vs. Novation and Affiliated Companies—a whistleblower lawsuit filed in Federal District Court, Dallas, TX on September 23, 2007	Novation executives accepted special benefits in terms of travel and entertainment to give preference to companies for contract awards. Examples: Shortly before announcing a bid for NOVAPLUS* exam glove contract, American Health Products—a large manufacturer of medical gloves—hosted a Riverboat recreational cruise on Lake Michigan. Several members of Novation contracting department were present at the cruise. Novation did not inform VHA and UHC, and HPPI members and customers about the role this event played in awarding a contract.

discouraged competition. Two of the largest GPOs, Premier and Novation, were involved. Mr. Joe E. Kiani, Masimo Corporation's CEO, stated before the U.S. Senate Judiciary Subcommittee on Antitrust, Competition Policy and Consumer Rights[5] that his product had been locked out of the market because his main competitor, Nellcor, paid fees to the two national GPOs.[6] Furthermore, both Premier and Novation had awarded sole source contracts to Nellcor. It also appeared that Nellcor was paying additional fees to the GPOs and disguising them as investments in venture capital partnerships or donations for health institutes or foundations.

The evaluation process for Masimo's oximeter by Premier was also riddled with irregularities. After issuing a promising evaluation of the product, Premier declared that the improvements weren't good enough to justify a contract. It also indicated that more study was needed. This study took more than two years and led to a final rejection of the product by Premier. By then Nellcor had come out with its own improved model. Premier also blamed high staff turn-over and Masimo's slow response to inquiries from its panel.[7]

Retractable Technologies, Inc.

Another case of questionable practices threatening competition involved Retractable Technologies, Inc. (RTI) and its pursuit of a contract with Premier and Novation in competition against Becton Dickinson & Company (BD), which is one of the largest suppliers to Premier and Novation. In December 1996, BD signed a 7.5 year multibillion dollar exclusive contract with Premier to supply Premier's member hospitals with needle devices.[8] A month later and after agreeing otherwise, Mr. Douglas Hawthorne, CEO of Presbyterian Hospitals (Dallas), said that there was no way he could buy VanishPoint devices, which was the brand name of automated retraction syringes from RTI. The company accused Novation and Premier of pressuring hospitals not to buy RTI's superior product. Some hospitals publicly confirmed their preference of RTI needle over the one offered via GPO contract, however the contract agreement was limiting their choice of single items. Representatives of the Texas based Shannon Medical Center stated that the hospital would loose more than $100,000 a year if it fails to but 95 percent of its medical supplies through Novation's VHA contract.[9]

RTI's president Thomas Shaw brought this example of GPOs' dealings to the national television. In his interviews with NBC *Nightly News* and CBS *60 Minutes*, Mr. Shaw stated that no-stick VanishPoint syringe can significantly increase the safety of patients and nurses. However, RTI's sales representatives weren't even allowed to make sales calls and demonstrate their products in hospitals affiliated to GPOs, that is, Premier and Novation.[10] Furthermore, doctors and nurses, who requested RTI products, were pressured to withdraw such requests.[11]

In 1998, in a meeting with Novation, a Novation representative proposed to RTI that the company put a private label on RTI's blood collection tube holder, increase the per unit price of 27 cents to $1.00, and split the difference. As it turned out, this was a common practice in the industry.[12] Novation first needed permission from BD, which never happened. The exclusive contracts that Premier and Novation had signed with BD called for tying and bundling products. Furthermore, in 1997, Premier suggested that RTI should have its devices evaluated at a Premier-BD testing facility. Later it was clear that a payment of $1,000,000 to "Premier Innovation Institute" would be necessary to be considered for a contract.[13]

In addition to obscure Innovative Institute donations, Premier was later reported to gain extra revenues through other questionable practices, such as collecting indirect marketing commissions from suppliers by offering special conference registration packages of $25,000 that would allow suppliers to advertise at the meetings and have private dinners with hospital representatives.[14] In 1998, RTI filed a civil antitrust suit against BD, Sherwood (later acquired by Tyco), VHA (Novation), and Premier challenging their contracting practices.[15]

Biotronik

Biotronik is a privately held U.S. company based in Oregon. It manufactures cardiac pacemakers and implantable cardiac defibrillators. Mr. Thomas Brown,

Biotronik's executive vice president, indicated that his company had been excluded from several contracts to supply its products because of its inability to pay extra fees to the GPOs.[16] He also stated in his written statement to the Senate Subcommittee that GPO's contracting decisions were influenced by large suppliers and the amount of money a supplier contract will generate for the GPO.[17] The system of administrative fees, payable by the suppliers, creates a strong incentive for the GPOs to buy large volumes of a particular product that would maximize their fee-generated revenue. This practice also discourages purchases of new and more effective devices that might reduce the GPOs fee-based revenues.

St. Jude Medical

St. Jude Medical is a maker of pacemakers. The company wanted to sell its product to Premier. However, its two main competitors, Medtronic and Guidant, already had contracts with Premier. To help evaluate St. Jude's claims that its technology represented a "breakthrough," Premier formed an expert panel of six cardiologists, including Dr. Anne Curtis of the University of Florida. St. Jude claimed its pacemaker could operate using less electricity, which would mean that the implanted battery would last longer. According to the *New York Times* investigation, on September 19, 2000, the panel concluded: "In light of the increased device longevity and ease of use, the expert panel agreed unanimously that St. Jude's breakthrough claim is substantiated." However, Premier reported to its contracting committee that the experts had found only a "theoretical breakthrough potential" and never mentioned the unanimous expert conclusion. In March 2001, Premier's contracting committee rejected St. Jude's request after concluding that the product's battery did not last significantly longer than the battery of its rivals.[18]

Applied Medical

Applied Medical was founded in 1987 in Orange County, CA. The company designs, develops, manufactures, licenses, markets, and sells specialized devices for cardiovascular, vascular, laparoscopy, urology, and general surgery. In 2000, Applied was invited to bid on a Novation contract for sutures, trocars, and other devices. Applied offered a price of $150 against $250 offered by Johnson & Johnson. Applied's bid was rejected even though it had the best price. It took months to get an audience with Novation to be informed that Applied didn't have the rest of the products that Johnson & Johnson and Tyco bundled with the trocars.[19]

Bunnel Incorporated

Bunnel Inc. had for many years produced a state-of–the-art newborn ventilator that helped in preventing chronic lung disease by delivering very fast and small ventilations breaths. The company, however, was unable to secure a supply contract with a GPO. Subsequently, when the company started work on developing an improved device with better monitoring system, it could not secure venture capital due to the fact that it did not have a contract with any of the GPOs.[20]

Conflicts of Interest, Nepotism, and Beneficial Business Practices

Neoforma

Novation charges its vendors for the required use of Neoforma, an e-commerce company whose largest shareholders are Novation's parent companies, VHA and UHC. Neoforma has lost hundreds of millions of dollars since its inception while adding little value to the member hospitals. It represents yet another layer of administrative costs imposed by GPOs.[21]

American Pharmaceutical Partners

Los Angeles-based American Pharmaceutical Partners (APP) received patronage from Premier, which helped the company to start and push hospital business and become one of Premier's elite "corporate partners" with favorable contract agreement. The price was $46 million of APP's shares given to Premier. One of the Premier's executives, William J. Nydam, received APP's options worth of $1.3 million. Another Premier executive, Mr. Palmer Ford, who worked in the venture capital unit, received an undisclosed number of APP's options for his consulting services.[22] In its response, "Premier officials stated that they did not know until an inquiry by The Times that another of its executives, William J. Nydam, received stock options as a director of a Premier contractor."[23]

Horizon Medical Products

In 1998, Horizon Medical Products (HMP), based in Manchester, GA, offered 500,000 of its shares to Premier as a form of "partial compensation" for the GPO's services. HMP also included some of Premier's executives to its board and offered generous stock options package.[24]

Although all these cases indicate specific issues of conflicts of interest, the primary conflict lies in the core structure of the GPO business model. A fundamental flaw in the government approved administrative fee, or government sanctioned kickback from the suppliers, gives GPOs the exclusive right to collect this fee from the suppliers while hospitals and other healthcare providers are prohibited from doing so. Moreover, this government-provided protection allows GPOs not to disclose financial aspects of their operations and further exacerbates hospitals' trust in the existing system. This lack of transparency, or rather nonexistence of it, puts the hospitals at the mercy of the GPOs and vulnerable to their exploitative practices.

Incurring Higher Costs for Member Hospitals: Failure to Deliver Best Available Products

The sole purpose of the GPOs is to negotiate on behalf of the healthcare providers the best possible prices for the best available medical products. However, even this core principle became questionable in the conduct of the major GPO groups.

General Accounting Office (GAO) Report on GPO Practices

At the request of Senators DeWine and Kohl, GAO conducted a pilot study on the role of large GPOs in the marketplace for medical devices used in hospitals. The GAO study concluded that the price savings have little relationship to the size of the GPO. For example, the two largest GPOs, that is, Novation and Premier, with a combined purchasing volume of approximately $60.0 billion, return only 22–40 percent of the revenues to the member hospitals. Conversely, a smaller group, Consorta, returns approximately 68 percent of its revenue to the hospital members. Dennis Hall, a chief executive of the Baptist health System that buys medical devices via Novation, in the interview to the *New York Times* said: "No, we are not satisfied with the amounts we are receiving."[25]

The findings of the study also indicated that in many cases prices secured through GPOs were higher than prices paid by hospitals directly to the vendors, in certain cases these prices were at least 25 percent higher.[26] This price differentiation became apparent to many hospitals and led them to go it alone by ending their relationships with GPOs. In 2000, Iowa Health System, a 10-bed hospital chain, discovered that by purchasing supplies directly from the manufacturers it saves 12–14 percent and they expect to increase these savings in the future.[27] A New Jersey hospital chain Virtua Health realized that the administrative fee and incentive payments that manufacturers pay to GPOs to secure a contract result in the end in higher prices. The hospital now makes all its purchases directly from the suppliers. The savings arising from direct purchasing are used to increase salaries and benefits to the medical personnel and expand operation facilities.[28]

According to Nicholas Toscano, who overseas purchasing department at Virtua Health, another price benefit of direct purchasing is the flexibility. GPOs' contracts are usually signed with the same supplier for an extended period. By signing shorter contracts Virtua Health can utilize savings from the drop in the prices for some medicine and equipment.[29] Extended contracts with sole-suppliers secured by GPOs not only prevent hospitals to gain extra savings from price fluctuations, but they also limit hospitals' access to the most innovative products available on the market. To secure the lowest price claimed by GPOs, hospitals are forced to purchase specific items in large volumes and/or for longer terms.

GPO representatives claim that they do not restrict hospitals from buying medical supplies elsewhere. However, the hospitals draw a different picture. Healthcare providers are led to believe that standardization of equipment across healthcare system is necessary because it guarantees both the lowest price and the highest quality. Hospitals and physicians are discouraged by GPOs from approaching vendors for in-hospital competitive trials.[30] Mitchell Goldstein, neonatologist from Citrus Valley Medical Center, in his testimony to the Senate Subcommittee described an incident when Utah Medical Product's newborn central line catheters were smuggled into hospitals and kept locked because they are prohibited under the GPO contract.[31]

Industry's Response

In response to the multiple allegations of GPOs' unfair business practices, on April 30, 2002 U.S. Senate Subcommittee on Antitrust, Business Rights, and Competition of the Committee on the Judiciary held a hearing on the issue of GPO business practices. It was the first congressional investigation of GPOs since 1986, when the exemptions from the federal anti-kickback laws were issued.

At this hearing, the CEOs of two largest group purchasing groups, Mark McKenna of Novation and Richard Norling of Premier testified and responded to the accusations of questionable conduct. Both Premier and Novation asserted that their companies did not engage in unfair practices by claiming that they had specific purchasing systems in place that allowed for fair selection of most needed products to be included in the GPO contracts regardless of the supplier's profile. Although both Novation and Premier stated that they procured diversified portfolios of products from multiple sources, they did support standardization to the extend that it simplified usage of medical devices, offered high quality, and ensured safety of patients and medical personnel.

In the specific case of Masimo, Mr. McKenna of Novation indicated that the oximeter was given detailed examination, but the company "did not find it at that time to be new or innovative."[32] Premier's representatives stated that Masimo's oximeter had not been approved by the purchasing group partly due to lack of evidence and objective peer-reviewed studies confirming oximeter's benefits.

When the issue of conflict of interest was discussed, both companies assured the subcommittee that they had detailed codes of conducts and conflict of interest policies in place that they adhere to. While Richard Norling did not deny his company's financial interest in its client companies, and Mark McKenna confirmed his ownership of stocks in the companies with which Novation did business, both CEOs claimed that they adhered to their companies' conflict of interest policies, which they found to be fair and true.

In response to the findings of GAO report, both Mark McKenna and Richard Norling expressed their concerns about the flaws and limitations of the "pilot" study. Both Novation and Premier stated before the subcommittee that their administrative fees did not exceed 3 percent. The companies also stated that besides administrative expenses, cost of equipment, and support of other programs offered by the companies, all remaining revenue funds are returned to the member hospitals.

*Further Investigations by GAO, Federal Trade Commission, and
the U.S. Department of Justice*

At the 2002 hearing, the Subcommittee's Chairman, Senator Herb Kohl (D—Wisconsin) requested that the Federal Trade Commission (FTC) and the Department of Justice (DOJ) start an investigation on GPOs' compliance with the federal antitrust laws. He also asked that GAO continue its examination of the GPOs financial dealings.

The second hearing before the Senate Subcommittee, entitled *Hospital Group Purchasing: Has the Market Became More Open to Competition?* was held on July 16, 2003, about 15 months after the first hearing. At this hearing, the U.S. GAO presented a draft report of its second GPO study "Use of Contracting Processes and Strategies to Award Contracts for Medical-Surgical Products."[33]

GAO examined business practices of seven GPOs, including Premier and Novation, and concluded that most of the GPOs were still utilizing questionable contracting strategies. The report also concluded that, under cover of offering discounts to the hospital members, GPOs limit competition and access to innovative technology. Both GPOs were found to be practicing bundle contracts, which constituted on average 40 percent of their revenues. Premier banned GPO-initiated commitment levels, but high commitment levels on the side of the vendors were still allowed. Novation's policies allowed commitment levels of up to 75 percent.

The GAO's investigation of the seven GPOs' practices found that administrative fees from medical-surgical manufacturers did not exceed 3 percent in 2003. However, this rule did not apply in the case of private label manufacturers, who generally paid 5 percent fee, and in the case of one of the major GPOs, the fee was as high as 18 percent.[34] Said Hilal, President of Applied Medical Resources Corp., claimed that GPOs routinely exceed 3 percent cap on administrative fees by disguising them as other types of payments.[35] In response to GAO report's findings and criticism of suppliers, Jody Hatcher, vice president of Novation, said: "Of course, there will always be some anomalies."[36]

The GAO investigative report as well as witnesses' testimonies showed multiple cases of noncompliance by GPOs with their own codes of conduct. Moreover, despite great fanfare with which the GPOs promoted their voluntary codes of conduct, they have shown little interest in creating measures that would ensure the general public of the true nature of their compliance effort. A good example of this point is California Senator Martha Escutia's proposal for Bill 749. The bill called for an adoption GPOs' code of conduct into legislation. While the bill provisions echo GPOs' own public commitments, Senator Escutia's effort met strong resistance on the part of many GPOs.[37]

Response of the GPO Industry

At the second hearing of the Senate Subcommittee, industry leaders indicated that GPOs had made considerable progress in addressing the issues discussed in the GAO report and also raised by the industry's critics. During his testimony at the first Senate Judiciary Committee's hearing on April 30, 2002,

Richard Norling, Premier's CEO, had promised to personally expedite the process of evaluation of Masimo's product under Premier's breakthrough technology program.[38] In less than six months after the hearing, Masimo was awarded a contract from Premier. RTI settled with Tyco, VHA (Novation), and Premier in 2003 for $55.5 million.[39] Biotronik's products submission was reexamined by Premier's through its new "Breakthrough Technology" program and received unanimous approval by the panel of physicians.[40]

Regarding corporate equity interests, Premier reported that the company sold its stake in American Pharmaceutical, reaping more than $20 million on the stock price increase.[41] Companies were also required to reinforce conflict of interest policies through the revised codes of conduct. Premier also made a commitment to disclose financial and salary information to general public starting September 2003.[42]

While GPOs agreed to tighten conflict of interest policies, the most fundamental issues of limited competition and access to innovative technology remained poorly covered in the GPOs' corporate and industry-wide codes of conduct. Healthcare Industry Group Purchasing Association's (HIGPA) new code of conduct did not provide any requirements for the process of product and vendor selection. Although, Premier's and Novation's codes included provisions on evaluation process and access to breakthrough technology, these provisions were broadly defined, inspirational by nature and limit hospital members' involvement in the selection process. For instance, in respect to clinical preference products, for example, products that healthcare providers identify as preferable for patients' needs, Novation's Operating Principles called for "relevant member councils or task forces to make the determination as to whether a particular product was a clinical preference product."[43] Robert Aromando, Vice President of Marketing at Bracco Diagnostics, company producing diagnostic imaging products used for x-ray and MRI procedures, in his statement before the Senate Committee expressed strong concern that a "council" or a "task force" were able to make an objective and meaningful decision on whether or not an individual healthcare provider's preferences are reasonable.[44] Furthermore, these evaluations could take a long time, for example, up to 18 months, to complete the process and thereby delay their availability to customers.[45]

Premier had previously promised to ban the practice of sole-sourcing with regard to physician preference items. However, according to the GAO investigation, the company continued to rely heavily on this practice. GAO report also found that despite the two companies' commitments and plans to reduce contract terms, their contract lengths generally exceeded 3 years.[46] Moreover, while GPOs codes provide for contract flexibility to meet hospitals' needs for innovative technology, evidence shows that the companies' practices do not follow such commitments.[47]

Safe harbor provisions clearly define the limit of administrative fees to GPOs to be 3 percent. Nevertheless, GPOs were generally blamed for charging fees much higher to the specified limit. Premier's corporate code of conduct provides for strict restrictions of the fees within legally allowed limits.

Novation's code of conduct, however, specifies administrative fee restrictions only on clinical preference items, leaving the door open for generic product contracts. Novation has also been known to fatten its fee structure by requiring vendors to sell their branded products to Novation's own private label brand at high mark ups, to which Novation would add another layer of administrative, marketing, and distribution fees before supplying these products to its member hospitals. Since Novation did not own or outsourced manufacturing to lower costs, the only purpose of this convoluted scheme was to enrich Novation to the detriment of its member hospitals. Industry-wide code of conduct prepared by HIGPA does not provide any specifications in regard to maximum level of fees charged by GPOs.

The government granted safe harbor for the GPO industry has remained the major concern for industry critics. Even after the settlement with Premier, Thomas Shaw, President and CEO of RTI, stated that there was no significant improvement in the GPOs' conduct. "There is no improvement, none." He said, "The only equitable solution would be for the GPOs to stop taking administrative fees from the manufacturers."[48]

GPOs Push and Pull

The period after the Second Congressional hearing can be characterized as a push and pull game between GPOs and the critics of the industry. Although there was growing public concern with the industry practices, the GPOs were primarily focused on shielding their industry from external assaults by making vague promises and broad generalizations about their progress toward reforms. For example, in the summer of 2004, HIGPA submitted comments to the Centers for Medicare and Medicaid Services (CMS) on an interim final rule concerning sales price data. In the comments, HIGPA claimed that GPOs imposed administrative fee does not affect medicine prices and, therefore, should be removed from the calculations of pharmaceutical manufacturers' average sales price.[49]

Many of GPOs practices that were generally believed to be anticompetitive and inefficient in delivering the best available products to the healthcare providers continued to be actively utilized in GPOs' purchasing contracts. According to Novation, hospitals' participation in the group's private label program NOVAPLUS increased 50 percent in the period of 1998–2003 and accounted for $1.5 billion in spending in 2003.[50]

Financial Disclosure

Following the second subcommittee's hearing, Premier disclosed on its Web site information on corporate ownership. While Premier had sold shares of American Pharmaceuticals for nearly $20 billion, it continued to own interest in APP's parent, American Bioscience, which is not publicly traded. Gina Clark, spokesperson for Premier said, "There is a fiscal responsibility we have as a partner, and in [2003], the market has not allowed us to (divest the interest)."[51] In addition to American Bioscience, Premier holds equity in four other vendor companies: Global Healthcare Exchange, provider of medical e-commerce systems; Healthcare Waste Solutions, waste management services company; Amerisource Bergen Corp., nation's largest drug distributor; and LXN, producer of blood glucose monitoring tests. Moreover, the list of companies, in which Premier holds equity interest, also include a number of "potential vendors"—medical companies, which are currently not involved in any business with Premier.[52]

VHA, which belongs to the second largest GPO Novation, also posted corporate financial information on its Web site. The company executives claim that the move was voluntary and not made under the pressure of congressional investigations. The company disclosed its net income, consolidated statements of cash flows, and balance sheets. The company also posted a statement of changes in patrons' and shareholders' equity.[53] However, VHA remained uncertain on whether it would disclose such information. The CEO of the company, Curt Nonomaque, said that VHA is currently reviewing its position on disclosure.[54]

Premier claims that it reports to its 200 shareholders in regard to the executive compensation. However, the company has retreated from its commitment to publicly disclose financial information and executive compensation. The spokesman for the company, Gina Clark, said that this decision was made based on the industry's unwillingness to follow Premier's example. "Because others in our industry are unwilling to make the same level of commitment, we decided that it would be anticompetitive for us to disclose executive (and board) compensation," she told *Modern Healthcare*.[55]

Small Manufacturers Remain Unsatisfied

Despite certain progress in resolving conflicts with GPOs, medical device manufacturers continued to be dissatisfied with the industry's practices. After settling with Tyco, Novation, and Premier, RTI's Vanishpoint syringe was distributed by most major GPOs. Nevertheless, RTI's market share in the market of needle products was minimal and the company continued its aggressive rivalry against unfair competition. Phil Zweig, spokesperson for RTI called Premier's technology breakthrough program nothing more than a "buzz phrase." He said, "They came up with this marketing thing that they are open to new technology, and there is nothing further from the truth."[56] In early February 2004, the U.S. District Court in Texarkana, Texas, held a hearing testimony in the civil trial of a lawsuit by RTI against BD.[57] RTI reached a settlement with BD for $100 million.[58]

Within two years from the settlement with Premier, circumstances again turned against Masimo. Premier had again decided to revert to sole-source contracting, which seriously limited Masimo's ability to sell their products in a competitive environment. Masimo was unable to get a contract with Novation up until summer 2004, when Novation opened up its sole-source contract and awarded a contract to Masimo. Problems followed because Novation sent letters to their member hospitals requiring them to continue to purchase between 75 and 95 percent of their requirements from Nellcor and thus leaving very little opportunity for Masimo to sell its device to the hospitals contracted by Novation.[59] Masimo filed lawsuits against two Tyco affiliates, Tyco Health Care Group, L.P. (manufacturer and distributor of Nellcor brand among others) and Mallinckrodt Inc., for violating antitrust laws.

VHA Health Foundation

In 2004, Service Employees International Union (SEIU) conducted an investigation of the questionable activities of an organization called VHA Health Foundation (VHAHF), which had received sizable donations from Novation's suppliers. In its testimony to the Senate Subcommittee on the impact of hospital GPOs, SEIU cited research that linked the VHAHF with receiving questionable donations from manufacturers affiliated to Novation, including $2.0 million donation from unnamed companies.[60]

VHAHF is a wholly owned Section 501(c)(3) tax-exempt not-for-profit subsidiary of Novation's parent, VHA Inc. (nationwide network of community-owned healthcare systems).[61] It receives nearly all of its support in the form of donations from the same manufacturers that have benefited from sole-source or bundled contracts with Novation. These manufacturers include among others, Abbott Laboratories, Baxter Health, Cardinal Health, Eastman Kodak, Johnson & Johnson, and Standard Textile.

According to IRS filings, VHAHF spends a small portion of its annual donations on activities that are appropriate or acceptable under 501(c)(3).[62] Substantial portions of VHAHF's annual contributions are paid back to its owner VHA Inc, in management fees, rent, and other miscellaneous and sometimes questionable payments.

On September 14, 2004, the SEIU (In an article published on September 27, 2004 in *Modern Healthcare* and titled "Lucrative Liaison? Critics Question VHA Foundation—Novation Connection," Cinda Becker investigated the charge made by the SEIU in the hearing.[63] Critics of the VHAHF contended that the foundation and its grant program was a way to solicit extra cash from vendors that do business with the hospitals' GPO, Novation.[64]

Money for the VHAHF's "Creating Better Health through Innovation" grants came from Novation suppliers. The SEIU had questioned the appropriateness of vendor donations to the foundation. The SEIU was looking into the donations that were redistributed to VHA executives as compensation.[65] However, as mentioned earlier in this section, VHA as well as other industry players, decided not to disclose executives' and board members' compensation. VHA's CFO explained that "we looked at the issue very carefully and the consensus was that there was not a lot to be gained from disclosing salaries."[66]

Federal Investigations and 3rd Congressional Hearing

On September 26, 2003, at the request of the U.S. Senate Judiciary Committee, FTC jointly with the DOJ held a hearing on the subject of GPOs' anticompetitive practices in the national hospital supply market. FTC and DOJ produced in July 2004 a report "Improving Health Care: A Dose of Competition."[67] Among the issues related to patient care, price of drugs, and insurance costs, the report also examined GPOs anticompetitive activities. Specifically, the report discussed the applications of the Health Care Statement 7, which provided government protection and safety zone to GPOs for making purchasing arrangements on behalf of the healthcare providers. Although multiple speakers criticized this safety zone provision at the 2003 FTC/DOJ hearing,[68] the report concluded that Statement 7 "does not preclude Agency action challenging anticompetitive contracting practices—that happens to occur in connection with GPOs."[69] The agencies stated that they would examine, on a case-by-case basis, the facts of any alleged anticompetitive contracting practices to determine whether the practice violates the antitrust laws. This conclusion left critics disappointed and even more eager to push for a new legislation overlooking GPOs' business practices.

Small manufacturers claimed that no significant change was seen in the GPOs conduct. Purchasing groups continued to enroll contracting practices that are believed to be unfair and anticompetitive. Former antitrust attorney for the FTC, David Baldo, stated in his testimony that "the voluntary codes are ambiguous, lack consistency, contain no enforcement mechanisms and don't authorize any organization to police compliance."[70]

A similar view was expressed by the Connecticut Attorney General, Richard Blumenthal. In his testimony, he stated: "The conduct revealed over the last two years calls into question whether some GPOs have at heart the best interests of the constituencies they were formed to serve." He also added that "there is a clear, compelling need for federal regulation of GPOs."[71]

Acceleration of Government Initiated Investigations

Despite the findings of the FTC/DOJ report, more GPO investigations were on the way. Novation was facing most of the troubles. The company received subpoena from U.S. attorney in Dallas to submit some documents. Novation was also under an investigation by Connecticut Attorney General, Richard Blumenthal, who noted that his investigation would be broadened to determine wither GPO purchasing practices defrauded the Medicaid program.

Senate Judiciary Committee shared the concern over the transparency of the revenue distribution and called for investigations to be conducted by the Office of Inspector General (OIG) of the Department of Health and Human Services on the subject of GPOs purchasing revenues and Medicaid cost rebates. The first report by Daniel Levinson released in January 2005 investigated three GPOs and their members. The investigation showed that member hospitals did not always correctly track and record rebates received from the GPOs. In five years, the discrepancies in record keeping accounted for hundreds of millions of dollars.[72]

The second OIG investigation of three additional GPOs was released a few months later. Deputy Inspector General of Audit Services, Joseph Vengrin, reviewed Medicare cost reports of 7 healthcare systems that represented 38 hospitals. The investigation found that one of the healthcare systems did not fully account for net revenue distribution and did not distribute all of the administrative fees to its six member hospitals. The second report reiterated earlier call for better monitoring and clarification of CMS instructions to hospitals.[73]

Small medical manufacturers have continued to criticize GPOs for their snail-like progress toward reform. RTI continues to face problems selling its products. In 2007, RTI again filed a lawsuit against BD claiming that BD had utilized anticompetitive contracts and limited RTI's participation in the medical devices market.[74] Masimo's case was again tried in February 2005; a month later the jury found that four of the five Tyco's practices were certainly anticompetitive and awarded Masimo $140 million in damages that were then tripled to $420 million under a federal antitrust statute.[75] However, almost a year later, on March 2006, Federal District Court Judge Mariana Pfaelzer in district court in Los Angeles, threw out the entire award and ordered a new trial.[76]

Connecticut's Attorney General, Mr. Richard Blumenthal, initiated an investigation of the Healthcare Research and Development Institute (HRDI) as part of a broader investigation of GPOs' practices.[77] HRDI is an arcane for-profit company, which serves as a network of healthcare corporate executives as well as manufacturers and suppliers of medical and healthcare related products. As stated by Connecticut's Attorney General Richard Blumenthal in his testimony before the Senate Subcommittee on March 15, 2006, HRDI dealings are not transparent leading him to believe that the purpose of this organization was to conceal questionable business practices from the public.[78] HRDI's meetings were not open to the general public or to vendors that were not members of the institute. Moreover, the rules of the institute limited membership to only two vendors in any product category.[79]

HRDI ownership structure is another issue of concern. CEOs of major hospitals and healthcare systems, many of whom sit on the boards that control the nation's largest GPOs, own the institute, and 45 or so corporate members apply for membership to HRDI. When accepted, these corporate members pay significant annual dues and extra fees. HRDI asserts that its goal is to get together healthcare executives, manufacturers, and suppliers of healthcare-related goods and services. This networking and idea exchanges would help them in improving the quality of hospitals and healthcare systems.[80] In practice, this turned out to be an indirect source for making large payments to hospital executives with the expectation of gaining additional sales from the hospitals controlled by these executives. Reports indicate that after consulting with a HRDI hospital executive, one of the vendors went from zero to $3.6 million in annual sales.[81] HRDI's vendors were stated to pay $40,000–$50,000 annually for two private consultation sessions with hospitals executives, which were usually held in luxury resorts.[82] The money collected through annual dues were used to pay "honorarium" for their services in the context of HRDI. HRDI Web site is inaccessible to the public.

In January 2007, HRDI agreed to stop selling "consulting advice" to vendors. According to the settlement signed by HRDI and the State Attorneys General in Connecticut and Florida, hospital members are no longer allowed to accept consulting fees, free trips to resorts, and other valuable gifts from suppliers. The settlement also included a $150,000 fine to be paid by HRDI.[83]

CHAPTER 6

Congressional Deliberations of GPO Operations

First Hearing: Hospital Group Purchasing: Lowering Costs at the Expense of Patient Health and Medical Innovations?

On April 30, 2002, the Senate Committee on the Judiciary Subcommittee on Antitrust, Business Rights, and Competition held its first hearing on the topic of Group Purchasing Organizations (GPOs). In his opening remarks Senator Herb Kohl (D-Wisconsin) stated:

> This subcommittee turns its attention to an issue affecting the health and safety of every American who has ever or will ever need treatment at a hospital, in other words, every one of us. This issue is how hospitals form buying groups to purchase nearly everything used by hospitals.... These buying groups, known as group purchasing organizations, or GPOs, are at the nerve center of our health care system. Because they determine what products are in our hospitals, they directly affect patient health and safety. Because they control more than $34 billion in health care purchases, they impact the cost we all pay for our health system. Because they represent more than 75% of the nation's hospital beds, they are a powerful gatekeeper who can cut off competition and squeeze out innovation.[1]

The focus of the first hearing was to discuss and deliberate on the operations and practices of GPOs. Media reports and governmental studies on the operations of GPOs had caused the committee to investigate the purpose of GPOs. The committee's three main concerns as put forth by the Chairman of the Subcommittee Senator Kohl were:

a. How critical health decisions regarding life-saving medical equipment were being influenced by GPOs financial agreements with suppliers.
b. How GPOs dubious contracting practices have stifled competition and innovation and physicians were limited by the availability of medical devices in providing critical care.

c. Findings of a General Accounting Office (GAO) study that reported on how GPO's did not achieve cost savings for hospitals.

Summing up the objective of the hearing, Senator Kohl said:

> Our goal should be to ensure that the GPO system truly achieves cost savings in the cost of medical equipment, and that these savings do not come at the expense of patient health or medical innovation.[2]

Although a majority of the senators sought answers to these concerns, they also saw the hearing as an opportunity to know more about the functioning of GPOs and their value addition to the healthcare industry. Senator Strom Thurmond (R-South Carolina) wanted to understand if the antitrust immunity enjoyed by GPOs reaped benefits for those seeking healthcare and requested the committee to study potential conflicts of interest. The hearing was well-attended with a cross section of representatives from various groups, that is, senior executives of GPOs, hospitals, companies alleging misdeeds by GPOs, academic researchers and industry analysts, and the news media.[3]

Industry's Response

Support for GPOs came mainly from the executives of the GPOs themselves. Mr. Richard A. Norling, Chief Executive Officer of Premier, Inc who spoke for the GPO industry pointed out the benefits of GPOs and Premier's efforts in particular, in improving the healthcare industry. He stated:

> Since being formally recognized by Congress, GPOs have produced tremendous savings for our nation's healthcare system. It has been estimated that GPOs save healthcare institutions between 10 and 15 percent of their non-labor health care costs...
>
> Equally important to the substantial savings are the increases in the quality of care and advances in treatment made possible by GPOs through their clinical improvement initiatives. As Congress and the Department of Health and Human Services have recognized, GPOs help hospitals secure better pricing for high-quality supplies and the most up-to-date technologies they want and need.[4]

Mr. Norling claimed that GPOs achieve savings either by leveraging the combined buying power of hospitals or by using their collective knowledge in selecting suitable products for patients. He recounted how Premier during the last five years of its operations had returned more than 80 percent of excess reserves to its not-for-profit members. He noted that Premier's Technology Assessment Group benefits hospitals by tracking advancements in technology, medical equipment and devices, features, costs and suppliers and keeps its members updated. He also asserted that Premier's contracting process was open to all suppliers and claimed that the company (1) "proactively seek out new technologies; (2) follow up on our members' expressions of interest in emerging products; and (3) respond through our Technology Assessment and Technology

Breakthroughs Programs to requests from manufacturers to consider possible contracting opportunities."[5] Furthermore, Mr. Norling stated that by contracting through GPOs, sellers spend less money on advertising, promotion, and sales of their products.

Finally, in defense of the administrative fees and Premier's policies, he stated: "Our administrative fees, which average 2.1%, fall within the guidelines established by the Department of Health and Human Services to reflect Congress's concern that fees not be excessive. In fact, we currently have no administrative fees over 3% for medical products and pharmaceuticals under group contracts."[6] Moreover, according to Premier's CEO, "hospitals and other healthcare systems—especially those not-for-profit hospitals that are the owners and members of Premier's GPO—continue to operate in a powerful cost squeeze and need the help provided by GPOs in the future even more than they have needed us in the past."[7]

Mr. Norling found a supporter in Mr. Mark McKenna, President, Novation who said: "We actually see ourselves as a champion for the small rural or community hospital that would have a difficult time providing these services on their own. Through our aggregated approach, small rural and community hospitals enjoy the buying strength of large health systems."[8] Mr. McKenna also claimed that by purchasing products through Novation, hospitals not only achieve cost savings but also considerable cost avoidance.

Criticism

Although GPO supporters touted the benefits of GPOs, physicians, companies condemning GPO actions, and venture capitalists described the reality from the other side of the fence. Dr. Mitchell Goldstein, Neonatologist, Citrus Valley Medical Center strongly opposed the practices adopted by the hospitals and GPOs and narrated how patients were deprived of access to the latest technology. Questioning the role of GPOs in patient care he stated: "Group Purchasing Organizations operate in the middle ground selectively contracting with manufacturers and supposedly providing discounted pricing to hospitals. However if the equipment available doesn't provide for the individual needs of the patient, at what price is cost savings achieved?"[9]

Drawing from his personal experience, he recounted how a scientifically proven medically advanced product was substituted for a less superior technology because of a GPO mandated contract and thereby affecting patient care. Critical of the process that physicians had no say in selecting appropriate medical devices for their patients, Dr. Goldstein stated: "Physicians are discouraged from 'officially' approaching the vendor for in-hospital competitive trials. Hospitals are falsely led to believe that they can rely on a consistent pricing schedule offered through the GPOs to meet physician expectations for choice and quality. Hospital costs can increase secondary to related complications, and again patient care suffers."[10]

Mr. Joe Kiani, President and CEO, Masimo Corporation described in his testimony how his company was victimized and excluded from the market by the two largest GPOs. Criticizing claims that GPOs save money for hospitals he stated:

> The title of this hearing is interesting. "Hospital Group Purchasing: Lowering Costs at the expense of Patient Health and Medical Improvements." This title assumes that GPOs are saving hospitals money. In many instances, the two biggest GPOs are eliminating competition, so it is hard to understand how they can be saving money. To exclude competition, the two biggest GPOs (Premier and Novation) who control over 70% of the nations hospital purchases have discovered how to use the kickbacks to work with the powerful companies to shut out their competitors. Their strategies maximize both the GPOs and their largest suppliers mutual revenues, at the expense of other vendors, hospitals, patients, and payers.[11]

According to Mr. Kiani economic penalties, threats of expulsion, bundling of products, and discount rebate schemes were some of the anticompetitive measures used by Premier and Novation. He went on to state: "Benefits are today being denied as a result of the distorting effect of kickbacks, sole source contracting and bundling and other anti-competitive practices that would be illegal if Congress had not legalized kick-backs in 1986 for the GPO industry."[12]

Ms. Elizabeth A. Weatherman, Managing Director, Warburg Pincus, LLC who represented the venture capitalist community stated that the anticompetitive practices of GPOs would discourage venture capitalists from funding scientific and medical projects since the risks were not matched by returns. "GPO practices such as contract exclusivity, substantial fee structures, and product bundling, if allowed to continue, will so constrict potential markets that product segments where these practices are widely adopted will simply not be considered for venture capital backing."[13] Stating that the anticompetitive practices and collusive tactics of GPOs cannot be justified, she expressed surprise that the government was tolerant with such malpractices in medical sector. She also questioned the assertion that GPOs save money for the hospitals. "The idea that the GPOs 'save' money for hospitals by extracting larger price discounts from producers than they could achieve by themselves is unprovable and most likely wrong—unprovable because no one knows what the 'real' market price would be in a truly competitive market among producers (in the absence of GPO gatekeeping)."[14]

Senator Kohl condemned reports of financial allegations and conflicts of interest, which claimed that the chief executive at Premier had received financial compensation in return for awarding contracts to a pharmaceutical company and urged the GPOs to "clean up its own house."

> Practices such as sole sourcing, high commitment levels—requiring a hospital to purchase as much as 90% of a product from one company in order to get the maximum discount—and bundling—giving hospitals extra discounts and bonuses for buying a group of products—can seriously damage the ability of doctors to choose the best products for their patients and for competitive manufacturers to survive and innovate . . . These practices are appalling and cannot be

tolerated. We cannot accept a situation where a decision on which medical device will be used to treat a critically ill patient could conceivably or even theoretically turn on the stock holdings of a GPO executive.[15]

Similar sentiments were expressed by Senator Orrin G. Hatch (R-Utah) and Senator Strom Thurmond (R-South Carolina) who condemned the actions of GPOs. Senators Hatch and Thurmond criticized how monopsonists Premier and Novation, the two largest GPOs, have the highest market share while others trail behind raising concerns. They stated that as a result of industry consolidation Premier and Novation control purchasing for 60 percent of the country's hospitals and this along with their dubious practices was a warning sign. Speaking for the small device manufacturers that had complained of GPOs' predatory tactics, Senator Hatch said, "Allegations that large suppliers have effectively 'bought' access to GPOs warrant further investigation to ascertain how widespread such activities are. Similarly worrisome are assertions that the products of favored suppliers are included in 'bundled' or 'sole source' contracts that create strong disincentives for hospitals to purchase competing products, effectively shutting smaller competitors out of the market."[16] Senator Kohl and Senator Patrick Leahy (D-Vermont) referred to the finding of the GAO report and expressed skepticism about GPOs' claims of saving money for hospitals.

Recommendations

Senator Kohl directed the GPO industry to work with the committee and draw up its own code of conduct addressing the ethical conflicts and contracting practices. His call was supported by Senator Schumer who expressed happiness that the GPO industry was on the path to self-reform and was willing to work under limited government intervention. Mr. Kiani proposed a list of solutions to eliminate conflict of interests that arise during GPO contracting processes.

- Repeal the anti-kickback exclusion for GPOs and do not let them be paid by the suppliers/vendors, when they are supposed to be representing the hospital members. The member hospitals should pay the fees directly and insure the loyalty of their group purchasing organizations.
- Eliminate sole-source and other committed volume contracts. Each hospital should have the ability to commit to any product it wants without facing bundling schemes designed to prevent their choice.
- Eliminate all product bundling so that clinicians are able to select products based on their individual merits.[17]

Requesting the subcommittee to scrutinize the antitrust immunity and anti-kickback exception that GPOs enjoy, Senator Thurmond stated: "We should not support policies that inhibit the abilities of smaller manufacturers to introduce innovative products into the marketplace. If patients are not benefitting from current practices, we should seek to implement reforms that free the marketplace to function unhindered by anti-competitive practices."[18] A similar demand was made by Ms. Weatherman who came out strongly in favor of legislation and stated that the special exemptions enjoyed by GPOs under the antitrust laws should be examined.

Senator Kohl was quick to issue warning bells stating that any delayed or ineffective self-regulation by the GPOs would draw congressional action. In view of the committee members requests to examine the immunity GPOs enjoy under antitrust laws, Senator Kohl claimed that Senator Mike DeWine (R-Ohio) and himself had written to the Department of Justice (DOJ) and Federal Trade Commission (FTC) to reconsider the rules that safeguarded GPOs from antitrust scrutiny.

Second Hearing: Hospital Group Purchasing: Has the Market Become More Open to Competition?

The Senate Subcommittee on Antitrust, Competition Policy, and Consumer Rights held its second hearing on July 16, 2003 to revisit the issue of GPO. The second hearing was called after an elapsed time period of 15 months since the first hearing.

In his opening statement, Subcommittee's Chairman, Senator Mike DeWine (R-Ohio) briefly reviewed the deliberations of the first hearing, which had revealed a number of instances that pointed to conflict of interest, self-dealing, anticompetitive behavior, impeding the flow of new technologies, and financial enrichment, among others, on the part of GPOs management. He also indicated that mostly these "concerns were aimed at Premier and Novation; the nations two leading GPOs."[19] In the wake of the testimony provided at the first hearing by various witnesses, both Senator DeWine and Senator Herb Kohl (D-Wisconsin) urged the GPO industry to adopt voluntary codes of conduct to address the concerns that were identified by the subcommittee's investigation.

The first hearing before the subcommittee called for GPOs' creation of codes of business conduct that would address the three major areas discussed at the hearing: (1) ensure that conflicts of interest do not exist, (2) ensure that contracting processes do not reduce competition and access to new technology, and (3) purchasing organizations guarantee best products at the best available price. In particular, the codes had to address five specific issues that raised concerns of unfair dealings:

1. corporate equity interests,
2. sole-sourcing,
3. high commitment level from hospitals (up to 95 percent of all products) to purchase through GPOs to receive discounts,
4. discounts for bundle of products purchased through a single contracts, and
5. administrative fees in excess of 3 percent.

The industry had indeed responded positively to the subcommittee's call for action and "after a great deal of work with the Subcommittee adopted codes of conduct reflecting a series of commitments regarding their ethical standards and their business practices"[20] In addition to fulfilling its main purpose of reviewing the codes of conduct created by GPOs, the second hearing also witnessed the presentation of the GAO report on the contracting practices and strategies used by GPOs in awarding medical contracts.

Summing up the objective of the hearing, Senator Kohl said "Today, we ask two questions. What progress has been made in the marketplace since Premier and Novation made their agreements nearly a year ago? And what remains to be accomplished?" The hearing was well represented by members from interested parties, that is, senior executives of GPOs, medical device manufacturers, hospital purchasing consultants, hospital suppliers, and venture capitalists.[21]

Industry Response

In response to the committee's call to self-reform, most of the GPOs created/revised their corporate codes of business conduct to address issues noted in the first hearing: conflict of interests, sole-sourcing, commitment levels, bundling, and administrative fees. The subcommittee specifically examined three codes: HIGPA, Premier, and Novation.

HIGPA

In July 30, 2002, Health Industry Group Purchasing Association (HIGPA), a trade group for group purchasing companies, announced its code of conduct that was later accepted by many industry players in lieu of their individual codes. The code addressed issues discussed at the First Senate Hearing, that is, conflict of interest provisions, vendor selection, product evaluation, purchasing system, and compliance.

Premier

In response to pressure and requirements of the U.S. Senate Judiciary Committee, the Board Audit Committee and CEO of Premier, Inc. decided to commission a study of the GPO industry and recommend the best practices to be adopted by the company. In March 2002, Premier engaged Prof. Kirk O. Hanson, executive director of the Markkula Center for Applied Ethics at Santa Clara University, to carry out the necessary inquiries and prepare the final report, which was released in October 2002. A detailed analysis of Prof. Hanson's report appears in chapter 8.

The draft report presented to the reviewing committee in June 2002 provided a set of 50 recommendations for the best practices in the GPO industry. All but one—dealing with the executive compensation disclosure—of the recommendations were accepted by the Audit Committee. These recommendations along with "Additional Commitments" set by Primer's executives laid the foundation for the company's code of conduct, which was announced in early August 2002.

Novation

On August 8, 2002 Novation submitted for the review of the subcommittee its new Operating Principles. The principles were designed based on the existing corporate code of conduct and conflict of interest policy. The company also worked together with HIGPA to ensure its compliance with the industry standards.

Critics of the industry recognized the companies' efforts in creating codes of conduct as an important first step in ensuring responsible business practices. They also pointed out that the codes in their current form had multiple deficiencies. Senator DeWine went on to say that while he gave credit to Premier and Novation for implementing some needed reforms, the overall assessment suggested a great deal more needed to be done before one could really say that industry's overall conduct had significantly changed.

Mr. Mark McKenna, President, Novation stated that the company in response to the committee's call had adopted a set of operating principles calling for change in seven core areas: innovative technology; sole, dual, and multi-source contracts; commitment levels; contract terms; private label contracting; vendor fees; and, code of conduct and compliance. He also emphasized that these principles were drawn in consultation with the Subcommittee and reaffirmed his company's commitment to further reforms.

It should be noted here that Mr. McKenna's public pronouncements of progress were not matched by the company's activities in the field. The details of the company's alleged sins of omission and commission were revealed in a recent whistleblower's lawsuit and are discussed in the epilogue of this book.

Mr. Richard A. Norling, Chairman and CEO, Premier Inc. announced to the subcommittee that the company had fulfilled its commitment by supporting the creation of the industry-wide HIGPA code and by implementing the 13 principles it created in August 2002. He stated:

> We at Premier have rolled-up our sleeves and plunged into the job of creating a set of practices and principles that will ensure the highest standards of ethical conduct. We made a strong commitment to set the pace of leadership for our industry. We lived up to that commitment by adopting the tough, comprehensive principles embodied in the Industry Code, the Premier additional principles, and the recommendations included in the Hanson report.[22]

Criticism

Recounting how the GPOs self-policing "Code of Conduct" act was brought about by the *New York Times* series of articles on GPOs[23] and the investigation by the U. S. Senate Committee on Antitrust, Competition Policy, and Consumer Rights, Mr. Thomas Brown, Executive Vice President, Biotronik, Inc. said: "These so-called 'Codes of Conduct' were to be established to (1) insure conflicts of interest do not exist, (2) insure contracting practices do not reduce or stymie competition or innovation in health care or narrow the ability of the physician to choose the best treatment for their patients, and

(3) insure health care cost is being reduced by securing the best prices through volume purchases."[24]

Mr. Brown claimed that areas of concern continue to exist. He believed that GPOs' administrative fees policies and practices act as effective barrier to entry for small companies that intend to penetrate the market. He proposed an alternative approach whereby GPOs' revenue should come from a fee paid by the member hospitals. The hospital would also share with GPOs by returning to them some portion of the savings realized by the member hospital through GPOs contracting operations.[25]

Mr. Said Hilal, President and Chief Executive Officer, Applied Medical Resources Corporation, could not be more skeptical of GPOs' assertions of creating benefits for the member hospitals and called Novation and Premier initiatives in response to the Senate hearings to be "temporary eye wash." He stated:

> If GPOs were fulfilling their original purpose—enabling hospitals to acquire the best products at the lowest cost—there would be no need for these hearings. Unfortunately, GPOs have mutated from their intended role as collective bargaining purchasing agents, acting on behalf of member hospitals, into sales agents protecting the interest of a select group of large and dominant multi-product suppliers of medical devices. This mutation is the product of incentives built into the current business relationships between GPOs and those dominant suppliers.[26]

Mr. Hilal explained that threats of economic sanctions, bundling practices, and GPO connections prevented hospitals from switching to Applied's products even though they were stated to be superior compared to other suppliers. GPOs used several methods like "bundling of unrelated products; sole-source contracting; high minimum purchase requirements to obtain discounts; prohibition of evaluations of competitive products; delayed payment of incentives; and forfeiture of rebates for being 'out of compliance' with the GPO contract"[27] to thwart new players. Mr. Hilal claimed that the actual market price of products sold to GPO members was comparatively lower than the inflated prices of products offered under GPO contracts.

Ms. Elizabeth Weatherman, Vice Chairman, National Venture Capital Association expressed concern that the voluntary codes of conduct adopted by GPOs were not adequate and may lose sheen in the absence of the committees supervision. She said,

> The GPOs may appear to be adhering to the "letter" of your April 2002 request, but we fear that the "spirit" is still lacking in some.... Unfortunately, from our perspective, the concept of "standard practices" allows too much latitude for interpretation by individual GPOs—many of whom have not impressed us in the past with their ability to police themselves.[28]

Contrary to Mr. McKenna's claims that Novation on 10 occasions had awarded dual or multisource contracts for clinical preference products, Senator Kohl stated that one-third of Novation's contracts for clinical preference products were still sole-sourced. Though Mr. Norling stated in his testimony that Premier had eliminated bundling the GAO report asserted that most GPOs use bundling and in one of the two largest GPOs product bundling contributes 40 percent of its revenue.

Recommendations

Most of the industry critics urged the subcommittee not to be influenced by the GPO promises of reform and instead called on the subcommittee to enact legislation that would bring about a permanent change. Mr. Hilal called on the subcommittee to exercise its power and responsibility to encourage anti-trust enforcement officials at the FTC and the DOJ to enforce laws to curb the actions of GPOs. Ms. Weatherman recommended the creation and enforcement of a comprehensive code of conduct in the GPO industry. She also stated that clear benchmarks were needed to measure the performance of the code.

Third Hearing: Hospital Group Purchasing: How to Maintain Innovation and Cost Savings?

The battle between antagonists and protagonists of GPO industry regulations continued at the third hearing before the Subcommittee on Antitrust, Business Rights, and Competition of the Committee on the Judiciary. The third hearing scheduled testimony from three witnesses. Two testimonies—one by David Balto, former FTC antitrust enforcer, and the second one by Joe Kiani, CEO of Masimo Corporation—representing views that were critical of the GPO practices. The third testimony was by Robert Betz, president and CEO of HIGPA, who presented the views of the GPO industry.

After two congressional hearing and two GAO investigations, the subcommittee was still unsatisfied with the progress made by the GPO industry. Senators DeWine and Kohl acknowledged progress made by GPOs in ensuring fair business conduct, but expressed their concern over the successful implementation of the codes provisions on the part of the GPOs in the future. "How can we be certain that these considerable gains will remain when the spotlight of a Senate hearing room fades away?" Senator Kohl said.[29]

The purpose of the hearing, according to the Senator DeWine, was to "decide if we can trust that the current reforms are sufficient, or if not, what pathways we can take to ensure that the current reforms are actively implemented and, in fact, long-lasting."[30] Senator DeWine concluded that there were three possible paths for the future: maintain industry's status quo, introduce new regulations, or proceed with industry self-regulation programs.[31]

As a result, the third GPO-related meeting of the subcommittee introduced a bill proposal that would end immunity of the GPOs from anti-kickback laws. The bill entitled Medical Device Competition Act of 2004 (S.2880) would allow limited cash payments to GPOs but would also give an authority to the federal Department of Health and Human Services to monitor such payments and require annual certification of all purchasing agents.[32]

Joe Kiani of Masimo Corporation told the subcommittee that over the last two years his hopes for improving GPO industry by introducing self-regulation mechanisms remained unrealized. He stated that large GPOs continued to engage anticompetitive practices of sole-sourcing and product bundling. He called for a legislation that would bring necessary oversight and open GPO market for fair competition.[33]

Mr. Kiani's view was supported by Mr. Balto, who claimed that while being on a neutral territory, that is, not representing either GPOs or small manufacturers, he commended for government regulations. Mr. Balto stated that at the time safe harbor provisions were granted, the problems in group purchasing industry were far less significant. But the problems grew over the recent years into a "serious gap" in addressing GPOs' anticompetitive behavior. The former antitrust lawyer spoke well of GPOs efforts in self-regulation. However, he also stated that, in his mind, these efforts will fail because they don't have "teeth." In his opinion, existing self-regulatory principles would fail for four main reasons:

1. Lack of clear and unambiguous rules.
2. Lack of any enforcement mechanisms.
3. Lack of penalties for noncompliance.
4. Lack of due diligence and transparency.

In regard to the issue of possible increase in healthcare costs and prices, Mr. Balto asserted the subcommittee that years of anticompetitive investigations had taught him that elimination of barriers to competition always brings greatest and long-lasting benefits in the form of innovation and lower competitive prices.[34]

On behalf of the industry, Dr. Robert Betz, assured the subcommittee—without offering justifiable proof—that GPOs continue to offer hospitals valuable services. He referred to the conclusion of the FTC/DOJ report that the industry does not need any additional regulations.[35] Dr. Betz stated in his testimony that FTC currently had adequate enforcement capabilities to address any cases of anticompetitive and illegal conduct. He noted, however, that all GPO members of HIGPA were in compliance with the industry code. In addition, several important steps had been taken by HIGPA to ensure GPOs' compliance with codes of conduct. However, in response to Senator Kohl's question, Dr. Betz also conceded that in case of noncompliance, GPOs could continue to do business, but would have to deal with significant market burdens by loosing membership in the trade association. This last statement was met with skepticism by Masimo's CEO, who pointed out that some large GPOs were not members of HIGPA, but nevertheless maintained their strong positions in the industry. He provided an example of HealthTrust that chose not to join HIGPA, but kept a leading position in the industry.

Fourth Hearing: Hospital Group Purchasing:
Are the Industry's Reforms Sufficient to Ensure Competition?

The third hearing did not resolve the problems of GPO conduct. However, under the threat of possible legislative reform, largest GPOs consolidated their efforts in building an alternative to the proposed regulation in a form of self-regulatory industry-wide code of conduct called Healthcare Group Purchasing Industry Initiative (HGPII). The effectiveness of the Initiative in regulating GPOs conduct was discussed at the fourth and the last hearing before the U.S. Senate Committee on the Judiciary held on March 15, 2006.

The fourth hearing set its focus on two issues:

1. The subcommittee proposed to examine three measures that might be considered toward reforming the conduct of Healthcare Group Purchasing Industry. These are "the Proposal for Enacting the Hospital Group Purchasing Organization Reform Act," "S.2880—Medical Device Competition Act 2004 (Introduced in Senate) 108th Congress, 2nd Session," and "Ensuring Competition in Hospital Purchasing Act."[36]
2. The subcommittee wished to discuss the GPO industry's new code of conduct called HGPII, and critically examine its scope, implementation procedures, and likelihood of success, both as proclaimed by the industry and also as viewed by the industry critics.

The three measures proposed by the subcommittee are analyzed in chapter 7. Our assessment of the HGPII is presented in chapters 8, 9, and 10.

Congressional Drive toward Regulatory Reform

The fourth hearing of the U.S. Senate Judiciary Subcommittee on Antitrust, Competition, Policy and Consumer Rights culminated in a discussion of the Healthcare Group Purchasing Industry Initiative (HGPII) both as to its then current status and future prospects. At the same time, the subcommittee proposed three measures as possible avenues for reform of the GPO operations. In this chapter, we provide a brief discussion of these proposals and our analysis of their potential impact on the GPO industry.[1]

It should be noted here that none of these bills came up for vote for lack of political will and also in the face of strong opposition from the GPO industry and its allies. Nevertheless, it is important that we analyze these proposals in the context of how they might impact the GPO-related issues in the future should the current approach, that is, the HGPII falls short of meeting its intended objective as delineated in the three hearings.

S.2880: Medical Device Competition Act of 2004

The bill called upon the Secretary of Health and Human Services, in consultation with the Attorney General and Federal Trade Commission (FTC), to establish procedures for annually certifying that GPOs are in compliance with the requirements promulgated in the bill (appendix 7.1). The rationale for the bill was

i. The compelling public policy goals of
   1. encouraging competition and innovation in the hospital supply and medical device markets, and
   2. reducing the cost of health care as a result of aggregating buying power;
ii. the potentially detrimental impact of certain anticompetitive contracting practices; and

iii the need to avoid conflicts of interests and other unethical practices by GPOs (appendix 7.3).

Analysis

There are a number of practical issues in S.2880 that would seriously undermine its effectiveness in achieving its intended goals, that is, to improve the competitive environment in which GPOs operate. It is unlikely that it would have the necessary "reform" effect on GPOs' current business practices.

The regulatory enforcement of this bill would be highly adversarial. The organizations to be regulated, that is, GPOs, would have a strong financial incentive to prolong and even scuttle all enforcement efforts because every delay and dilution translates into substantial financial gains. An adversarial regulatory environment would require substantial commitment of financial and professional resources on the part of the regulatory authorities. S.2880 does not provide any additional resources to the Department of Health and Human Services (DHHS). Nor does it make any specific regulatory demands to be implemented by the DHHS. Therefore, implementation of these regulations would be highly vulnerable to DHHS's own changing priorities and to the changing political climate in Washington. Thus while the GPOs' current practices will continue, their effective regulation could not be ensured even with the passage of this S.2880.

The current effort at regulating GPOs is vulnerable to unequal financial, political, and organizational leverage. GPOs, who are the primary beneficiaries of the status quo, are a highly focused, amply financed, and well-organized industry. It could and certainly would mobilize significant financial resources to dilute and delay effective enforcement of S.2880. If this bill is enacted into law in 2006, GPOs would have two years to continue business as usual and also devise other ways, which would allow them to maintain their stranglehold on the purchasing process, without violating this law. Moreover, these groups have the will and the means to persist in their efforts over a long period of time.

Conversely, the groups that stand to gain from a strong and effective regulatory oversight are widely dispersed and not as well organized. They include, among others, smaller hospitals, nursing homes, other healthcare providers, the vast patient population, and ultimately the American public. In their current mode, they lack adequate financial and informational resources, effective organizational mechanisms, and political muscle with which to counterbalance the potential power and influence of GPOs.

Another problem with S.2880 is that it is nonspecific as to what constitutes "reasonable costs." This issue is left to future rulemaking by the DHHS. The regulatory history of the FTC, Consumer Product Safety Commission (CPSC), and other similar bodies is replete with instances where larger companies would dump truckloads of documents asserting that this information supported the companies' position while fully knowing that FTC or CPSC did not have the resources to evaluate and analyze those documents. This situation invariably leads to a settlement in terms that are at best face-saving on the part of the regulators without necessarily bringing about significant changes in the conduct of the companies' conduct.[2]

Adequate enforcement requires sufficient staff and financial resources, which are not always available given our history of budget tightening in the arena of health and human services. There would always be pressure to cut back in one area to meet other "more important" priorities.[3] It should be apparent that GPOs would have every incentive in the world to overplay the so-called unnecessary cost of this regulation.[4]

Hospital Group Purchasing Organization Reform Act

This bill was intended to amend title XI of the Social Security Act to ensure full and free competition in the medical device and hospital supply industries (appendix 7.2). This proposal has two components.

The first one pertains to the establishment of a Hospital Group Purchasing Organizations Ethics and Business Practices Compliance Office (hereinafter called the Office) in the DHHS. This Office would monitor and ensure compliance-related activities of hospital group purchasing organizations that meet certain minimum criteria as to their size and scope and would be covered under the proposed act.

The second component, which would be the main activity of the Office, pertains to the certification by the Office to the effect that the covered GPOs have complied with the industry's code of conduct. The act and the Office also stipulate as to the major components of such a code of conduct and the manner in which the covered organizations (GPOs) would comport themselves in their compliance with the industry's code of conduct.

Analysis

This proposed act provides only a broad framework for creating a code of conduct for the GPO industry. However, it leaves the entire process of code creation, implementation, monitoring, and compliance assurance to "self-regulation" on the part of the GPOs. This is an unrealistic assumption given the fact that GPOs are adamantly opposed to any code of conduct that goes beyond generalities as to standards of performance and does not have meaningful assurance of compliance with code standards no matter how ambiguous and vague they might be. In the absence of compliance standards that are outcome-oriented and not merely process-oriented, and a compliance verification system that is independently monitored and certified, the proposed act would fail to achieve any of its intended objectives. Instead, it would result in negating any potential benefits that might come from the establishment of the Office and its certification of GPOs.

The conditions outlined in the act for the GPOs' code of conduct do not mention any requirements for creating standards that would specify minimum levels of compliance. The act also does not specify activities that would be strictly proscribed. There are no provisions in the act requiring that a GPO would be legally liable, and subject to civil and even criminal penalties, for making false and inaccurate claims as to its performance under the code.

The establishment of this Office is quite important in that it would create a venue for highlighting the problems associated with the current modus operandi of the GPOs and their new Initiative. It would also provide a forum where GPO activities and performance can be presented with some external assurance as to their accuracy and transparency. This would allow those groups and individuals—who are adversely affected by the activities of GPOs—to have a venue for airing their complaints and seek redress. As such, it should serve as a first line of "preventive" deterrence.

The quality of regulation is greatly influenced by (a) the willingness to cooperate on the part of those who are to be regulated; (b) the quality and accuracy of the information provided to the regulators by the organizations that are to be regulated, and their willingness to do so; and (c) the resources—financial and professional—available to the regulators to perform their duties under the proposed act.

Furthermore, to be effective, an industry code of conduct must also have a governance process that is independent of the GPOs whose activities it is supposed to monitor and verify. It would also be beneficial to separate the primary activities of GPOs, that is, manage negotiations of group purchasing contracts with suppliers, from the role of collecting and disbursing the proceeds of administrative fee received from the suppliers.

An industry code of conduct must have significant representation in its governance and oversight structure from the beneficiaries of the group purchasing system, in whose sole interest the GPOs are supposed to operate. Otherwise, the code content and its implementation would be reduced to the self-serving claims by the GPOs.

An effective measure to overcome this situation would be to treat the official reports by the GPOs as "implied contract"[5] and thus any false claims made in these reports would be subject to legal proceedings and penalties. The new act should specifically allow private action by injured parties against GPOs where their reports based on the self-evaluation of compliance with the industry's code of conduct would be considered factual statements of the GPOs activities.[6]

Ensuring Competition in Hospital Purchasing Act

The objective of this bill was "to repeal a safe harbor with respect to vendors in order to ensure full and free competition in the medical device and hospital supply industries."[7] In our view, this is perhaps the most significant and effective action that the Congress can take to bring greater efficiency, reduced costs, and increased transparency in an otherwise opaque area of costs-benefits related to the operations of GPOs, hospitals, nursing homes, and other healthcare providers (appendix 7.3).

Analysis

For obvious reasons, GPOs are adamantly opposed to the elimination of the safe harbor provision. Because of the enormous amount of money involved, even a small reduction in the GPO costs would yield substantial benefits to the healthcare providers that are covered by the GPO-contracted and managed purchasing programs. In defending their role and justifying their modus operandi, GPOs make a variety of unsubstantiated and unverifiable assertions concerning the savings they achieve and pass on to hospitals, nursing homes, and other healthcare providers.[8] They also make claims for their economic efficiencies in negotiating lower prices from their suppliers, which are then passed on to the GPOs' beneficial owners. They further raise the specter of hospitals being deprived of savings and surpluses distributed by the GPOs in the event that the safe harbor is repealed and the administrative fee is phased out.[9] The impression invariably created but never supported with data and facts from the GPOs is that the repeal of safe harbor would amount to financial catastrophe for a large number of hospitals, nursing homes, and other healthcare providers.

It is worth repeating that there are good reasons for the hospitals, nursing homes, and other healthcare providers to combine their purchases and thereby leverage their buying power to negotiate lower prices and volume discounts. However, the benefits of combined purchasing power are considerably reduced because of the middleman, that is, GPOs, control the entire process through restrictive arrangements with suppliers and customers. These arrangements allow the GPOs to capture a large portion of the gains from the group purchasing activities. These excessive agency costs, that is, compensation for the GPOs, are further facilitated through GPOs' control of all relevant financial information; and, where the governance and accountability structure of these activities is largely, if not entirely, controlled by the GPO management.

The current business model provides the GPOs with the most opportunity and also the maximum incentive to structure their operations in a manner that would maximize their income and management rewards. Under these circumstances, seeking lower prices from the suppliers takes a back seat to higher returns generated by products that maximize revenue for GPOs through administrative fee and other direct and indirect payments. An illustrative example of the variety of ways by which GPOs can enrich themselves, and to the detriment of their intended beneficiaries can be found in a recently filed whistleblower's lawsuit against Novation. Details of this lawsuit are provided in the epilogue of the book.

The current system of administrative fee has no relation to the cost of running GPO operations. Nor is it related to the efficiency and cost of products contracted by different suppliers. Instead, it has become a system of "pay to play" where the middlemen, GPOs, attempt to maximize their revenue by increasing the total size of purchases. And, all other things being equal, a higher priced product would yield a higher level of revenue to the middleman.

Conclusion

The three proposals are good, albeit partial steps, that aim to remedy some of the problems that are embedded in the current business model of GPOs and their protective umbrella, which inhibits competition and also protects them from the consequences of their anticompetitive behavior. Therefore, any reform proposals, whether mandatory or voluntary, must foster a business environment which ensures that

a. the agent's financial incentives are closely aligned with the economic interests of the master, that is, hospitals, nursing homes, and other healthcare providers;
b. the agent's rewards are closely tied to clearly defined and measurable performance targets;
c. there are effective measures of oversight and governance to monitor the agent's activities and to hold the agent accountable for predefined performance targets; and
d. the agent's performance orientation must be shifted away from self-enrichment of the GPOs and their management, and toward the notion of stewardship of resources for the benefit of the GPOs' principal clients, that is, hospitals, nursing homes, and other healthcare providers.

Appendix 7.1

S.2880

Medical Device Competition Act of 2004 (Introduced in Senate)

S 2880 IS

108th CONGRESS

2d Session

S. 2880

To amend title XI of the Social Security Act to ensure full and free competition in the medical device and hospital supply industries.

IN THE SENATE OF THE UNITED STATES
October 1, 2004

Mr. KOHL (for himself and Mr. DEWINE) introduced the following bill; which was read twice and referred to the Committee on Finance

A BILL

To amend title XI of the Social Security Act to ensure full and free competition in the medical device and hospital supply industries.

Be it enacted by the Senate and House of Representatives of the United States of America in Congress assembled,

SECTION 1. SHORT TITLE.

This Act may be cited as the 'Medical Device Competition Act of 2004'.

SEC. 2. FINDINGS.

Congress finds the following:

1. Given the increasing costs of health care in the United States, there is a compelling public interest in ensuring that there is full and free competition in the medical device and hospital supply industries so that the best and safest products are available to physicians and patients at a competitive price.
2. By aggregating purchases, hospital group purchasing can reduce the cost of acquiring medical equipment and hospital supplies so long as such purchasing is done in a manner consistent with antitrust law and free competition.

3. Some practices engaged in by certain hospital group purchasing organizations have had the effect of reducing competition in the medical device and hospital supply industries by denying some suppliers and device makers access to the hospital marketplace.

4. There is a compelling public interest in having the Secretary of Health and Human Services, in consultation with the Attorney General and Federal Trade Commission, engage in oversight and supervision of the current Federal health care program anti-kickback exemption (also known as the safe harbor) provided to group purchasing organizations under subparagraphs (C) and (E) of section 1128B(b)(3) of the Social Security Act (42 U.S.C. 1320a-7b(b)(3)). This oversight and supervision should ensure that the safe harbor does not shield conduct that harms competition in the hospital supply and medical device industries.

SEC. 3. ENSURING FULL AND FREE COMPETITION.

(a) IN GENERAL—Section 1128B(b)(3)(C) of the Social Security Act (42 U.S.C. 1320a-7b(b)(3)(C)) is amended—

(1) in clause (i), by striking `, and' at the end and inserting a semicolon; and

(2) by adding at the end the following new clauses:

`(iii) the contracting, business, and ethical practices of the person are not inconsistent with regulations promulgated by the Secretary pursuant to subsection (g)(1);

`(iv) the person has been certified by the Secretary under subsection (g)(2) to be in compliance with the regulations promulgated pursuant to subsection (g)(1); and

`(v) the amount to be paid the person does not exceed a total of 3 percent of the purchase price of the goods or services provided by that vendor;'.

(b) REGULATIONS- Section 1128B of the Social Security Act (42 U.S.C. 1320a-7b) is amended by adding at the end the following new subsection:

`(g)(1)(A) The Secretary, in consultation with the Attorney General and the Federal Trade Commission, shall, not later than 1 year after the date of enactment of the Medical Device Competition Act of 2004, issue proposed regulations, and shall, not later than 2 years after such date of enactment, promulgate final regulations, specifying contracting, business, and ethical practices of persons described in paragraph (4) that are contrary to antitrust law and competitive principles, to ethical standards, or to the goal of ensuring that products necessary for proper patient care or worker safety are readily available to physicians, health care workers, and patients.

`(B) In issuing and promulgating regulations under subparagraph (A), the Secretary shall take into account—

`(i) the compelling public policy goals of—

`(I) encouraging competition and innovation in the hospital supply and medical device markets; and

`(II) reducing the cost of health care as a result of aggregating buying power;

`(ii) the potentially detrimental impact of certain anticompetitive contracting practices; and

`(iii) the need to avoid conflicts of interests and other unethical practices by persons described in paragraph (4).

`(2) The Secretary, in consultation with the Attorney General and the Federal Trade Commission, shall establish procedures for annually certifying that persons described in paragraph (4) are in compliance with the final regulations promulgated pursuant to paragraph (1).

`(3) The Secretary, in consultation with the Attorney General and Federal Trade Commission, shall, not less than 6 months after the date of enactment of the Medical Device Competition Act of 2004, issue proposed regulations, and shall, not later than 1 year after such date of enactment, promulgate final regulations, to clarify its regulations promulgated pursuant to section 14(a) of the Medicare and Medicaid Patient and Program Protection Act of 1987 to specify that the definition of `remuneration' under this section with respect to persons described in paragraph (4)—

`(A) includes only those reasonable costs associated with the procurement of products and the administration of valid contracts; and

`(B) does not include marketing costs, any extraneous fees, or any other payment intended to unduly or improperly influence the award of a contract based on factors other than the cost, quality, safety, or efficacy of the product.

`(4) A person described in this paragraph is a person authorized to act as a purchasing agent for a group of individuals or entities who are furnishing services reimbursable under a Federal health care program.'

(c) DEFINITION OF PURCHASING AGENT- Section 1128B of the Social Security Act (42 U.S.C. 1320a-7b), as amended by subsection (b), is amended by adding at the end the following new subsection:

`(h) For purposes of this section, the term `purchasing agent' means any individual, organization, or other entity that negotiates and implements contracts to purchase hospital supplies or medical equipment, devices, products, or goods or services of any kind for any group of individuals or entities who are furnishing services reimbursable under a Federal health care program, including organizations commonly known as `group purchasing organizations.'

(d) EFFECTIVE DATE- Clause (v) of section 1128B(b)(3)(C) of the Social Security Act (42 U.S.C. 1320a-7b(b)(3)(C)), as added by subsection (a), shall take effect 1 year after the date of enactment of this Act.

Appendix 7.2

108th CONGRESS

2D SESSION

S._____

To amend title XI of the Social Security Act to ensure full and free competition in the medical device and hospital supply industries.

_____

IN THE SENATE OF THE UNITED STATES

introduced the following bill; which was read twice and referred to the Committee on

_____

A BILL

To amend title XI of the Social Security Act to ensure full and free competition in the medical device and hospital supply industries.

Be it enacted by the Senate and House of Representative of the United States of America in Congress assembled,

SECTION 1. SHORT TITLE.

This Act may be cited as the "Hospital Group Purchasing Organization Reform Act".

SEC. 2. FINDINGS.

Congress finds the following:

I. Given the increasing costs of health care in the United States, there is a compelling public interest in ensuring that there is full and free competition in the medical device and hospital supply Industries so that the best and safest products are available to physicians and patients at a competitive price.

1. By aggregating purchases, hospital group purchasing has the potential to reduce the cost of acquiring medical equipment and hospital supplies so long as such purchasing is done in a manner consistent with antitrust law and free competition.

2. Some practices engaged in by certain hospital group purchasing organizations have had the effect of reducing competition in the medical device and hospital supply industries by denying some suppliers and device makers access to the hospital marketplace.

3. There is a compelling public interest in having the Secretary of Health and Human Services engage in oversight and supervision of the current Federal health care program anti-kickback exemption (also known as the safe harbor) provided to hospital group purchasing organizations under section 1128B(b)(3)(C) of the Security Act (42 U.S.C. 1320a-7b(b)(3)). This oversight and supervision should ensure that the safe harbor does not shield conduct that harms competition in the hospital supply and medical device industries.

SEC. 3. ENSURING FULL AND FREE COMPETITION.

(a) IN GENERAL.—Section 1128B(b)(3)(C) of the Social Security Act (42 U.S.C. 1320a—7b(b)(3)(C)) is amended—

(1) In clause (i), by striking ", and" at the end and inserting a semicolon; and

(2) By adding at the end the following new clauses:

"(iii) in the case of an applicable organization whose volume of sales resulting from contracts negotiated by that organization exceeds $10,000,000 annually, the person is certified by the Secretary under subsection (g)(2); and

"(iv) in the case of an applicable organization, the amount to be paid the person does not exceed a total of 3 percent of the purchase price of the goods or services provided by that vendor;"

(b) HOSPITAL GROUP PURCHASING ORGANIZATIONS ETHICS AND BUSINESS PRACTICES COMPLAINCE OFFICE.—Section 1128B of the Social Security Act (42 U.S.C. 1320a-7b) is amended by adding at the end the following new subsection:

"(g) HOSPITAL GROUP PURCHASING ORGANIZATIONS ETHICS AND BUSINESS PRACTICES COMPLAINCE OFFICE.—

"(1) ESTABLISHMENT. —The Secretary shall establish within the Department of Health and Human Services a Hospital Group Purchasing Organizations Ethics and Business Practices Compliance Office (in this subsection referred to as the 'Office').

"(2) ACCOUNTABILITY PROCESS WITH ANNUAL CERTIFICATION. —The Office shall establish and oversee an accountability process with respect to applicable organizations whose volume of sales resulting from contracts negotiated by that organization exceeds $10,000,000 under which the Office annually certifies that—

"(A) the code of conduct which governs the ethical and business practices of the organization contains the minimum requirements described in paragraph (4); and

"(B) the organization is in substantial compliance with such code of conduct.

"(3) SUBMISSION OF ANNUAL REPORTS. —The process established under paragraph (2) shall require that in order to be certified for a year, the applicable organization shall submit an annual report to the Office describing in detail the contents and administration of its code of conduct which govern ethical and business practices. Such a report shall be submitted to the Office at such time, in such manner, and containing such information as the Office may require.

"(4) MINIMUM REQUIREMENTS FOR A CODE OF CONDUCT.— At a minimum, a code of conduct which governs ethical and business practices of an applicable organization shall contain provisions that—

"(A) prevent conflicts of interest and other unethical practices;

"(B) ban the acceptance of payments from vendors other than payments reasonably associated with the procurement of products or the administration of valid contracts;

"(C) ban the acceptance of payments from vendors intended to unduly or improperly influence the award of a contract based on factors other than the cost, quality, safety, or efficacy of the product;

"(D) prevent business practices which are contrary to the goal of ensuring that the best and safest products are available to physicians, health care workers, and patients at a competitive price;

"(E) establish training programs for all employees to ensure compliance with the code of conduct;

"(F) create a mechanism for employees to report violations;

"(G) discipline employees who do not follow the code of conduct;

"(H) establish internal or external audits, as appropriate;

"(I) designates and internal compliance officer to monitor compliance with the code of conduct; and

"(J) establish any other provisions that the Office deems necessary or appropriate.

"(5) REVIEW. —The Office shall annually publish a review of the codes of conduct which govern the ethical and business practices of organizations that submitted reports under paragraph (3) in order to provide a reflection of best practices.

"(6) SOLICITATION OF VIEWS OF INTERESTED PARTIES. — The Office shall solicit the views of tall interested parties, including suppliers or manufacturers of medical products, medical equipment, or medical devices, when—

"(A) certifying that an applicable organization is in substantial compliance with its own code of conduct pursuant to paragraph (2)(B); and

"(B) drafting the annual review pursuant to paragraph (5).

"(7) SOLICITATION OF VIEWS OF THE DEPARTMENT OF JUSTICE AND THE FEDERAL TRADE COMMISSION. — The Office shall solicit the views of the Antitrust Division of the Department of Justice and of the Federal Trade Commission regarding procompetitive and anticompetitive business practices when—

"(A) certifying that an applicable organization is in substantial compliance with its own code of conduct pursuant to paragraph (2)(b); and

"(B) drafting the annual review pursuant to paragraph (5).

"(8) ANNUAL BEST PARCTICES SEMINAR. —The Office shall sponsor and oversee an annual best practices seminar for applicable organizations described in paragraph (1)."

(c) DEFINITION OF PURCHASING AGENT AND APLICABLE ORGANIZATION. —Section 1128B of the Social Security Act (42 U.S.C. 1320a-7b), as amended by subsection (b), is amended by adding at the end the following new subsection:

"(h) DEFINITIONS. —In this section—

"(1) PURCHASING AGENT. —The term 'purchasing agent' means any individual, organization, or other entity that negotiates and implements contracts to purchase hospital supplies or medical equipment, devices, products, or goods or services of any kind for any group of individuals or entities who are furnishing services reimbursable under a Federal health care program, including organizations commonly known as 'group purchasing organizations'.

"(2) APPLICABLE ORGANIZATION. —The term 'applicable organization' means a purchasing agent, but excludes an entity whose primary purpose is the purchasing of pharmaceuticals or the management of a pharmaceutical benefits program."

Appendix 7.3

109th CONGRESS

1ST SESSION

S._____

To amend title XI of the Social Security Act to repeal a safe harbor with respect to vendors in order to ensure full and free competition in the medical device and hospital supply industries.

IN THE SENATE OF THE UNITED STATES

introduced the following bill; which was read twice and referred to the Committee on

---

A BILL

To amend title XI of the Social Security Act to repeal a safe harbor with respect to vendors in order to ensure full and free competition in the medical device and hospital supply industries.

Be it enacted by the Senate and House of Representative of the United States of America in Congress assembled,

SECTION 1. SHORT TITLE.

This Act may be cited as the "Ensuring Competition in Hospital Purchasing Act".

SEC. 2. ENSURING FULL AND FREE COMPETITION.

(a) IN GENERAL.—Section 1128B(b)(3) of the Social Security Act (42 U.S.C. 1320a-7b(b)(3) is amended by striking subparagraph (C).

(b) TECHNICAL AND CONFORMING AMENDMENTS. —

(1) Section 1128B(b)(3) of the Social Security Act (42 U.S.C. 1320a-7b(b)(3)) is amended—

(A) by redesignating subparagraphs (D) through (G) as subparagraphs (C) through (F), respectively;

(B) in subparagraph (F), as so redesignated, by striking "and" at the end;

(C) in subparagraph (H), as added by section 237(d) of the Medicare Prescription Drug, Improvement, and Modernization Act of 2003 (Public Law 108-173; 117 Stat. 2213) —

(i) by moving such subparagraph 2 ems to the left; and

(ii) by striking the period at the end and inserting ";and";

(D) by redesignating such subparagraph (H) as subparagraph (G); and

(E) by moving subparagraph (H), as added by section 431(a) of the Medicare Prescription Drug, Improvement, and Modernization Act of 2003 (Public Law 108-173; 117 Stat. 2287, 2 ems to the left.

(2) Section 1860D-31(g)(4)(A) (42 U.S.C. 1395w 141(g)(4)(A)) is amended by striking "section 1128B(b)(3)(G)" and inserting "section 1128B(b)(3)(F)".

(c) EFFECTIVE DATE. —The amendments made by this section shall take effect 1 year after the date of enactment of this Act.

CHAPTER 8

The GPO Industry's Efforts in Creating a Voluntary Code of Conduct: The Hanson Report

On April 7, 2005 the GPO industry announced its voluntary principles or code of conduct called the "Healthcare Group Purchasing Industry Initiative" (hereinafter referred to as the Initiative) or HGPII. The creation of the HGPII was not inspired by the industry's self-realization of its obligations to the industry's principal beneficiaries, or to better align industry members' self-interest with those of their beneficiary clients. This Initiative was the industry response to (a) call for voluntary action by the Senate Judiciary Subcommittee on Antitrust, Competition, Business and Consumer Rights, and (b) to forestall any legislative action for greater governmental oversight and reporting requirements. The industry was also responding to the rising media criticism and regulatory concerns, lawsuits, and federal and state investigations of certain practices that were found to be prevalent among GPOs and their management. These practices were considered to be inconsistent with ethical and professional norms of business conduct in the healthcare industry.[1]

In this context, it is important to examine the antecedents that led to the creation of the HGPII because they establish a baseline or threshold, which the industry members must exceed with regard to code components, implementation procedures, independent compliance verification, and transparency in public disclosure. In general, an industry's credibility and public trust are likely to be lower where the antecedents to the code creation are negative. Therefore, for such a code to be credible, the industry leaders must provide convincing evidence of their good faith to earn public trust and regulatory dispensation in evaluating the "voluntary" and "self-regulatory" characteristics of their code of conduct or ethical principles.

An analysis of the antecedents to the creation of the "Initiative," its content, governance structure, compliance reporting, and public disclosure, suggests that the goals of the industry in creating the Initiative appeared to be the opposite of those advocated by the Senate to make GPOs' operations more accountable and transparent. Although the industry has given the impression of responding to public concerns in a constructive manner, it has created a system that completely controls the type of information to be generated, the degree of specificity it would contain, and the manner in which it would be reported to the public. And finally, through its absolute supremacy of the governance process and accountability, it has removed all possibility—if indeed there was any—of providing information to the public, which would enable third party independent observers to evaluate its comprehensiveness, veracity, and usefulness in understanding the operations of GPOs and their impact—both positive and negative—on the healthcare industry in the United States.

Premier's Report "Best Ethical Practices for the Group Purchasing Industry"

In response to the pressure and demands of the Senate subcommittee, the Board Audit Committee and CEO of Premier, Inc. decided to commission an independent study of the GPO industry and to recommend the best practices to be adopted by the company. In March 2002, Premier engaged Prof. Kirk O. Hanson, Executive Director of the Markkula Center for Applied Ethics at Santa Clara University, to carry out the necessary inquiries and prepare the final report.

The report, which was released in October 2002, outlined as its goals: (a) to examine the structure and business practices of the GPO industry, (b) to examine the current ethical practices of the industry, (c) to identify best ethical practices for the industry, and (d) to compare these best practices to the current policies of Premier, Inc.

The publication of this report led to certain questions and even criticism from within the industry as to the thoroughness of the data gathering process. It also cast doubt as to the supposed independence of the author in preparing his report and recommendations.

The HGPII was announced with great fanfare to the public where it made unwarranted and unsupportable claims as to the quality and comprehensiveness of the initiative and the commitment of its major sponsor, Premier. For example in comments to the press Prof. Hanson claims, "This GPO initiative is the most extensive voluntary disclosure of ethical and business practices undertaken by any industry in the country. The steps taken by these GPOs represent a new standard in ethical business practices and challenge others in the healthcare supply chain to operate with similar transparency."[2] In another statement, he lauds Premier by saying "There's no question Premier's practices are better than any other GPO." Overall, the company has been "extraordinarily wise," in his view. They were singled out in the newspapers as a symbol of the problem for "an appearance of bad faith."[3]

However as we shall point out in chapters 9 and 10, the description of the GPO Initiative by Prof. Hanson is exaggerated and appears to be in the nature of a public relations exercise than a meaningful dialogue. One is also puzzled by Prof. Hanson's assertions about Premier's conduct in the most laudatory terms as if they were established facts. Even a cursory review of the vast body of literature on this topic would have demonstrated that HGPII fails to meet even the minimal requirements that would give the code a patina of legitimacy and credibility.[4]

Professor Kirk Hanson's Investigation and Recommendations Leading to the Creation of HGPII

Prof. Hanson began his work in late March 2002 and presented his final report to the Audit Committee and Board of Directors on October 18, 2002.[5] Prof. Hanson's report was a significant effort involving a consultative process that included Premier's board members, conferences with a cross-section of Premier's employees, CEOs, and other top officers of member hospitals in the Premier family, and four academic experts in the area of applied ethics, who are affiliated with major universities in the United States.

The final report was released in October 2002. Prof. Hanson indicated that in the preparation of this report, he was given full freedom to access any company documents; to communicate with anyone inside or outside the company; and to consult with other experts deemed necessary. The report's author also had the final determination as to the report's content and its release to the public. The report contained 50 recommendations for the best practices in the GPO industry. These recommendations along with "Additional Commitments" set forth by Premier's executives laid the foundation for the company's code of conduct, announced in early August 2002.

The findings of the report are important. They provide a framework that has been emulated in the HGPII. But the report is even more important for what it does not cover, which in our opinion, seriously undermines its potential regarding the effectiveness and credibility of the Initiative. In his final report, Prof. Hanson states that the study does not examine the past practices of Premier or other GPOs. Nor does it seek to examine the charges that "compromises" have been made. The report does not indicate where it draws the line between past practices that it has excluded and current practices (which it has included in the "Terms of References" for the inquiry). The report does not specify any current activities that it considers objectionable and the extent to which these practices are at variance with past practices.

It is difficult to understand Prof. Hanson's decision not to examine past activities and accusations of misconduct against Premier and other GPOs. It is hard to conceive of a situation where a new set of ethical practices is being suggested while ignoring all prior circumstances and incidents of unethical and possibly unprofessional conduct on the part of the companies involved and whether these activities were unique to the company or were a common pattern in the industry. This situation is comparable to a physician's prescribing medication to a patient while deliberately ignoring the patient's past history of diseases and symptoms of current ailments. If this decision was based on sound logic, the public is entitled to an explanation.

The report's discussion of the current industry practices does not provide any specifics. Instead, it includes a list of "unavoidable and ever-present tensions" that shape (GPO industry and Premier's) ethical practices.[6] This approach robs the report of its essential product, that is, the evaluative analysis and professional judgment on the part of Prof. Hanson that would inform the reader as to the extent and scope of embedded conflicts of interest that have permeated the industry and how they might be contained, if not eliminated. For example, in the section on relationships, Prof. Hanson states that

a. GPOs' primary obligations are to its owners and members.
b. Some GPOs have had additional and simultaneous relationships with vendors, including joint investments, supplementary marketing and representative agreements, and private-labeling agreements. These additional relationships may generate additional revenue for the GPO and could give a GPO the incentive to contract with vendors willing to engage in these additional relationships.
c. GPOs have at times permitted their executives to invest in, serve on the board of, and receive compensation from vendors and potential vendors. Similarly, this practice raises significant ethical concerns.
d. GPOs make extensive use of advisory groups composed of employees of member hospitals. Some of these advisors have, or may have, equity ownership in vendors, or may have received gifts or compensation from vendors.[7]

Prof. Hanson has decided not to elaborate on these relationships and their adverse impact on their principal clients, that is, hospitals and ultimately the patients. For example, he states that GPO's primary responsibilities are to its owners and members. Left unsaid is the challenge of resolving an inherent conflict in fulfilling these responsibilities to the GPO's owners and members. In other sections, Prof. Hanson eludes to the "inherent tensions" in the GPO industry. However, another description of these tensions could be described as "avenues and opportunities" for protecting and enhancing GPO interest at the expense of their principal clients. One may legitimately argue that these so-called tensions represent those very aspects of the GPO conduct that has elicited public criticism and regulatory inquiry.

Some of the tensions described are:

a. The tension between standardization of medical procedures (and therefore supplies and equipment) and the need to adopt rapidly technologies that improve medical outcomes. Standardizing equipment in operating and hospital rooms clearly saves lives. Having clinicians work on equipment with which they are familiar reduces errors and improves performance. Standardization also helps reduce inventory and materials handling costs. Yet, at some point, improved technology or opportunities for reduced cost by switching vendors or products warrants paying the "costs" in dollars and errors to adopt improved products and technologies.

b. The tension between whether to adopt technological and other performance innovations based on initial information and vendor representations or to wait for performance data based on actual use before new contracts are written and adoption is recommended.

c. The tension between the cost and other advantages of working with "familiar vendors" and the need to direct buying to vendors with the best prices and the latest technologies.

d. The tension between being a private for-profit organization that must sustain its own financial strength and being owned by nonprofit organizations.

e. The tension between negotiating stable multiyear contracts and buying on the spot market.

f. The tension between being solely a GPO and the interest the member's have in the GPO taking on a variety of other functions that serve the members and improve their supply chain management and overall performance. With these other activities comes the possibility of conflicts of interest and more complex relationships with vendors and potential vendors.[8]

Professor Hanson indicated that he interviewed in person and by telephone almost 100 individuals including company executives and employees, directors, and advisors. He also interviewed member hospital CEOs and staff of Premier member hospitals, vendor representatives, venture capitalists, trade associations' executives, journalists who have written about the industry, and Congressional staff.[9] The report does not identify that other GPOs, in addition to Premier, were consulted in the preparation of the report. The goals of the study were to examine the GPO industry and its current ethical practices and then identify best ethical practices for the industry. The final report does include a short overview of the industry and current GPO practices. However, the report does not list what companies, other than Premier, participated in the study and which executives were interviewed, or the extent to which the report represents industry-wide report. As Curt Nonomaque, executive vice president, chief financial officer, and treasurer of VHA (one of the co-owners of Novation), said in an interview with *Modern Healthcare*: "I am surprised [the study] was couched as an industry report. Nobody from our organization was contacted about it."[10]

Although the study was meant to create a set of "best practices" that would be applicable to all industry members, the author himself admits that "no matter how detailed a list of ethical principles and practices might be, there will still be work adapting and applying the principles to a specific organization." He also states that he has "drafted these ethical practices with Premier in mind."[11] This is puzzling. Clearly, reported unethical practices that gave rise to the Senate hearings and other governmental investigations were not limited to one or two GPOs, but were endemic to most of the major companies in the GPO industry. Otherwise, there would be no point in creating an industry-wide code of conduct. Instead, the report focuses on the future design of best ethical practices that "will enable Premier and other GPOs to maximize their contribution to these twin goals of health care, and to avoid conflicts of interest."[12]

The above-quoted description of the research process fails to indicate the participation of any public interest groups, advocates of healthcare consumers, and other interested parties, such as healthcare insurance companies, with a vital interest in the conduct of GPOs. The committee, which was set up to review the first draft of the report, consisted of four independent academic scholars and four top managers of Premier. No other representatives of other GPOs, vendors, hospitals, or public interest groups were asked to provide their views on the preliminary findings of the study.

The report lists 18 general ethical principles, which "seek to resolve or at least balance these inherent tensions and other dilemmas of operating efficiently and profitably in the GPO industry."[13] These are

- A GPO should manage its ethical practices deliberately and with care. Management and the Board of Directors should share the responsibility for maintaining an effective ethical management system.
- A GPO's first obligation is to serve its members' interests, which includes the twin goals of good medical outcomes and cost containment, and through its members, the ultimate customers, the patients.
- GPOs should provide ongoing assistance to their members in critical supply chain issues such as product safety and efficacy.
- A GPO should ensure that its employees and non-employee directors and advisors do not have conflicts of interest that would compromise the decisions they make on behalf of the hospitals.
- A GPO itself should avoid conflicts of interest arising from ownership of equity in vendors or other business relationships with vendors, where these relationships do not directly serve the members and their interests.
- No contracting decision should be based primarily on the amount of administrative fees or fees for other services paid by a vendor. Total value to the members must be the criterion.
- A GPO employee or non-employee director or advisor should recuse himself or herself from any decision that represents a conflict of interest or may appear to be a conflict of interest.
- A GPO should seek broad engagement and input from member hospitals and their employees, particularly clinical staff, in contracting and technological assessment decisions.
- No vendor should be permitted to own or control a GPO.
- GPO employees and non-employee directors and advisors must protect the confidential information they possess.
- GPOs should conduct their business with maximum practical transparency, making extensive information about their operations available to their members and to the public.
- GPOs should conduct ongoing studies on the value they create for their members.

- GPOs should make all contracting decisions based on the interests of the members.
- GPOs should create a process for evaluating products and services that is as objective as possible.
- GPOs should provide members with maximum choice in purchasing, consistent with capturing maximum value from the contracting process and aggregation of demand.
- GPOs should provide hospitals with a greater range of choice in those areas where the individual choice of products or services by the clinician is strongly related to good medical outcomes.
- GPOs should write contracts of the shortest duration feasible when all economic considerations are included, thereby providing future opportunities to adopt breakthrough technologies and to improve the products and terms of contracting.
- GPOs should promote the use of minority and women owned vendors where practicable.

These are indeed good ethical and aspirational principles, which not only GPOs but all companies should follow. However, from the perspective of this author, they leave everything to the discretion of the companies without indicating any specificity as to actions, accountability and transparency in compliance verification. In the absence of meaningful, transparent, and independent verification, the rationale of voluntariness and expectation of public trust falls on its face.

The author further elaborates on these general principles into 50 specific ethical policies, which are in the nature of practical guidelines. They were developed jointly by the author and Premier executives to "assure that they can be implemented in Premier."[14] Details of these practical guidelines are provided in appendix 8.1 to this chapter.

The issue is not about balancing these "inherent tensions" but to prevent GPOs from abusing their market power and information control for their benefit and at the expense of their primary clients. If all we can hope for is to seek a "balance" then the "voluntary principles" cannot be the solution when the scope, implementation, and performance evaluation of these principles are controlled entirely by the GPOs. In this context, it should be noted that the 50 ethical measures recommended in the report are in the form of exhortations of "what thou shalt not do" and have no mention of any outcome-oriented standards against which GPOs' conduct could be measured.

Another issue which we consider potentially damaging is the report's complete omission of the structural issues that lie at the core of the industry's past questionable activities and potential future misconduct. These structural issues comprise the system of revenue generation, that is, the so-called administrative fee, which is the source of a substantial number of GPO abuses. The problem is further compounded by the opaque accounting systems used by GPOs to justify their operational expenses and the criteria they use to distribute the so-called revenue surplus to the member hospitals. In conclusion, and in the absence of an objective and forthright analysis of these two factors, any recommendations based on this report would be of dubious validity and questionable effectiveness.

The final irony of the report, which raises another question regarding its objectivity, is found in Prof. Hanson's "General Observations Regarding Premier, Inc." These are suffused with laudatory comments about Premier's management and its commitment to exemplary ethical conduct. In particular, this is the only area where Prof. Hanson diverges from his emphasis on non-judgmental description. Instead, he offers comments about the proactive and forward looking character of Premier's management. Among his other observations, he states:

a. Premier's management has demonstrated that it is committed to implementing best practices in ethical management and the specific recommendations made in this study. The author received complete cooperation throughout this study. Discussions during the final phase of the project regarding the practical problems to be encountered in implementing these recommendations were conducted in good faith. Management is proceeding to develop implementation plans regarding the changes recommended in this report.

b. Many of the practices that were of greatest public concern were already being addressed when this study was commissioned. For example, Premier's management had revised or was revising policies regarding employee ownership of equity in vendors and Premier's own equity in vendors. During the past six months, several equity positions in vendor companies were sold, eliminating relationships of concern. Much of the press attention during 2002 referred to Premier practices that had been changed 12 or more months ago.

c. Premier's management demonstrated a nimbleness regarding ethics policies when it prepared and communicated a set of "Additional Premier Commitments" on August 5 to Senators Kohl and DeWine. Combining its own thinking and several themes addressed in the first draft of this report, management showed a capacity to adopt change rapidly.[15]

Prof. Hanson has since relinquished his position as the Initiative's coordinator although he remains actively involved with the Initiative as advisor. The new coordinator of the HGPII is Mr. Richard Bednar of the law firm Crowell & Moring in Washington, DC. Mr. Bednar also holds a similar position with the Defense Industry Initiative. Mr. Bednar offered strong defense of the Initiative during his recent testimony before the U.S. Senate Committee on the Judiciary, on March 15, 2006: "I am very pleased to report that this GPO Initiative is off and running on a path destined for success."[16]

Appendix 8.1: Recommendations for Best Ethical Practices

General Ethics Policies

1. *Commitment to Its Members and to the Goals of Quality Medical Care and Cost Containment*[17]: A GPO should emphasize in its values or mission statement that it acts first and foremost as a representative of its member hospitals, and pursues two primary goals, quality medical care and cost control.
2. *Code of Ethics*: A GPO should have a comprehensive code of ethics or code of conduct covering the points in this report and other common ethical policies. [18]

Conflict of Interest Provisions

3. *No Gifts to GPO Employees*: No GPO employee[19] should accept gifts, entertainment, favors, honoraria, or personal services payments, other than of nominal value, from any participating vendor.
4. *No Equity Ownership by GPO Employees*: No GPO employee should own equity in any participating vendor.[20]
5. *No Vendor Equity in GPO*: No participating vendor should be permitted to own equity in a GPO.
6. *No Gifts to Non-Employees Who Can Influence Contracting*: No non-employee director, officer or advisor of the GPO who is in a position to influence the GPO contracting decisions should accept any gift, entertainment, favor, honoraria, or personal services payment (except of nominal value) from any participating vendor.[21] (For advisors on purchasing committees, this restriction may be limited to vendors in the area in which they advise.)
7. *Non-Employees to Recuse Themselves If They Have Received Gifts*: Non-employees who are in a position to influence GPO contracting decisions should recuse themselves from any negotiations or decisions relating to a vendor from whom they have received such items.
8. *Disclosure by Non-Employees of Equity Interests*: Non-employees who are in a position to influence GPO contracting decisions should be required to disclose any equity interests in any participating vendor.
9. *Non-Employees to Recuse Themselves If They Have Equity Interests*: Non-employees who are in a position to influence GPO contracting decisions and have such equity ownership should be required to recuse themselves from any negotiations or decisions relating to that vendor.
10. *No Non-Employee Advisors with Extensive Equity Interests*: No non-employee director, officer, or advisor who is in a position to influence the GPO contracting decisions shall serve as advisor in an area in which they hold extensive equity investments.
11. *Limitation of Equity Investment by GPO in Vendors*: No GPO should hold a corporate equity interest in any participating vendor, unless the acquisition of the equity interest demonstrably benefits the GPO's

members by creating a source of a product or service where there is no other source, or very limited sources. Further, board approval should be required for any such investment.

12. *Disclosure of Equity Investments in Vendors*: Any corporate equity interest in any participating or potential vendor should be fully disclosed to GPO members and publicly disclosed on the company Web site.

13. *No Commitments Permitted if GPO Has Equity Investment*: No GPO should impose an obligation, commitment, or other requirement that in any way obligates a member to purchase goods or services from such a Participating Vendor in which the GPO has an equity investment.

14. *Limitation on Other Business Relationships with Vendors*: No GPO should have other business relationships with Participating Vendors unless those relationships are necessary to achieve core GPO goals. Such relationships shall be disclosed to members, fees will be reasonably related to the value received, and vendor participation shall have no bearing on GPO contracting decisions.

15. *Insider Trading*: GPOs should explicitly prohibit insider trading by employees based on any knowledge of vendors or their prospects gained through their employment.

Contracting Practices

16. *Goals of Contracting*: GPO policies and procedures should state and promote contracting arrangements that achieve both a high quality of medical care and competitive pricing.

17. *Statement of Vendor Rights and Responsibilities*: The GPO should adopt and make available a statement of the rights and responsibilities of bidders and vendors.[22]

18. *Right to Communicate Directly with Vendors*: GPOs should permit members to communicate directly with all vendors and to assess products or services provided by all vendors.

19. *Right to Purchase Clinical Preference Items Off Contract*: GPOs should permit members to purchase clinical preference items directly from vendors who do not contract with the GPO.

20. *Notice of Pending Bidding Processes*: GPOs should implement a contracting process that informs potential vendors of the process for seeking and obtaining contracts and provides interested vendors the opportunity to solicit contracts. Upcoming contracting processes should be listed on a publicly available Web site. (Updates which do not extend existing contracts need not be pre-noticed.)

21. *Fair Technology Evaluation Process*: GPOs should conduct technology assessments in a fair, timely, confidential, and unbiased manner, with an opportunity for review of decisions by vendors whose products or services are evaluated. GPO should provide an opportunity for all members to have input to the technology assessment process.

22. *Technology Breakthrough Procedures*: GPOs should operate a breakthrough technology evaluation process in a fair, timely, confidential,

and unbiased manner, with an opportunity for review of decisions by vendors whose products or services are evaluated. All contracts should include a clause permitting cancellation or the addition of new contracts in a category if breakthroughs are verified.

23. *Vendor Grievance Procedures*: GPOs should adopt policies and procedures that endeavor to address vendor grievances related to access for innovative clinical products or services. GPO will maintain a bidder and vendor grievance procedure actively disclosed to prospective and participating vendors.

24. *Limitation on Sole-Source Contracts*:[23] All GPO contracts for Physician Preference Products and Services[24] should be multisource.

25. *Limitation on Commitment Levels*: All GPO contracts for Physician Preference Products should be written without GPO-imposed commitment levels.

26. *No Bundling of Unrelated Products*: No GPO contracts should have bundling of Physician Preference Products with unrelated products.

27. *No Bundling of Products across Vendors*: No GPO contracts should have bundling of any products across different vendors.

28. *General Limitation of Contracts to 3 Years*: GPO contracts should be for 3 years or less, unless economic conditions require longer term agreements in the best interest of hospital members.[25]

29. *Cap on Administrative Fees*: No GPO contract should require administrative fees in excess of 3 percent.

30. *Standardization of Administrative Fees*: Administrative fees should be standardized for each bid process and product or service category and stated in advance to all bidders in that category.[26]

31. *No Up-Front Administrative Fees*: No GPO contract should charge up-front administrative fees from participating vendors.

32. *No Administrative Fees in the Form of Vendor Equity*: No GPO contract should permit administrative fees to be paid in the form of vendor equity.

33. *No Marketing or Other Fees from Vendors*: No GPO should receive marketing fees from participating vendors.

34. *No Private Label Programs*: No GPO should conduct private label programs that produce additional fees from Participating Vendors.

35. *Notice to Vendors of Ethical Standards*: GPOs should inform all vendors and prospective vendors of the ethical standards and practices of the GPO and seek the vendors' adherence to the same standards.

36. *Promotion of Minority Vendors*: GPOs should offer or participate in programs that promote diversity among vendors to include women and minority-owned vendors.

Disclosure and Reporting

37. *Disclosure of Contracts to Members*: Detailed data on existing contracts and on current contracting processes shall be readily available to members, including administrative fees paid for each contract.

38. *Disclosure of Contracts to the Public*: General data on existing contracts, specifying vendors and general categories of products on contract from those vendors, will be made readily available to the public.

39. *Annual Financial Reporting*: GPOs should prepare and distribute to all shareholders, members, and the public an annual financial report. Public reporting should be similar to that required nonprofit financial reporting and should include the compensation of the five highest paid GPO executives and of the corporate directors. Shareholder reporting should be more detailed.

40. *Disclosure of Vendor Payments*: GPOs should make full disclosure to GPO members of all vendor payments to the GPO, whether allocatable to a specific member or not.

41. *Cooperation with Cost Studies*: Each GPO should support authoritative surveys and studies on the value of GPOs and to disclose these studies to the public.

Governance

42. *Designated Ethics Officer*: GPOs should appoint or designate a member of the executive team to be lead ethics advocate, to raise policy and strategic issues of ethical significance with the management and board.[27]

43. *Designated Compliance Officer*: GPOs should designate a compliance officer to oversee compliance with the HIGPA code and other ethics commitments, and to do annual reporting, and to raise other policy issues of ethical significance with management and the board.[28]

44. *Review by Audit Committee*: The Audit Committee of the GPO should meet at least annually without management present to hear from the ethics and compliance officers and to discuss any issues brought forward by these officers.

45. *Annual Report on Ethics Performance*: GPOs should make an annual report to its audit committee, board, and members regarding its compliance with its own ethical policies. A summary of the report should be made available to the public.

Ethics Standards for Parent and Related Entities

46. *Parent Company—Conflict of Interest*[29]: All management employees of a parent organization to a GPO and any other employees in a position to influence the contracting process should follow the same conflict of interest rules that guide employees of the GPO itself. Similarly, non-employee directors, officers, and advisors of a parent organization should follow the same rules as they would if they directly served the GPO.

47. *Parent Company—Limitation on Business Activities*: The parent organization of a GPO may not engage in any type of business activity that would be prohibited for the GPO itself under these rules.

48. *Directors and Advisors to Non-GPO Subsidiaries of Parent Company—Conflict Of Interest*: All employees and non-employee directors, officers, and advisors of a non-GPO subsidiary controlled by Premier who are in a position to influence the contracting process should follow the same conflict of interest rules established separately for employees, directors, and advisors of the GPO.

49. *Non-GPO Subsidiaries of Parent Company—Limitation on Equity Investments*: No non-GPO subsidiary should hold a corporate equity interest in any participating vendor, unless the acquisition of the equity interest demonstrably benefits the GPO's members by creating a source of a product or service where there is no other source, or very limited sources. Further, board approval should be required for any such investment.

50. *Non-GPO Subsidiaries of Parent Company—Limitation on Business Activities*: A non-GPO subsidiary may have business relationships with participating vendors, but these relationships must be disclosed to members and must not influence contracting decisions. It is impossible to anticipate the many types of business relationships that may be developed in the future. The corporate ethics officer and the board must examine such relationships on an ongoing basis to insure that there is no influence on contracting decisions.[30]

CHAPTER 9

Theoretical Underpinnings for Creating Effective Industry-wide Voluntary Codes of Conduct

General Structure, Governance, and Intended Outcome of the Healthcare Group Purchasing Industry Initiative ("Initiative")

The drive for the Initiative was spearheaded by Premier, the industry's largest GPO. The founding members included the nine leading GPOs in the industry with a combined market share of 85 percent.[1] The declared purpose of the Initiative was to engage and sustain "best ethical and business conduct practices in the GPO industry."[2] The nine founding members and initial signatories of HGPII are Amerinet, Inc., Broadlane, CHCA, Consorta, Inc., GNYHA Ventures, Inc., HealthTrust Purchasing Group, MedAssets, Novation, and Premier, Inc. Of the nine GPOs covered by the HGPII, four GPOs, namely CHCA, Consorta, GNYHA, and Premier serve exclusively not-for-profit hospitals. Two others (HealthTrust and MedAssets) serve exclusively for-profit hospital alliances. The remaining three GPOs (Amerinet, Broadlane, and Novation) serve both not-for-profit and for-profit hospital alliances.

In announcing the Initiative, industry representatives praised their ground-breaking document, which they claimed would be a role model for other industries. The Initiative, they asserted, would provide improved benefits to hospitals, nursing homes, and other healthcare providers. They claimed that these benefits could not be duplicated through any other means, including greater regulatory oversight. Industry representatives further asserted—without any substantiating logic or factual data—that any change in the existing operating structure of GPOs would be quite harmful to the principal beneficiaries of the current system, that is, hospitals, nursing homes, and other healthcare providers.[3]

In describing their Initiative, the GPO groups made a number of claims. These covered both the benefits of the "voluntary" and "self-regulating" character of the Initiative, and also pointed to the harm that would be inflicted on the healthcare industry if any regulatory or mandatory changes were imposed on the industry.[4]

The Initiative is intended to encourage best ethical and business conduct practices by requiring each signatory company to pledge to follow six core ethical principles; to report annually on adherence to these principles using an Annual Accountability Questionnaire; and to participate in an Annual Best Practices Forum to discuss best ethical and business conduct practices with other GPO representatives and with representatives from government and other organizations.

Notwithstanding the industry's exaggerated claims as to the innovative character and far-reaching scope of the Initiative, and its assertions as to the industry voluntary code of its type, the GPO Initiative is neither innovative nor far reaching. Creation of industry-wide voluntary principles or codes of conduct has been a growth industry for the last two decades. As a matter of fact, any self-respecting industry would be found to have one or even multiple codes of conduct. These codes or sets of principles purport to address public concerns about some aspect of an industry's behavior or enhance public image of the industry's persona as a good community citizen and socially responsible industry.

In its current form, the Initiative falls considerably short of even the minimal criteria that such a voluntary code must meet. Therefore, before analyzing the specific content of the Initiative, it is important that we understand the parameters of established economic theory, which delineates the underlying conditions that need to be met if an industry-wide code is effective in (a) creating necessary incentives for the industry members to comply with the code and (b) engender public trust in the industry's assertions of upholding high standards of business conduct.

There are two important considerations required of any analysis of an industry's code of conduct. The first has to do with the code principles and how they are to be implemented. The second pertains to the assertions made by the code's proponents concerning the anticipated changes in the industry members' ethical conduct and their business operations, and the enhanced benefits that would accrue to the industry's primary clients and public-at-large. These benefits must be significant, and the industry's claims of enhanced performance more credible, when a code of conduct has been created in response to allegations of prior improper conduct on the part of the industry members and when the industry is contesting the need for additional regulatory oversight as unnecessary and counter-productive.

In analyzing the potential effectiveness of the Initiative to deliverer on its promises, we have used a two-pronged approach.

1. In this chapter, we provide a generalized framework that sets forth the situation with regard to competitive dynamics of the marketplace

surrounding an industry and the industry structure that must be addressed for an industry-wide code to have a reasonable chance of meeting its performance standards.

2. In the next chapter, we examine the extent to which the HGPII has been structured to anticipate and overcome the challenges emanating for competitive market conditions and intra-industry competitive structure, and thus ensure that the Initiative's performance expectations are likely to be fulfilled.

A Generalized Theoretical Framework for Analyzing Industry-Based Codes of Conduct

Industry-based codes of conduct are neither a recent phenomenon nor a radical innovation. Most business organizations would develop voluntary arrangements that aim to standardize technical and quality standards for products, contracts, and other arrangements, which create economies of scale and reduce transaction costs.[5] The economic case for voluntary cooperation among business enterprises in this area is clear and compelling. Such voluntary arrangements often involve the adoption of industry-wide codes that are designed to advance and protect the interests of member companies from market–based competition by companies in other industries. They are also used to present a unified defense against regulatory changes that adversely affect the industry members' operating environment and financial well-being.

This form of industry cooperation has been most successful in creating a pro-business and pro-industry regulatory and financial environment in the United States. In its extreme form, regulatory regimes that are created to protect consumers and other groups that may be adversely affected by industry action, often end up protecting the industry, a phenomenon that has been described as the "capture theory of regulation" and widely discussed and analyzed in economics, political science, and other pertinent fields of social inquiry.[6]

Experience in the United States regarding the power and influence of lobbying by industry groups can be gauged from the large number of trade associations and their registered lobbyists in the nation's capitol and in those of the 50 states in the Union. Notwithstanding their vociferous support of competitive markets and free enterprise, these trade associations are single-minded in their pursuit of regulations, subsidies and tax incentives that protect their market position from competition and create a playing field that is tilted in their favor.[7]

Another dimension of the benefits of industry coalitions is the protection of companies from the cost of negative externalities by transferring them to other segments of society, and thereby reducing industry members' operating costs and improving returns on investment.[8] Examples of such externalities include air pollution, untreated waste water, and so on. Individual companies and industries mobilize their combined efforts to minimize their cost burden for such externalities by pushing them on to other segments of the community.

The business case or the economic justification for corporate social responsibility (CSR)-related codes of conduct or ethical principles for business conduct, is infinitely more complex when compared to the conventional codes of conducts for business groups. In direct contrast to the conventional principles or codes, CSR-related codes of conduct call for the industry or group members to voluntarily assume some of the costs associated with the industry's negative externalities.

The past two decades have witnessed an enormous growth on the part of industry groups to create various types of statements of principles or codes of conduct that would establish the sponsoring organization's bona fides as a socially responsible organization. Available data, although not comprehensive, suggests that these codes have become de rigueur among corporations and industry groups all over the world.[9] Unfortunately, the widespread creation of such codes by corporations and industry groups has not gone beyond the rhetorical stage. Sponsoring organizations, in general, have failed to take adequate steps to implement their codes of conduct and to make more transparent their efforts toward compliance and improved performance. Nor do business organizations as yet view them as a means of building public trust. The inevitable result of this state of affairs has been that these principles or codes of conduct are treated with disdain and largely dismissed by knowledgeable and influential opinion leaders among various stakeholder groups, the news media, and even the public-at-large. Instead of gaining public trust and credibility for their efforts, the sponsoring organizations suffer from the backfire effect of poor public relations and potential damage to their institutional reputation.[10]

CSR-related codes of conduct or voluntary ethical principles have become a staple of large industry groups, large corporations, and especially multinational corporations.[11] Generally categorized under the rubric of principles or codes of CSR, they are established by industry or group-based organizations that protect and advance the groups' shared interests. They allow an industry the flexibility to create responses that are cost-effective, maintain member companies' discretion to conduct their business without outside intervention and oversight, and project the industry's performance in the most positive manner. Another subset of this category includes codes whose primary focus is to burnish the industry's image as a socially responsible and member companies as good corporate citizens.

An industry-wide code must create a set of standards that would improve industry's conduct from its current status, which has been perceived by its external stakeholders as failing to meet societal expectations. Therefore, to be viable to both the industry members and society-at-large, an industry-wide code of conduct must narrow the credibility gab between societal expectations and industry performance. Nevertheless, in examining the efficiency of such a code, we must also recognize the fact that industry members would resist any call for changes in their conduct, where these changes are perceived to be costly and contrary to their economic interest. A distinction, however, needs to be made here between economic costs that would accrue to the industry members because of unrealistic expectations from external groups and the economic costs that industry members should have incurred but were able to avoid because of their oligopolistic structure, market power, and other related factors.

Structural Problems Associated with
Industry-Based Voluntary Codes of Conduct

Industry-based codes of conduct seek to create and sustain a common position by industry members from challenges by nonindustry stakeholders concerning their normal business practices, which have been viewed as adversely affecting other segments of society. These codes are invariably created as "voluntary initiatives" by the industry and are designed to deflect public pressure for further regulation and mandatory conduct on member companies in the industry.

An industry-based CSR-related code of conduct consists of a set of activities that industry members voluntarily commit themselves to undertake to minimize, if not completely eliminate, sources of real or perceived conflict member companies' conduct and societal expectations. HGPII falls in this category of industry-codes. As such, it is subject to structural and operational constraints that are embedded in this form of voluntary code and the obstacles that these codes must overcome if they are to succeed in narrowing the credibility gap between societal expectations and industry performance.

In the final analysis, a code of conduct is only as good as the results it produces. Therefore, code planners must create a process that would ensure proper implementation, internal monitoring and control, and accountability for achieving preestablished performance standards. Otherwise, the code would produce the opposite of its intended purpose. It would also create unintended consequences, which would worsen the situation. One of the most difficult, and potentially costly, situations from society's perspective is to allow those who benefit from a weak or ineffective code to take control of the process of code creation and implementation. Unfortunately, the proponents of the GPOs code of conduct have made this so-called self-governance as the pillar of the uniqueness of their Initiative and, from the perspective of public interest, doomed it to failure.

To be effective and credible, industry-based voluntary codes of conduct must contend with three issues that are embedded in the code structure. These are (a) the free rider problem (b) the problem of adverse selection, and (c) the notion of "best business practices." The magnitude and severity of these problems would adversely affect their collective operation.

Overcoming the Problems of Adverse Selection, Free Rider, and
Diminution of Best Business Practices

CSR-related industry codes of conduct must contend with the vexatious problems of adverse selection, free rider, and a diminution of best business practices. Adverse selection occurs when the companies with poor performance records join the industry-group thereby tainting the industry's reputation and public distrust of the industry's code of conduct. It also discourages high-performing companies from joining the group for fear of adversely affecting their current reputation.

The industry's desire to enroll the largest number of companies in the code effort gives rise to the free rider problem because of the reluctance of the poor performing companies to improve their performance. There is no need to do so because they can enjoy higher reputation by riding on the coat trails of high-performing companies. Similarly, a desire to include the largest possible number of companies in the industry-wide code gives the recalcitrant and poor performing companies an effective veto toward any changes in best business practices, which may add to their operational costs. Their participation would also result in undermining the credibility and reputation of the companies that have better track records and stronger commitment to compliance with the code of conduct. The net result is that poor performing companies drag down the so-called best business practices to the lowest common denominator.

Adverse selection results in discouraging good companies from joining the group and thereby undermining the industry-based code's potential effectiveness in creating improved industry conduct that would narrow the gap between societal expectations and industry performance. An industry's effort to improve "best practices" invariably suffers when the group is dominated by free riders and companies with bad performance (adverse selection). These companies exert pressure on other members to keep a lid on the costs associated with improving compliance as the price of ensuring their participation in the industry's code of conduct. The notion of constantly improving "best practices" also suffers from the twin elements of the free rider problem and adverse selection. Innovative companies cannot benefit from improving their practices under the guise of standardization. Scholarly research in economics and management literature shows that industry practices are most likely to improve under conditions of highly competitive markets where insiders must continuously improve to gain competitive advantage. Improvement in the "best business practices" is unlikely where the "improvements" might increase costs through absorption of negative externalities, which the least efficient and most recalcitrant members are unlikely to accept.

Private Law Character of CSR-Related Voluntary Codes of Conduct

A voluntary code does not reduce the burden of compliance on the member companies, it increases it. Unlike mandatory regulatory requirements where noncompliance may subject the companies to civil and legal penalties, voluntary codes shift the entire onus of compliance on the companies, which must provide strong proof of compliance to a skeptical society. The nature of "voluntariness," and by implication the flexibility afforded to companies, also depends on the basic premise that the sponsoring organizations and their critics share a common interest in improving the underlying conditions of the affected groups and that it is in the interest of all parties to resolve these issues within the realistic constraints of available financial resources, competitive market conditions, and the adverse societal impact of current business practices.[12] This is a proactive stance and perhaps the best practice in all possible worlds. It provides scope for experimentation and building consensus, and where necessary and desirable, facilitates the enactment of public law.

Another potentially volatile, highly unpredictable, and often miscalculated, factor has to do with the nature of adverse public reaction and regulatory response if the industry's code fails to meet societal expectations of the industry's reform efforts. Industry-wide CSR-related codes that depend on voluntary compliance and rarely incorporate enforcement measures are most vulnerable to the problems of free rider and adverse selection. The need to keep the largest number of companies in the group pushes performance standards to the lowest common denominator. Companies with the weakest records can force standards down to what they are willing to live with. This situation suits the poorly performing and recalcitrant companies, that is, adverse selection, which stand to gain from enhanced public approval—at no or little cost to themselves—as a result of the time and resources expended by the best-performing companies. At the same time, the best-performing companies suffer from the taint caused by the actions of recalcitrant companies.

This situation is further exacerbated under conditions where the most recalcitrant members are also industry leaders. The fact that a voluntary code lacks any independent external monitoring and compliance verification invariably contributes to this tendency because the industry members can conceal their motives against making any changes in their business practices from public and regulatory scrutiny. The combined effect of the three structural flaws, that is, the free rider problem, adverse selection, and inherent disincentives in improving the current business practices in the operations of the voluntary industry codes, is further exacerbated when the control of the code's governance structure is held exclusively or primarily by the industry members, and where there is no system of independent outside monitoring and compliance verification, the prevailing situation with HGPII. Such a code, when stripped of its self-serving verbiage, is reduced to a hapless piece of public relations exercise, which no one takes seriously either inside the industry or outside among the industry's critics.

Creating Internal Cohesiveness and a Commonly Shared Vision

Industry-wide voluntary codes of conduct that deal with societal concerns also face major challenges in transforming this need "to do something" into active strategies. Their difficulties, including those described in the following text, arise from conflicts among member companies within the industry and a lack of trust by external constituencies in the industry's external sociopolitical environment.

a. Many companies are philosophically opposed to creating voluntary codes that they view as giving-in to the industry's critics.
b. There is the inherent difficulty of finding common ground among member companies that otherwise compete vigorously against each other.
c. Another set of difficulties emanates from individual companies' operational constraints, financial concerns, and above all, corporate culture

and management orientation toward responding to social and environmental challenges.[13]

d. The long-term benefits of industry-wide cooperative effort, nevertheless, carry short-term costs, which must be compensated through improved productivity. This takes time and requires structural and organizational changes that are not always easy to accomplish.

A more serious, albeit negative, outcome of this approach lies in its lack of credibility with the industry's external stakeholders. Most current industry-based codes, which fall in the category of "principles," suffer from a low level of community trust. Most industry groups offering codes make similar claims regarding their effectiveness and yet are unable and unwilling to satisfy industry critics with credible performance measures.

This phenomenon is generally described in the economic literature as a problem of asymmetric information and is best illustrated by the example of selling used cars, as discussed by the Nobel laureate economist George Akerlof.[14] Just as in the case of used cars (pejoratively called "lemons"), industry-groups find it difficult to persuade their external stakeholders that they are telling the truth about their code elements and performance standards. As in the case of used cars, each seller knows the quality of his or her offerings. Since the products are not similar, the customer must have sufficient and believable information about the claims made by each seller. Each seller immediately matches the claims of every other seller, while these sellers however, are unwilling or unable to provide verifiable or trustworthy information. Since the buyer has no means to compare the truthfulness of competing claims, he/she treats each seller's information as equally false and thereby debases the quality claims of all sellers.

The situation discourages the companies willing to offer greater compliance toward a code's broader principles because they cannot improve their credibility with the public. At the same time, the enhanced effect on their reputation arising from the efforts of the forward-looking companies is shared equally by the recalcitrant companies in the group who benefit at the former's expense. Conversely, any public reprobation of the recalcitrant companies taints the reputation of the forward-looking companies because they belong to the same group.

Positive Aspects of Industry-wide Voluntary Codes of Conduct Dealing with Societal Issues

Industry-based CSR codes of conduct, nevertheless, can serve an important business and social purpose. From the business viewpoint, these codes provide industry members with the opportunity to develop solutions that are focused, economically feasible, and cognizant of the industry's special needs. They engender public trust through "reputation effect" and avoid being tainted by the actions of other companies.[15] From the public's perspective, voluntary codes also serve an important purpose. They obviate the need for further governmental regulation. They also allow the moderate elements among the affected groups to seek reasonable solutions to the issues involved.[16]

Unfortunately, most industry groups, advancing CSR-related codes, have not gone beyond the rhetoric stage with the result that well-informed segments of population and industry critics treat business assertions with disbelief. The success of this system depends largely on the industry's ability to create and sustain a high level of public credibility. Public trust, under these circumstances, is highly fragile and transitory. It must be continuously and consistently nurtured to build a reservoir of goodwill. This would be a kind of invested social capital, which yields a regular flow of social dividends in the form of public trust.

Preconditions for Creating an Effective Industry-wide CSR-Related Voluntary Code of Conduct

Based on our research and field work in monitoring code compliance, we have identified eight conditions that must be met for an industry-based code to demonstrate measurable and credible compliance with the industry's voluntary initiative.

1. The code must be *substantive* in addressing broad areas of public concern pertaining to industry's conduct.
2. Code principles or standards must be *specific* in addressing issues embodied in those principles.
3. Code performance standards must be *realistic* in the context of industry's financial strength and competitive environment. The industry should not make exaggerated promises or claim implausible achievements.
4. Member companies must create an effective *internal implementation system* to ensure effective code compliance.
5. Code compliance must be an integral part of a management performance evaluation and reward system.
6. The industry must create an *independent governance structure* that is not controlled by the executives of the member companies.
7. There must be an *independent external monitoring and compliance verification system* to engender public trust and credibility in the industry's claims of performance.
8. There should be maximum *transparency and verifiable disclosure* of industry performance to the public. Standards of performance disclosure should be the sole province of the code's governing board.

In our analysis of the potential effectiveness of HGPII (see chapter 9), we would apply these standards to test the viability of the Initiative's six principles, their operative mechanism, and governance structure to deliver on the promises of enhanced ethical conduct made by the GPO industry.

CHAPTER 10

Healthcare Group Purchasing Industry Initiative (HGPII)

The GPO industry's voluntary code of conduct, HGPII, or the Initiative, was introduced in April 2005. During the fourth Senate Subcommittee hearing[1] the industry's sole spokesperson, Mr. Richard Bednar made strong assertions to the committee as to the scope of the Initiative and the prospect of its effective implementation. It was also stated that this Initiative was one of the most innovative and far-reaching efforts on the part of the GPO industry and that this Initiative could serve as an exemplary role model of cooperative voluntary effort toward self-regulation on the part of the private sector organizations. The industry also claimed that the involvement of the top management of the industry's leading GPOs would ensure maximum compliance and thereby make any mandatory, government sponsored, monitoring unnecessary.

For the record, it should be stated that Mr. Bednar does not hold a managerial position in the GPO industry. Instead, he was speaking from his position as the coordinator of HGPII, a position that he had occupied for less than three months at the time of the hearing. The industry now has had more than three years of compliance effort and progress in implementation. Therefore, an analysis and evaluation of the industry's reform effort through its Initiative should yield a better understanding of the prospects and promises of the Initiative. In undertaking this analysis, three points should be kept in mind.

1. The Initiative was a direct response to the established fact that some of the major GPOs and their management had engaged in practices that indicated conflict of interest and actions contrary to the best interest of the industry's primary beneficiaries, that is, hospitals, nursing homes, and other health services providers.
2. The GPOs operated under a regulatory environment that offered the industry special protections from anticompetitive conduct and ensured a predictable stream of revenue (income) with little downside risk.

3. The GPOs derived a significant part of their income from the services that were paid for—to a large extent—from public sources, that is, tax supported funding.

The combined effect of these three factors places extra burden on the industry and requires that the industry:

a. must adhere to a higher standard of ethical conduct;
b. its operations must be directed first and foremost for the benefits of its beneficiary clients and only secondarily for the benefits of its owners and managers; and
c. must display a high level of transparency in all aspects of its operations to engender public trust, which is paramount for companies that impact public health and well-being.

The creation of the HGPII was announced by the industry leaders on April 7, 2005. Its nine founding members are the leading companies in the GPO industry with a combined market share of 85 percent.[2] The declared purpose of the Initiative was to engage and sustain "best ethical and business conduct practices in the GPO industry."[3]

The HGPII consists of six principles:

1. Each Signatory shall have and adhere to a written code of business conduct. The code establishes the high ethical values expected for all within the Signatory's organization.
2. Each Signatory shall train all within the organization as to their personal responsibilities under the code.
3. Each Signatory commits itself to work toward the twin goals of high-quality healthcare and cost effectiveness.
4. Each Signatory commits itself to work toward an open and competitive purchasing process free of conflicts of interest and any undue influences.
5. Each Signatory shall have the responsibility to each other to share their best practices in implementing the Principles; each Signatory shall participate in an annual Best Practices Forum.
6. Each Signatory shall be accountable to the public.[4]

In announcing the Initiative, industry representatives praised their groundbreaking document. The Initiative, they asserted, would provide improved benefits to hospitals, nursing homes, and other healthcare providers. In his testimony before the Senate Judiciary Subcommittee on Antitrust, Competition Policy, and Consumer Rights, Mr. Richard Bednar, the new coordinator of HGPII, made further claims about the benefits of the new Initiative. He asserted that the HGPII, which had been modeled after the Defense Industry Initiative (DII) holds a similar promise of enhanced industry performance, which would yield benefits that could not be duplicated through any other means, including greater regulatory oversight.[5] Industry representatives also asserted—without any substantiating logic or factual data—that any change in the existing operating structure of GPOs would be quite harmful to the principal beneficiaries of the current system, that is, hospitals, nursing homes, and other healthcare providers.[6]

The Initiative is intended to encourage best ethical and business conduct practices by requiring each signatory company to pledge to follow six core ethical principles, to report annually on adherence to these principles using an Annual Accountability Questionnaire, and to participate in an Annual Best Practices Forum to discuss best ethical and business conduct practices with other GPO representatives and with representatives from government and other organizations.

Analysis of the Initiative and Its Components

In describing their Initiative, the GPO groups made a number of claims. These covered both the benefits of the "voluntary" and "self-regulating" character of the Initiative. They also pointed to the harm that would be inflicted on the healthcare industry if any regulatory or mandatory changes were imposed on the industry.[7]

In chapter 9, we described eight preconditions that are essential in determining the measure of an industry-wide voluntary code of conduct. These preconditions require that a voluntary industry-wide code must be substantive, specific, and realistic in addressing issues of broad public concern as to industry's conduct. It must contain systems for internal compliance, management performance evaluation and compensation. It must have an independent governance structure to ensure that those evaluating the code's performance are not controlled by the companies whose performance is being evaluated. And finally, the code and its implementation system must be subjected to independent external monitoring for compliance verification and transparency in verifiable disclosure.

In the following sections, we analyze the Initiative using the yardstick of the preconditions for creating an effective industry-wide voluntary code of conduct.

Principles 1, 3, and 4: Core Values of the Initiative

Principles 1, 3, and 4 embody the mission and goals of the Initiative. They call for the signatories to create and adhere to a written code of conduct that establishes the high ethical values of the industry, work toward the twin goals of high-quality healthcare and cost effectiveness, and commit their companies toward an open and competitive purchasing process that is free of conflicts of interest and undue influences.

These principles are at best aspirational and exhortative. They lack specificity as to what business practices would meet the so-called high ethical standards. Nor do they provide any outcome-oriented yardsticks by which the external community would be able to judge the efficacy and veracity of the claims made by the signatories in meeting societal expectations underlying these principles.

Importance of External Input

Creation of ethical standards by a company or industry must have strong input from sources outside the company and industry. These sources must represent the perspective of those groups, and society at-large, where public good was supposed to have been adversely affected by the industry's prevailing practices. Absent such a caveat, an industry or company created code of conduct is unlikely to offer more than what the company-industry itself considered "ethical enough" rather than what societal elements would consider the deficiencies in a company/industry's current practices. Such a gap is quite normal in a dynamic business-society environment.

Good business conduct cannot be judged outside the competitive environment in which a business operates. Therefore, whether we like it or not, business standards of ethical conduct must have an independent, external component code of conduct. Industries and companies that ignore this obvious situation are likely to end with codes of conduct that are no more than meaningless paper exercises and just as useless.

Good ethics is not always good business. If it were otherwise, we would not need any codes of conduct—whether voluntary or mandatory—because business organizations would do their utmost to become more ethical since it would serve their business interests. Even under conditions of free and competitive markets, ethical conduct cannot be guaranteed. Competitive markets may make businesses efficient; they do not necessarily make them virtuous because highly competitive markets drive businesses to exploit every possible opportunity or risk losing business to their competitors.[8]

The case of promoting ethical conduct among businesses and industries under conditions oligopolistic structures are infinitely more complex. And yet, ironically enough it is the inefficient markets that provide the largest opportunities for unethical conduct, greatest needs for ethical standards, and most intense industry resistance to acquiesce to compliance with meaningful ethical standards that would reduce their opportunities for maximizing their exploitative gains. We maintain that this state of affairs admirably describes the GPO industry and, therefore, its promises of good conduct should be examined with a great deal of caution and skepticism.

Industry Structure and Its Relevance in Creating an Effective Voluntary Industry-wide Code of Conduct

An industry-wide code of conduct is easily established and effectively implemented where all industry members share a common purpose and a common adversary. Successful examples of these codes are the multitude trade groups and industry associations where companies join together to lobby the government, and otherwise protect the interests of their members in the group.

An industry-wide code that deals with societal concerns, which emanate from the business operations of member companies, is more difficult to implement without significant outside pressure. Since the extent and nature of undesirable conduct would vary among different companies, their cost of compliance to a uniform code would also be different, hence the reluctance of individual companies to comply with a common code. This situation is quite similar to the case of the GPO industry. Testimony by industry representatives at the Senate subcommittee's hearing provided ample examples of these differences, which should be a warning to those who would depend on the companies to "define" their highest ethical standards and expect them to "demonstrate" good faith effort toward compliance.

Therefore, to be effective and credible, industry-based voluntary codes of conduct must contend with three issues that are embedded in the code structure. These are (a) the free rider problem, (b) the problem of adverse selection, and (c) the notion of "best business practices."

Free rider problems arise when some type of pressure and coercion is necessary to ensure that member organizations, which benefit from the collective effort, also share the cost of maintaining such effort in proportion to the benefits derived by them.[9] Adverse selection occurs when companies joining the industry group have a lower level of acceptable ethical conduct than is called for under the proposed voluntary code of conduct. In that case, they stand to gain immediate credibility by their association with the code. These companies are likely to exploit the benefits accruing from their participation in the industry's voluntary code while inflicting harm (through bad reputation) on other members of the group.[10]

Structural Flaws in the HGPII

The current conduct of GPOs can best be understood in the context of external environment that provides GPOs with the opportunities to maximize agency revenues without regard to commensurate benefits to the agency's beneficiary clients, that is, extract rewards that are far in excess of reasonable compensation. However, market-based opportunities for revenue generation are not sufficient by themselves. There is the attendant risk of being caught and punished for unethical or illegal conduct. Therefore, self-enrichment on the part of GPOs, funded directly by exorbitant agency costs, would be influenced by a confluence of the twin factors of external opportunities and risk-adjusted possibilities of self-enrichment. These are illustrated in exhibit 10.1.[11]

The first dimension, S_0S_1, of the framework deals with GPOs' external, market-based environment and opportunities that it provides for the middlemen to maximize agency profits. The second dimension, T_0T_1, indicates the magnitude of incentives available to GPOs, or the middlemen, and the extent to which these middlemen can exploit available opportunities for self-enrichment because of low risk of apprehension and punishment.

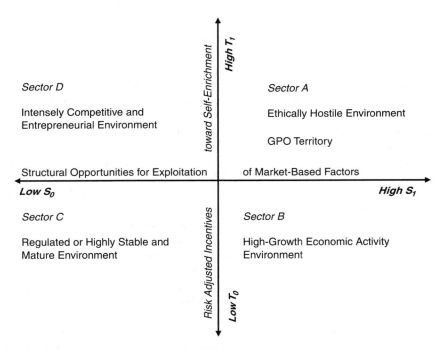

Exhibit 10.1 Influencing ethical conduct in GPOs

An analysis of GPOs' operational environment clearly suggests that GPOs fall in the sector delineated by T_1 and S_1. As an industry, GPOs are a highly concentrated oligopoly where two top companies commanded nearly 60 percent of the market share in 2004.[12] The nine companies, which are signatories of the HGPII, account for 80 percent of the total market share.[13] The industry's oligopolistic structure provides the suppliers with built-in incentives to work only through GPOs. It also makes it unnecessary and unproductive for the industry leaders to compete with each other. Instead, they maximize their market control and revenues through consolidation via mergers and acquisitions and thereby minimize intra-industry competition. This situation—where opportunism is not legally or economically controlled—leads to a disregard of ethical conduct even under conditions of normal business operations.

The second dimension of GPO sector T_1 should also be apparent. GPOs exercise strong control over the information regarding sources and amount of revenues, supplier relationships, and revenues beyond the 3 percent administrative fee; justification for their operating expenses and management compensation; and determination of the size and distribution of the surplus revenue to the member hospitals.

The benefits of combined purchases would be greatly reduced under conditions where the middlemen, that is, GPOs, control the entire process through restrictive arrangements with suppliers and customers. These arrangements would allow them to capture a large portion of the gains from group purchasing activities. These excessive agency costs, that is, compensation for the GPOs and their managers, are further facilitated through GPOs' control of all relevant financial information; and where the governance and accountability structure of these activities is largely, if not entirely, controlled by the GPO management.

To the extent that GPOs are profit-making organizations and largely self-governing, the current arrangement provides them with the most opportunity for self-enrichment, and maximum incentive to structure their operations in a manner that would maximize their income and management rewards. Under these circumstances, seeking lower prices from the suppliers would take a back seat to higher returns generated by products that would maximize revenue for GPOs through administrative fee and other forms of payments. Consequently, the member hospital group is both large and highly diffused. Individual hospitals generally have neither the expertise nor the resources to exercise effective oversight and governance over GPO operations.

Therefore, for the Initiative to succeed under these operating conditions, two things must follow.

1. The Initiative must create internal mechanisms to lower the risk-adjusted incentives toward self-enrichment. This would mean that member companies would create positive incentives for employees that strive for a higher level of ethical conduct and also punish employees that refuse to do so. This would apply equally to the employee conduct undertaken for personal gain or for the benefit of the employee's organization.
2. The second aspect is external and implies that industry's macro external environment is modified to reduce the structural opportunities for exploitation based on market factors. This would mean creating a system where a company's deviation from the industry's professed ethical standards results in loss of company's reputation, increase in regulatory oversight, and even civil and criminal penalties.

Unfortunately, the GPO industry has strongly resisted any demand for effective external monitoring. The result of this state of affairs, when combined with weak and ineffective internal monitoring must be a failure of the Initiative as a viable mechanism to improve the GPOs' performance and enhance public trust in the industry's reputation.

Principle 2: Employee Training Principle

One is hard pressed to understand as to why "employee training" has been elevated to the level of a principle in the GPO Initiative and, what if any, ethical norm underlies such training. Implementing ethical principles and integrating them in an organization's culture involve more than mere training. An organization must develop a system of "rewards and punishments" that would align an employee's personal goals and self-interest with those of the organization's needs and core values. In this framework, training can indeed be an important activity. Conversely, employee training could be an exercise in futility and degenerate into employee cynicism if the training is seen as mere window dressing where employees observe the lessons of training to be in sharp contrast to business practices that are rewarded by the management.

Principle 5: Sharing of Best Practices among Member Companies

At a superficial level, this principle makes good sense. However, when applied to real-life situations, this principle also fails for lack of an understanding of the competitive dynamics and industry structure that drives business conduct. The logic of constantly improving best practices and their sharing with other industry members suffers from the twin elements of the free rider problem and adverse selection.

An industry's effort to improve "best practices" is harmed when the group is dominated by free riders and companies with bad performance (adverse selection). These companies exert pressure on other members to keep a lid on the costs associated with improving compliance as the price of ensuring their participation in the industry's code of conduct (See chapter 9). Improvement in best practices cannot be sustained when companies involve are unable to benefit from improving their practices since they would be shared by other companies that have not incurred similar costs.

It follows, therefore, that "best practices" must have an element of external input and guidance. Otherwise, it would reduce itself to those practices that are supported by all industry members, or a very large majority thereof. Otherwise, the least ethical member companies would hold a veto power over other companies that wish to improve their standards and thus undermine industry's aura unanimity and cohesiveness. This point was vividly mentioned by Premier as its reason for discontinuing disclosure of top management compensation because other GPOs had declined to do so.[14] The situation is further exacerbated when the process of self-professed compliance and reporting is substituted for independent third party monitoring and full transparency in public disclosure.

Unfortunately, the Initiative in its current formulation meets all the negative conditions that would inhibit creation, dissemination, and advocacy of constantly improving best practices. The consequences of this state of affairs on the failure of the Initiative in creating and sustaining best practices should be quite apparent and just as easy to predict.

Principle 6: Accountability to the Public

This principle, like all the others has no definitional content and also lacks specificity. As such it is no principle at all. The concept of accountability has two components. The first one pertains to the elements a company's performance or Lack thereof that meets societal expectations of a company's performance, that is, the substance of a company's performance for which it holds itself accountable to its primary stakeholders. The second element pertains to the transparency in the company's external communications. None of these components have been satisfied in the so-called public accountability by the Initiative's sponsors.

Fatal Flaws in the Initiative

In our opinion, the Initiative suffers from two fatal flaws that render the Initiative totally irrelevant as to what it promises to the community by way of performance improvement.

1. The first one deals with the process of implementation and compliance with the Initiative's principles, and the system of governance that ensures the integrity of the process and also engenders public trust as to the veracity of claims made by the GPO Industry.
2. The second one deals with the Initiative's omission in addressing issues that underpin its business model and its adverse consequences for the industry's beneficiaries. They pertain to a clear and transparent explanation of how the GPOs generate revenue and how those revenues are allocated to expenses, management compensation, and distribution of any surplus or savings to the member hospitals.

Implementation Process

All member GPOs are required to complete a questionnaire every year for submission to the coordinator of the Initiative. The questionnaire merely asks the company to certify that it has complied with the requirements of the six principles. The companies do not provide any details or financial information. Nor do they discuss any issues where they found short falls in their compliance efforts. A review of the detailed questionnaires furnished by the first round of member companies further supports this observation. These questionnaires provide us with extensive details on individual GPO's policies and procedures, but there are no details on how these policies are being implemented, incidents of failure to comply, and the corrective actions, if any, taken by the management.

Furthermore, there is no independent process within the company, for example, internal audit department or external public auditing firm, to verify the accuracy of the information. Even where the company collects this information, it is not made public. The role of the Initiative's coordinator is exactly what the title suggests, that is, to receive and coordinate such information.

The governance structure of the GPO initiative does not provide any mechanism for independent external monitoring and verification of member companies' self-reported performance. Such an assertion would be untenable given the industry's current record.

The industry's vehement defense of voluntary self-regulation, evils of regulation, and independent monitoring is so deterministic as to exclude any room for doubt. The real world, however, is quite different. Even the most ardent advocates of free enterprise recognize the need for some form of oversight both to protect the industry from its own excesses and the public from the unintended consequence of industry's action.

The document also defends the inherent merits of a voluntary code when compared with the alternative of governmental regulation and alludes to the agile and dynamic nature of member companies' management in responding to the evolving needs of the healthcare marketplace. The document further argues that "an additional regulatory solution is much less likely to be successful. Faced with a complex regulatory scheme, companies inevitably turn primarily to lawyers to try to ensure that they are meeting the letter of the law. Any aspiration to best practices tends to be extinguished by regulatory complexity and burden."[15] Furthermore, any "attempt to regulate the industry would take several years, and would be unlikely to keep up with the structure of the industry. A voluntary system can require extensive ongoing transparency and respond most effectively to the changing structure of the industry."[16] Underlining these value-loaded assertions are such terms as complex regulatory schemes, where companies "inevitably" turn to lawyers, and where aspiration to best practices "tends to be extinguished by regulatory complexity and burden." Left unstated is the question as to what happens when industry members fail to meet their commitments.

Mr. Bednar's defense of a system of voluntary compliance, self-regulation, self-monitoring, and self-selected reporting in an oligopolistic industry suffering from public reprobation flies in the face of reality and historical evidence. If the industry is so confident of the integrity of this governance process, the substantiveness of its achievements, and the veracity of its information, why is it so adamant against any requirement that its actions, communications be externally monitored and their accuracy verified by a credible third party?

If voluntary self-regulation, with any external oversight, could be successful, as Mr. Bednar asserts, there would be no need for agencies like Consumer Product Safety Commission, Environmental Protection Agency, Occupational Safety and Health Administration, and Food and Drug Administration, to name a few. We would all then be able to live happily in the Nirvana of private enterprise and dispense with interfering and unproductive regulatory bureaucrats.

There is ample evidence in the history to show that political leaders seldom initiate or succeed in creating regulatory oversight to prevent potential problems. Instead, most of regulatory reforms come about to correct the problems that have already been created in the market economy and the regulation is designed to limit the broad economy and to safe the "markets" from the adverse consequences of their poor judgment.

This point was poignantly made by Mr. Vikram Pandit, the current CEO of Citigroup in a recent Op-Ed piece in the *Wall Street Journal*. Commenting on the collapse of the financial system arising from the sub-prime lending debacle, he states:

> In my view, three principles in particular—transparency, a level playing field and systemic oversight—are the essential elements we need to consider...Markets cannot clear without transparency...We all know that and yet we're seeing again the consequences of a lack of full transparency...Yet transparency is difficult to achieve. It requires continual vigilance...Moreover, transparency means that systemically significant institutions—essentially any institution whose

uncontrolled failure would impact the financial system in a significantly adverse way—should meet robust information requirements set by the overseeing regulatory agency...[The third principle suggests] is a need for oversight for systemically significant institutions. We cannot and should not legislate away an institution's ability to lose shareholders' money. But none should have the right to impose externalities on the rest of the financial system.... In order to realize all the possibilities in the global trends reshaping our world and our financial systems, we welcome a more robust regulatory architecture that embraces standards broad and clear enough to apply to all participants, but is flexible enough to be adaptable to unforeseeable changes in a dynamic market.[17]

Mr. Bednar's references to Sarbanes-Oxley and U.S. Sentencing Guidelines are also misplaced. Under the Sarbanes-Oxley, the top managers of a company are held responsible for any misstatements or omissions of material facts, which they have certified as accurate. Similarly, the Sentencing Guidelines consider a company's diligence in installing and monitoring control systems. The guidelines, however, do not absolve managers for their illegal conduct in any way. It should be apparent that no such provisions exist in the HGPII and hence any comparison between the two is inaccurate and unjustified. Mr. Bednar also states that insofar as the sanctions are concerned, "this Initiative is not designed to tee up penalties for misconduct. It is designed to encourage ethical conduct."[18] Mr. Bednar goes on to state that "CEOs believe in ethical leadership as the best way to introduce ethical business conduct within their organizations. The CEOs do not believe in out-sourcing this responsibility." Mr. Bednar places his confidence in the integrity of the CEOs of the member companies and thus asks us to commend the Initiative's system of self-governance, one in which the same group of people whose performance is being evaluated are the people who are doing the evaluation.

Mr. Bednar's assertions as to the effectiveness of the self-governance, which means no outside watchdog of any kind, were also dismissed by two senior law enforcement officials who had investigated GPO conduct. For example, during the third hearing of the Senate subcommittee on GPO operations, Connecticut's Attorney General Richard Blumenthal stated that his investigation over the last two years makes him question as to whether some GPOs were at all committed to serving the best interest of their constituencies, and added that "there is a clear, compelling need for federal regulation of GPOs."[19] In a similar vein, Mr. David Baldo, former antitrust attorney at the Federal Trade Commission concluded that voluntary codes of the type of the HGPII ineffective and meaningless because they are "ambiguous, lack consistency, contain no enforcement mechanisms and don't authorize any organization to police compliance."[20]

Governance Structure

The governance structure of the Initiative is comprised of a Steering Committee whose members are the CEOs of the major GPOs that account for more than 80 percent of the industry's revenue. Therefore, for all intents and purposes the control of the Steering Committee rests in the hands of the very CEOs whose companies are to be monitored by the Initiative. From the public policy perspective, the Initiative's governance structure is the worst that could be designed to engender public trust in an industry's performance, which had hitherto suffered from public disapproval for its business practices, self dealings, and other instances of conflict of interest. And yet, it is the best form of governance structure, if the intent was to control and protect all "sensitive" information from the prying eyes and ears of the industry's critics and public-at-large. What is even more preposterous is the industry's claim that this governance structure would ensure full commitment of the CEOs to the Initiative. The statement, however, begs the question that if each CEO is fully committed to the code, why is there a need for a collective industry effort.

In his testimony before the Senate Judiciary Subcommittee on Antitrust, Competition Policy, and Consumer Rights, the Initiative's coordinator, Mr. Richard Bednar alludes to recent developments in corporate governance, that is, the Sarbanes-Oxley Act and U.S. Sentencing Commission Guidelines for Organizations,[21] both of which urge companies to install in-house training and monitoring processes, whose effectiveness would be considered as mitigating factors when companies are found to be in noncompliance with required legal or regulatory standards of conduct.

There are two serious problems with Mr. Bednar's assertions. The six "principles" are nothing more than a set of exhortations that these companies would fulfill as they see fit. All measures of substance are left entirely to the member companies. Industry members also set their own criteria regarding compliance, performance evaluation, implementation assurance, and public disclosure.

In asserting the potential benefits of the voluntary Initiative, an industry document states: "Achieving exemplary ethics and business practices across an industry is something that will occur only if the leadership of the industry makes a significant commitment to achieve the articulated standards. With this Initiative, each CEO is pledging that his or her organization will achieve the ethics and business conduct standards that are addressed in the core principles and the questionnaire."[22]

Reduced to its bare essentials, the final product of this process is nothing more than a compilation of reports provided by the member companies based on their own self-evaluation. Member companies are asked to be accountable and transparent. What is left unsaid, however, is the mention of specific standards for which they should be held accountable. What are the specific requirements of transparency that they are expected to meet?

The Money Trail

As stated earlier, the Initiative is conspicuously silent regarding the issues that are related to how GPOs earn their revenues and how they spend them. Since money is the source of most of business practices where GPOs have been charged with questionable conduct, these issues must be made an integrate part of the Initiative's principles. Otherwise we would end up trying to fight the symptoms and ignore the underlying problem.

Administrative Fee and Safe Harbor

HGPII is conspicuously silent in its discussion of two important problems, that is, administrative fees and anti-kickback safe harbor that lie at the core of practically all questionable practices attributed to GPOs. The questionnaires, which establish the accountability system and transparency in disclosure, also do not deal directly with these issues. One of the most contentious items in this regard is the GPOs' collection from their suppliers of an administrative fee, rebates, and charges for various services.

The safe harbor protection give the GPOs almost total discretion in the use of this fee to cover their operating costs, and the distribution of any residual surplus to their member hospitals. This fee is intended to cover the cost of providing contract negotiations and management services by the GPOs. The administrative fee, however, has become a primary source of self-enrichment on the part of GPO management and to the detriment of their beneficiary clients.

Principal–Agency Conflict

There are three problems with the fixed fee arrangement, which cause them to lose any direct and meaningful relationship to the cost of service that it is intended to cover. First, instead of creating incentives to lower costs and better efficiencies, a constant fee rate creates incentives that do the opposite; the prices paid remain constant without regard to whether actual costs go down. A constant fee will eliminate the possibility of earning lower revenue from the administrative fee by the GPOs. Second, the fee structure generates rewards that further retard the process of innovation and cost efficiencies because the current system of administrative fee has no relation whatsoever to the cost of running GPO operations. Nor is the fee related to the efficiency and cost of products contracted by different suppliers. Instead, the fee has become a key part of a system of "pay to play" where the middlemen, that is, GPOs, strive to maximize their revenues by increasing the total size of purchases. And, all other things being equal, a higher priced product—given the same volume and a percentage fee—will yield a higher level of revenue to the middleman.

Third, the most important factor for the hospitals to understand and recognize is that the administrative fee is not some "free good" delivered by the suppliers out of the goodness of their hearts. For them, it is just another cost of doing business. Someone must pay this cost and it is reflected in the price, at which these goods are sold by the suppliers. It should be apparent to everyone that GPOs' current suppliers are not running a charity and that any fee that they have to pay, no matter what it is called, eventually would have to be added to their costs and reflected in the prices they charge for their products. When this fee is eliminated, the money saved does not evaporate into thin air. It would either be reflected in lower prices charged by the suppliers, or someone else would reap the profits. The inevitable result of a buyer's lack of control is that middlemen continue to earn enormous profits, and their managers excessive compensation, while hospitals struggle to make ends meet through excessive cost cutting that often endangers the quality of service and patient care.

When All Is Said and Done, It's Mostly Said Than Done

In this section, we briefly examine the proceedings of the Third Annual HGPII "Best Practices Forum" that was held in Washington, DC on January 15–16, 2008. Our intention is to understand and appreciate the progress that HGPII has made since its inception in April 2005.

The Initiative Progress Report

The discussion by the forum's participants was focused on the following issues:

1. The continued public distrust in industry's actions and statements.
2. The need to restore industry's reputation.
3. A sense of alarm that the industry show measurable progress or risk regulatory action especially in view of the fact that the next Congress may be controlled by the Democratic party.

Mr. Norling, CEO of Premier, referred to the increasing number of "headlines" in national periodicals related to myriad conflicts of interest, a lack of transparency, and litigation brought by the federal government. He also stated that the industry only has itself to blame for the current wave of investigations and legislation introduced on Capitol Hill this he attributed to the current behavior, questionable practices, and collusive relationships among various parties in supply chain transactions as the key contributors to these legislative issues.

Mr. Jerry Walsh of Hospital Purchasing Services (MedAssets Affiliate) stated that the greatest challenge faced by the healthcare industry is an overall lack of trust and an erosion of the public's confidence particularly in certain sectors of the healthcare industry.

Mr. Richard Bednar, Coordinator of HGPII, in his opening remarks praised members for their ability to function as a cohesive unit to develop an ethical framework of codes and business practices that could be held up to public scrutiny and be considered transparent, whilst at the same time maintaining their inherent competitiveness. He commented the group for their help in expanding the six core principles comprising the Initiative code of conduct. Mr. Bednar also noted the critical need for expanding the Annual Accountability Questionnaire to facilitate transparency within the industry (See table 10.1). Given below is the enhanced set of principles approved by the forum:

Table 10.1 Enhancement to HGPII's six core principles now "code of conduct principles"

HGPII's Six Core Principles (Before September 21, 2007)	HGPII's Code of Conduct Principles (September 21, 2007)
Each Member Shall:	Each Signatory Shall:
(1) Have and adhere to a written code of business conduct. The code establishes the high ethical values expected for all within the Signatory's organization.	(1) Each Signatory shall have and adhere to a written code of business conduct. The code establishes high ethical values and sound business practices for the Signatory's group purchasing organization.
(2) Train all within the organization as to their personal responsibilities under the code.	(2) Each Signatory shall train all within the organization as to their personal responsibilities under the code.
(3) Work toward the twin goals of high quality healthcare and cost effectiveness.	(3) Each Signatory commits itself to work toward the twin goals of high quality healthcare and cost effectiveness.
(4) Work toward an open and competitive purchasing process free of conflicts of interest and any undue influences.	(4) Each Signatory commits itself to work toward an open and competitive purchasing process free of conflicts of interest and any undue influences.
(5) Have the responsibility to each other to share their best practices in implementing the Principles; each Signatory shall participate in an annual Best Practices Forum.	(5) Each Signatory shall have the responsibility to each other to share their best practices in implementing the Principles; each Signatory shall participate in an annual Best Practices Forum.
(6) Be accountable to the public.	(6) Each Signatory, through its participation in this Initiative, shall be accountable to the public.

Source: http://www.healthcaregpoii.com/, October 30, 2007; HGPII Annual Report 2006.

And finally there were frequent mentions of the need for contracting an external assessor to audit the code was attained. The Initiative's governing body will aggressively pursue the contract of such a person, or body over the next few months notably in light of the greater transparency demanded by regulators and industry members.

The deliberations of the HGPII Third Best Practices Forum makes evidently clear that the industry recognizes that the problems and challenges confronted by the industry are unlikely to go away anytime soon. It is also apparent that the Initiative as presently constructed and implemented is unlikely to provide much help in either resolving the issues or enhancing public trust and confidence in the industry. Unfortunately, the GPO industry has been unable to provide the forward looking leadership to address the issues emanating from the oligopolistic structure of the industry and the inherent conflict of interest embedded in its business model that misaligns its financial incentives from the best interest of its beneficiary clients.

Concluding Remarks

Our discussion and analysis in the preceding sections effectively demonstrates that the HGPII is not structured to achieve its professed objectives. It has built-in structural characteristics that are designed to prevent it from attacking the problems, which initially gave rise to public controversy and pressure for additional regulatory oversight.

The GPO Initiative is weakened by a lack of specificity, nonexistent performance standards, an internally controlled and self-serving governance structure, and an absence of genuine independent external monitoring. Given its current structure, it is difficult to see how it can or will make any meaningful improvement in the system of GPO operations and in delivering benefits to the hospitals, which must be their principal beneficiaries. Conversely, the realization of these benefits is entirely feasible, if and when GPO operations are independently monitored and GPOs are held accountable for their conduct.

The Initiative needs to be enhanced by requiring the GPOs to make full and complete disclosure of their finances. Moreover, the financial disclosure would be certified and independently verified by an outside auditing firm. The information to be provided would include:

1. All sources of income and their connection with GPO operations.
2. Disclosure of operating expenditures in meaningful categories.
3. Details of compensation packages for top executives.
4. Distribution of surplus revenue to member hospitals and the criteria used to determine allocations.
5. Disclosure of ownership interests in GPOs by their managers and also by the managers of member hospitals.

Appendix 10.1: The Healthcare Group Purchasing Industry Initiative Code of Conduct Principles

1. *Each GPO shall have and adhere to a written code of business conduct. The code establishes high ethical values expected for all within the Signatory's organization.*
   a. Each GPO's distribution of code of business conduct ("Code") shall include
      i. distributing the Code to all new employees during their employee orientation; and
      ii. making available the Code to all clinical advisory committee members, contractors, directors, agents, and vendors.
   b. Each GPO's oversight of its Code shall include
      i. a compliance officer to be responsible for overseeing compliance with the Code;
      ii. a compliance committee or similar committee to advise the compliance officer and assist in the implementation of the Code;
      iii. a mechanism whereby employees can report possible violations of the Code without fear of retribution;
      iv. a mechanism to evaluate, investigate, and resolve suspected violations of the Code;
      v. a process to monitor on a continuing basis, adherence to the Code;
      vi. a process whereby adherence to the Code is measured in job performance;
      vii. a process to inform its Board of Director's committee or other appropriate committee regarding its adherence to its Code and its commitment to The Healthcare Group Purchasing Code of Conduct Principles; and
      viii. a process to continually measure and improve upon the value of the GPO's Code by evaluating best practices within the healthcare group purchasing industry.
2. *Each GPO shall train all within the organization as to their personal responsibilities under the code.*
   a. Each GPO's Code training shall include
      i. providing all new employees training on the Code and any applicable law; and
      ii. providing periodic compliance training, guidance, and education on the Code and any applicable law to employees, committee members, directors, officers, and any applicable contracting agents.
3. *Each GPO commits itself to work toward the twin goals of high-quality healthcare and cost effectiveness.*
   a. Each GPO's policies supporting high-quality healthcare and cost effectiveness shall include

      i. a policy that encourages a competitive marketplace for healthcare procurement;

      ii. a policy that encourages members to purchase future medical technology and products determined to be innovative;

      iii. a policy that promotes the evaluation of innovative medical technology and products; and

      iv. a policy that promotes purchase of safe medical products.

4. *Each GPO commits itself to work toward an open and competitive purchasing process free of conflicts of interest and any undue influences.*

    a. Each GPO's conflict of interest policies related to individuals shall include

      i. a requirement that employees in a position to influence the GPO contracting process not accept any gifts, entertainment, favors, honoraria, or personal service payments other than those of a Nominal Value from any participating vendor;

      ii. a policy prohibiting its employees who are in a position to influence the GPO contracting decisions from having an Individual Equity Interest in any participating vendor in the contract areas they influence;

      iii. a policy that requires that any employee not covered under Section 4(a)(ii), and any officer, director, or a member of an advisory board of a GPO who accepts any gifts, favors, honoraria, or personal services payments other than those of Nominal Value from any participating vendor to disclose such transactions to the appropriate governing body and for that individual to be recused from any negotiations or decisions related to such participating vendor;

      iv. a policy that requires that any employee not covered under Section 4(a) (ii), officer, director, or a member of an advisory board of a GPO to disclose Individual Equity Interests in any participating vendor to the appropriate governing body and for that individual to be recused from any negotiations or decisions relating to such participating vendor; and

      v. a policy that requires all employees, directors, officers, and members of advisory boards to disclose information regarding any conflict of interest described in its Code on at least an annual basis.

    b. Each GPO's conflict of interest policies shall include a policy to ensure that it does not have any Corporate Equity Interest in any participating vendor unless the acquisition of such Corporate Equity Interest demonstrably benefits the GPO's members, the GPO discloses such equity interest to its members in writing, and the GPO imposes no obligation, commitment, or other requirements or restrictions that in any way obligates a member to purchase goods or services from such participating vendor.

    c. Each GPO's conflict of interest and disclosure policies related to administrative fees shall include

      i. a policy that ensures that the receipt of administrative fees from vendors do not encroach upon the best interests of the GPO's members,

      ii. a policy that requires it to have a written agreement with each member authorizing it to act as their purchasing agent to negotiate contracts with vendors to furnish goods or services to each member,

      iii. a policy to disclose in writing to each member or member's agent that it receives payments from participating vendors with respect to purchases made by or on behalf of such member,

      iv. a policy that requires it annually to disclose all administrative fees received from vendors for contracting activities with respect to purchases made by the respective member, and

      v. a policy that requires it annually to disclose all payments received from any vendor in the course of the GPO's group purchasing activities, but not allocable   or otherwise reported with respect to the actual purchases of that or any other member.

  d. Each GPO's policies to ensure an open and competitive purchasing process shall include

      i. a requirement to publicly post on its Web site or through other appropriate means information about its contracting process and contract opportunities;

      ii. a policy to ensure a fair and unbiased system for evaluating healthcare products and services being considered for procurement;

      iii. a policy that allows its members to communicate directly with all vendors and evaluate their products, regardless of whether the vendor has a contract with the GPO;

      iv. a policy that allows its members to purchase medical products from vendors that do not contract with the GPO;

      v. a policy that establishes a vendor grievance procedure;

      vi. a policy to ensure the appropriate use of bundling, length of contracts, and sole or dual source contracts; and

      vii. a policy that promotes diversity among vendors to small, women and minority-owned vendors.

5. *Each GPO shall have the responsibility to each other to share their best practices in implementing the Principles; each Signatory shall participate in an annual Best Practices Forum.*

  a. Each GPO's Best Practices Forum participation shall include sending an appropriate number of participants including senior executives to actively participate in the annual Best Practices Forum.

6. *Each GPO shall be accountable to the public.*

  a. Each GPO's responsibilities shall include

      i. ensuring its CEO and Compliance Officer annually certify to the Initiative that it is in compliance with The Healthcare Group Purchasing Code of Conduct Principles,

ii. submitting its response to the Initiative's Annual Public Accountability Questionnaire on a timely basis, and

iii. ensuring its CEO and Compliance Officer annually certify to the Initiative that these individuals have reviewed and approved the GPO's Public Accountability response.

Approved and Adopted by the Initiative Steering Committee: September 21, 2007.

Epilogue: A Whistleblower Files a Law Suit against Novation

This is like deja vu all over again
—Yogi Berra

On September 23, 2007, the plaintiff Ms. Cynthia Fitzgerald filed a complaint ("Complaint")[1] against the defendants, Novation, LLC. ("Novation"), VHA, Inc. ("VHA"), University HealthSystem Consortium ("UHC"), and Healthcare Purchasing Partners International, LLC ("HPPI") for action to recover damages and civil penalties on behalf of the United States of America and the State of Texas, and complainant Cynthia I. Fitzgerald.[2]

The defendants in this action are charged with false statements and claims made, presented, and caused to be presented by the defendants and/or their agents, employees and coconspirators in violation of the Federal Civil False Claims Act,[3] and the Texas Medicaid Fraud Prevention Act, Texas Human Resources Code.[4]

The defendants in this action are VHA and UHC, two nation-wide hospital networks consisting of 2,200 community-owned hospitals and 100 teaching hospitals. Novation is the nation's largest group purchasing organization (GPO) founded and wholly owned by VHA and UHC to provide purchasing services to their collective 2,300 member healthcare organizations, and HPPI, another VHA-UHC joint venture and GPO that markets Novation purchasing agreements to more than 5,000 healthcare organizations that do not belong to the VHA or UHC hospital networks.[5]

At all times relevant to this Complaint, meaning from 1993 to present, the member hospitals of Defendants VHA and UHC and the healthcare organizations that were customers of Defendant HPPI, purchased under the Novation group contracts supplies and services that were used in providing medical care to beneficiaries of state and federally funded health insurance programs, costs of which were reimbursed by the government health insurance programs, including Medicare, Medicaid, and TRICARE/CHAMPUS.[6]

Medicare is a federally funded health insurance program primarily for the elderly. Medicaid is a state and federally funded health insurance program for low-income patients. In Texas, the Medicaid program—known as the Texas Medicaid Program—is funded with 60 percent federal funds and 40 percent state funds. The Civilian Health and Medical Program of the Uniformed Services, now known as TRICARE ("TRICARE/CHAMPUS"), is a federally funded health insurance program for individuals with family affiliations to the military services.[7]

During all times covered in this Complaint, defendant Novation (and its predecessor VHA Supply Company), was in the business of securing on behalf of the VHA and UHC Members and HPPI customers group contracts with manufacturers, suppliers, and distributors (collectively "vendors")[8] for supplies and services. The VHA and UHC Members and HPPI customers purchase more than $19.6 billion in supplies and services annually under Novation's group contracts and collectively comprise 22 percent of the national market of staffed beds, 29 percent of total admissions, and 30 percent of total surgeries, Consequently, Novation wields considerable power in determining which manufacturer will be awarded one of its more than 600 group contracts and which distributors will be authorized to distribute products under these contracts.[9]

The Complaint alleges that throughout this period, defendant Novation, with the assistance of VHA, UHC, and HPPI, used its contracting power to secure kickbacks and other illegal remuneration from the vendors as payment for awarding them coveted Novation contracts. It further argues that defendant Novation, and its affiliates engaged in these fraudulent practices knowing that such payments would inflate the costs of the contracted supplies that the VHA and UHC Members and HPPI customers purchased and would ultimately cause them to submit to the government health insurance programs—in the invoices and annual cost reports—claims for reimbursement for supplies and services that were higher than they would have been had Novation not solicited and received these illegal payments.[10]

Defendant Novation, with the assistance of VHA, UHC, and HPPI, also engaged in these fraudulent practices knowing that, by awarding contracts to those vendors willing to pay Novation the biggest kickback (and not necessarily those able to supply the best product at the lowest price), it would be routinely excluding smaller manufacturers with safer and more innovative products from supplying to hospitals and other healthcare institutions served by Novation and its affiliated companies. Further, these innovative products would have obviated or reduced the need for treatment of Medicare, Medicaid, and TRICARE/CHAMPUS beneficiaries and, in so doing, caused the government health insurance programs to incur increased healthcare costs.[11]

Under the Federal FCA and Texas MFPA, *Qui Tam*, Cynthia I. Fitzgerald, Plaintiff/Relator ("Relator") seeks to recover damages and civil penalties arising from defendants' actions in soliciting and receiving kickbacks and thereby causing the VHA and UHC members and HPPI customers to present false records, claims, and statements to the United States Government, the state governments (including the State of Texas) and their respective agents' claims for excessive reimbursement for supplies and services provided to beneficiaries of the Medicare, Medicaid, and TRICARE/CHAMPUS programs.[12]

Relator (Cynthia Fitzgerald) has information and believes that the fraudulent practices described herein were typical of defendant Novation and Novation's predecessor VHA Supply Company at all times material to this action and that VHA, UHC, and HPPI aided and abetted Novation and VHA Supply in these activities. Relator has information and believes that defendants have engaged in these fraudulent practices from at least 1993 to present.[13]

The Plaintiff

The Plaintiff Fitzgerald, a Texas resident, was employed by Novation from July 1998 to February 1999 as a Senior Product Manager for Medical/Surgical products in their Irving, Texas office. In this capacity, Fitzgerald negotiated with manufacturers of medical supplies from syringes to trash bags, extracting the lowest price for the highest-quality goods for healthcare consumers. During the period of her employment, Relator was responsible for negotiating and managing a portfolio of group contracts for medical/surgical supplies and services that was worth $243 million. In this connection, she became privy to the inner workings of Novation's contracting process, including the criteria Novation utilized to determine the vendors to whom it would award contracts.

Over the months, however, she found her job description turned on its head, as Novation executives asked her to look the other way as deals were cut with vendors that led to high prices for questionable items.[14] From her interactions with her superiors Sherry Woodcock and John Burks, among others, she quickly realized that her performance would be judged not merely by her ability to deliver to VHA and UHC members contracts for the best supplies at the lowest prices, but also by the amount of revenue she was able to generate for Novation in the form of up-front payments and other illegal remuneration, of which the members were not apprised.[15]

Shortly after Ms. Fitzgerald began to complain to senior management at Novation about these fraudulent practices, Novation terminated her employment in retaliation for her questioning their propriety. After mere seven months on this job, Cynthia Fitzgerald was out of work—fired, she says, because she raised questions about her company's business practices, including pressure to steer millions of dollars in business to a former official of the buying group's predecessor.[16]

"I don't look good in orange or in stripes," Ms. Fitzgerald said she told her supervisor after objecting to the way another contract was handled. After raising concerns about these practices with Novation's Human Resources staff, Senior Management and In-House Legal Counsel and having those concerns summarily dismissed, Relator realized that these fraudulent practices were not unique to the Medical/Surgical Division but instead pervaded Novation's business.[17] Before long, the company, Novation, arranged to have her "escorted off the property by guards." Ms. Fitzgerald, 44, made her comments recently under oath in a sealed deposition obtained by the *New York Times*.[18]

The two groups, which negotiate contracts for about two-thirds of the nation's hospitals, deny the accusations and are contesting them in court.

"We can, however, state that any decision to end Ms. Fitzgerald's employment was based on her work performance only," the statement added.[19]

Alleged Fraudulent Activities by Novation and Its Affiliates

From the details provided in the Complaint, it would seem that safe harbor protection and administrative fee are the core elements that provide both the *raison d'être* and the means by which GPOs alleged illegal activities are facilitated. Safe harbor provisions protecting GPOs from the Anti-Kickback Act[20] defines what constitutes as appropriate administrative fee (see chapter 4) and requires that (a) The GPO must have a written agreement with each of its members under which the fee and its terms are disclosed; (b) the fee must be 3 percent or less of the purchase price, and where it is more than 3 percent, the total amount to be paid by each vendor; and (c) the GPO must provide each member with an annual report listing the amount the GPO received from each vendor in administrative fees based on the member's purchases.[21] At the same time, "Federal law makes it a felony to "solicit [ ] or receive [ ] any remuneration (including any kickbacks, bribe or rebate) directly or indirectly, overtly or covertly, . . . in return for purchasing, . . . ordering, or arranging for or recommending purchasing, . . . or ordering any good, facility, service, or item for which payment may be made in whole or in part under a Federal health care program."[22]

The Complaint charges that during the period covered under the complaint, Novation (and its predecessor VHA Supply) had solicited and received from the vendors to whom it awards contracts kickbacks and other illegal remuneration as payment for awarding them group contracts. Unlike the administrative fees vendors pay to GPOs, which are condoned by Congress, these kickbacks and other illegal remuneration are in no way tied to the administrative costs Novation incurs in managing the contract. Nor are they calculated based on clearly defined, objective criteria such as the volume of purchases made under the contract by Novation's customers. Instead, they are simply payments Novation requires vendors to pay up-front or throughout the life of the contract for the privilege of being awarded a group contract and thereby gaining access to Novation's 7,300 customers.

The Complaint charges that Novation regularly chooses among the competing vendors based on who is willing to pay the most. Under this guiding business principle, Novation has awarded the majority of its more than 600 contracts to large vendors, who have been able to pay the biggest kickbacks. The vendors, in turn, inflate the prices they charge under the contract to recoup the costs of paying Novation the kickbacks and other illegal remuneration necessary to win the contact. These increased costs are ultimately borne by the insurers, both government and private, who reimburse the VHA and UHC members and HPPI customers for the costs of treating their insureds/ beneficiaries. Novation (and its predecessor VHA Supply) has concealed the existence of these kickbacks and other remuneration from the VHA and UHC members and HPPI customers, disguising the proceeds in "slush funds," secret accounts, and unrelated business ventures. The overwhelming majority of the monies/remuneration received from these kickbacks is retained by Novation, typically as lavish bonuses and "incentive" compensation for its officers and executives[23] or as capital for financing new ventures, such as the e-commerce company Neoforma, Inc.[24]

Types of Allegedly Fraudulent Schemes Engaged in by Novation and Its Affiliates

In her complaint, Ms. Fitzgerald indicated a number of unfair and illegal contracting practices by Novation employees. She recalled that companies bidding for Novation contracts were systematically proposing package deals that included opportunities for rebate, frequent-buyer discounts, "loyalty" rewards, baskets of products tied together, and even shares of stock, project sponsorship, and simply cash. The Complaint details a large number of instances where Novation audits affiliates have engaged in fraudulent activities. These are classified into four categories. They are (a) up-front payments to buy the contracts, (b) administrative/marketing fees, (c) payments for products offered under Novation's Private Label Brand, and (d) conflict of interest/beneficial business relations.

Buy the Contract or Pay to Play

These schemes involved Novation's seeking potential vendors to make up-front payments to ensure that their bids would be successful. On their face, these payments appear to have no relationship to the quality or pricing of the products being offered. And yet, they concealed a plethora of ingenious devices by which Novation would fatten its coffers.

Johnson & Johnson's attempt to buy the IV Catheter Contract
One of the first assignments given to Ms. Fitzgerald in her position as Senior Contract Manager was a three-year contract for "IV Standard and Safety Catheters and NOVAPLUS®IVStartKits." Under this contract, Novation was seeking a vendor to supply IV Catheters as well as IV Start Kits under Novation's private label brand. This was the first contract for IV Catheters and Start Kits put out for public competitive bid since Novation was formed. Ms. Fitzgerald was first alarmed by an incident around a private meeting with Johnson & Johnson (J&J), one of the companies whose bidding was still pending at the time. According to Novation's rules of ethical conduct, employees are not allowed to hold private meetings or to have any unrecorded communications with bidding companies. Ms. Fitzgerald claimed that she was deeply disturbed when J&J representative asked her "how much will it take to get the contract." She was also assured by J&J that it was a normal practice and others before her had done it.[25]

Fitzgerald made repeated efforts to seek guidance from her immediate supervisor Sherry Woodcock failing which she contacted other top officials at

Novation, including John Burks, former, head of Novation's Medical/Surgical Division. Burk indicated that while Johnson & Johnson's actions may have been unethical, he did not consider them to be illegal. Burks believed that Relator's suggested action—disqualifying Johnson & Johnson's bid—was too harsh a punishment. After Burks refused to take action against J&J, Fitzgerald took the matter to Novation's Human Resources staff, William Laws, Jr. and Shirley Lopez, and in-house counsel, Gerry Rubin, but was similarly rebuffed. Nevertheless, she ended up denying the contract to J&J because of its inferior bid and instead granted it to Becton Dickinson and Company (BD). This was the first and last contract Relator ever negotiated for Novation. Ms. Fitzgerald's refusal to play by these rules in the course of her work negotiating the IV Catheter Contract (and later the Can-Liner Contract) represented an un-expected (albeit short-lived) departure from the norm. Shortly after voicing her concerns about Novation's contracting practices, Ms. Fitzgerald began to receive criticism about her job performance, was ostracized by her co-workers, and quickly terminated.

Becton Dickinson's $100,000 "Donation" to Novation in
Connection with Winning the IV Catheter Contract
Having selected BD for offering a better value-price package on the IV Catheter contract, Fitzgerald was pressured by her managers to consider what revenue each bidder would be able to provide Novation. In response, Fitzgerald created a program of "sponsorships" at three levels, that is, gold, silver, and bronze to provide Novation's latest information technology project, "VHAseCURE. net" an intranet developed by VHA to enable VHA members to communicate with one another over the Internet. Although to the objective observer, these sponsorship payments appear wholly unconnected to the underlying contract, both Novation and the bidders understood that such "sponsorships" would buy favorable consideration from Novation in making its bid award. These "sponsorship" payments were over and above the administrative/marketing fee (expressed as a percent-of-total sales made under the contract) that vendors like BD had agreed to pay Novation to cover its costs for administering the contract.[26] BD agreed to make a contribution of $100,000 to become a sponsor of the program. Soon thereafter, Novation awarded BD the contract, and BD sent Novation a check for $100,000. At no time did Novation ever disclose the existence, amount or purpose of these "sponsorship" payments to the VHA and UHC members and HPPI customers.[27]

Becton Dickinson's $1 Million Payment in Connection with
Winning the Needle Contract
This case involved a payment of $1 million by BD to Novation as a "Special Marketing Fee" to get a three-year contract for needles and syringes. This $1 million fee was over and above the administrative/marketing fee BD had agreed to pay Novation over the life of the contract based on a percentage (3 percent) of the total sales made by VHA and UHC members under the contract. In the Complaint, Fitzgerald indicated that she had information and

believed that Novation never disclosed to the VHA and UHC members and HPPI customers the fact that it had received this payment from BD in connection with awarding BD the needle contract.[28]

Fee Enhancements by Distributors

In addition to choosing the manufacturers to whom it will award contracts, Novation also controls the distribution channels for the products purchased under its contracts. These exclusive rights are awarded to whom Novation calls "Authorized Distributors." For their services in distributing the products, Authorized Distributors are paid "distribution service fees" by the VHA and UHC members and HPPI customers. The distribution service fees, also known as "the Distribution Mark-Up Fees," are added to the price of the products/services and are calculated based on the total volume of distributed purchases made by the Novation customer. On the surface, Invitations-to-Bid to manufacturers, are supposed to be a public competitive bid process. However, in practice, Novation awards the distribution contracts based on which distributors are willing to pay Novation the largest kickback or other illegal remuneration.[29]

Like the "administrative/marketing" fees it charges manufacturers for the cost of administering the contract (described in the following text), Novation also requires distributors to pay it a monthly fee based on the total purchases of products made by its customers. Although Novation provides distributors with a minimum percentage for what this fee must be, Novation leaves it to the distributor's discretion to propose the amount of the percentage. Under such liberal contracting guidelines, Novation has regularly solicited and accepted lavish fees from distributors in exchange for awarding them an authorized-distributor contract.

In addition to the monthly fee, Novation also encouraged bidders to propose fee enhancements-ways for distributors "to enhance the fee paid to Novation." The Complaint alleges that Novation has routinely awarded distribution contracts to large distributors like Cardinal Health, Inc., Allegiance Corporation, and Owens & Minor, Inc., who were willing and able to pay Novation the largest fee enhancement, "additional fees," or other illegal remuneration.[30]

Administrative/Marketing Fees

In its Invitations-to-Bid, Novation requires all prospective bidders to include information on "marketing fees" to be paid to Novation and to calculate these fees as a percentage of sales made under the contract. Novation does not prescribe any limits on the size of the marketing fee that it is willing to accept (or that bidders may offer). According to a Novation "Contract Administration Fee Report," as of November 18, 1999, Novation had accepted administrative/marketing fees above 3 percent on at least 186 or 31 percent of its 600 contracts. For many of these contracts, Novation received administrative/marketing fees as high as 30 percent of total sales made by Novation's customers under the contract. Contrary to the safe harbor requirements regarding appropriate GPO fees, Novation routinely has solicited and accepted marketing fees that greatly exceeded the 3 percent-of-sales threshold and failed to inform the VHA and UHC members or HPPI customers of the amount received by Novation from such fees.[31]

Major Pharmaceutical Manufacturers Pay Novation Some of the Highest "Administrative/Marketing Fees"

Pharmaceuticals are the largest product line in Novation's contract portfolio. Of Novation's 600 contracts, 275 or 46 percent are contracts with major pharmaceutical manufacturers for the sale of a wide array of pharmaceutical products. Some of the pharmaceutical companies paying administrative/marketing fee ranging from 14 to 30 percent included: Nycomed, Inc. and Bedford Laboratories (30 percent), Dupont Nuclear (25 percent), Bristol-Myers (18 percent), and Abbott Laboratories (18 percent). The Complaint alleges that it has reason to believe that Novation has failed to inform the VHA and UHC members and HPPI customers of the amount of any of these administrative/marketing fees that it has received and continues to receive from pharmaceutical companies.[32]

Novation's Preference for Higher Priced Goods because They Serve to Increase Its "Administrative/Marketing Fees"

In the summer of 2001, Novation received two bids from J&J and U.S. Surgical for endo-mechanical products. Novation's internal evaluation found these products to be comparable while the U.S. Surgical prices were significantly lower than J&J. Nevertheless, the contract was awarded to J&J because U.S. Surgical's lower prices would significantly reduce the marketing fee that Novation would receive.[33]

Payments for Products Offered under Novation's Private Label Brand, "NOVAPLUS®"

Novation encouraged its vendors to supply some of their products to be sold under Novation's private label called NOVAPLUS®. This approach created one more opportunity for Novation to increase its revenues at the expense of its members. Under this arrangement, which is quite different from generics, neither Novation nor the supplier had any cost advantage. Instead, Novation's private label would end up creating an artificial middleman and thereby earn revenue for Novation at two different points of the supply chain. Since Novation is in the business of negotiating contracts from independent suppliers, there can be no justification for Novation to engage in self-dealing and otherwise conceal its conflict of interest from its members under Novation's private "NOVAPLUS®" label. Although, in its bid, Retractable Technologies inc. (RTI) had offered to sell its tube holders for 27 cents per unit, Novation proposed that RTI could sell the same tube holders to Novation's customers for $1 per unit—a 270 percent mark-up—simply by changing the label to Novation's NOVAPLUS® brand. In exchange for RTI's cooperation in this joint venture, Novation agreed to share with RTI a percentage of the profits from the 270 percent mark-up. Although

RTI rejected Novation's offer, Fitzgerald indicated that she had information and believed that Novation consummated many similar deals with other less scrupulous vendors.[34]

Conflicts of Interest/Beneficial Business Relationships

Nepotism/Cronyism with Heritage Bag

In 1998, Novation consolidated its contracts for can liners and awarded them to Heritage Bag Company. Among the reasons cited was the fact that Heritage Bag was offering Novation a payment of 8.19 percent of total sales, which was 6 percent higher than being offered by another supplier, Baxter Tennaco.[35] The information of extra fee paid to Novation was not disclosed to its members.[36] In a discussion with Fitzgerald, her supervisor Sherry Woodcock stated that can-liner contract would always go to Heritage Bag because the company was represented by John M. Doyle, the founder and former president of VHA supply.[37]

Complainant Fitzgerald had "specifically complained that Novation for years had given special treatment to Heritage Bag, a garbage bag company in Texas represented by the former official of the buying group's predecessor, John M. Doyle. Mr. Doyle is the founder and former president of VHA Supply, a buying group that in 1998 merged with a smaller group to form Novation." She was quoted in the *New York Times* in stating, "The only explanation that I ever received was that the contract belonged to Heritage Bag, it was going to belong to Heritage Bag, and that the last person who tried to remove that contract from Heritage Bag was in jeopardy of losing their job."

In response, company officials stated that Novation has spent approximately $11 million a year on Heritage Bag's products. "We give them as high a quality liner as there is in the industry, and the most competitive pricing in the industry." Heritage Bag declined to answer questions about Ms. Fitzgerald's accusations. The *New York Times* reporter, however, was not satisfied and made further inquiries. Her report:

So how good is Novation's contract? For one thing, Novation recommends Heritage Bags to its hospitals as a good buy. Even so, individual hospitals, consultants and smaller buying groups surveyed by The Times reported that if hospitals shop around they can get better deals on many of those same Heritage bags or on comparable bags made by other companies. One medium-sized hospital in the Midwest found, for example, that if it were to switch to Novation's products, it would add about $10,000 a year, or about 11 percent, to its garbage-bag budget. The hospital executive who analyzed the prices asked not to be named because of a confidentiality agreement. There is much better bag pricing outside the Novation-Heritage agreement—sometimes more than 20 percent better, said Bob Bissell, a principal of CoalesCo Ltd., which sets up purchasing cooperatives for small groups of hospitals. Two smaller buying groups separately compared their prices with Novation's prices for identical bags and each reported that its products were about 3 to 5 percent cheaper, on average, when the numbers were weighted to reflect the most frequently purchased bags. Both of these groups requested anonymity for fear of angering Heritage. Some critics of Novation believe that products like the garbage bags may cost more because of the fees manufacturers must pay in connection with contracts, which are then built into their prices.[38]

Owning Stock in Vendors to Whom Novation Awarded Contracts

There could be no more blatant conflict of interest than the situation where GPO executives have financial interest in the companies that are awarded contracts by the GPO. The Complaint cites numerous examples where Novation, VHA, and UHC, as well as top executives at these companies, owned significant stock holdings in and had mutually beneficial business dealings with the vendors. Several of these executives also sat on the vendors' Board of Directors. Rather than award contracts based on objective criteria like quality and price, Novation routinely awarded contracts to vendors in which Novation, its parent companies VHA and UHC, and officers of these companies had a personal financial and/or business interest.[39] These included, among others, J&J, Tyco International Ltd. (Tyco) and its subsidiaries, for example, Sherwood Medical, Kendell Sherwood-Davis & Geck, and Kendell Healthcare Products Company. Other companies similarly situated and receiving preferential treatment were Neoforma, Inc., and Genetech.[40]

Excessive Conference Fees

The Complaint charged that Novation regularly organized and hosted conferences on topics of interest to the VHA and UHC members and HPPI customers. In connection with these conferences, Novation routinely would approach large vendors whom it expected to be bidding on upcoming contracts and solicit from them exorbitant fees to attend segments of the conference sponsored by high-profile keynote speakers. These fees typically were well in excess of Novation's costs in putting on the conference. Moreover, Novation did not inform the VHA and UHC members and HPPI customers about the existence or amount of these fees and charges paid to Novation and kept by the company.[41]

Travel and Entertainment Costs

The Complaint charges that Novation (and its predecessor VHA Supply) accepted lavish trips, meals, and other entertainment from vendors who regularly bid on Novation contracts and to whom Novation subsequently awarded contracts. These trips, meals, and other entertainment had little if any legitimate business purpose. For example, shortly before Novation was expected to issue Invitations-to-Bid for its NOVAPLUS® exam glove contract, American Health Products (AHP)—a large manufacturer of gloves for medical use—hosted a Riverboat cruise on Lake Michigan with drinks, dinner, and dancing for Relator. Fitzgerald, her supervisor Sherry Woodcock, and other members of the Novation contracting staff were responsible for awarding this contract. Edward Marteka, President of AHP, Rick Feady, and AHP sales representative, and several other members of the AHP sales staff were present. Throughout the evening, little to no business was conducted. Fitzgerald also claimed that Novation failed to inform the VHA and UHC members and HPPI customers about any of these vendor-sponsored trips, meals, and other entertainment, the fact that such events had little to no legitimate business purpose, or the role these vents played in awarding contracts.[42]

Notes

Prologue: Hearing of the U.S. Senate Subcommittee on Antitrust, Competition Policy, and Consumer Rights

1. The Prologue is adapted, in its entirety, from the *Hospital group purchasing: Are the industry's reforms sufficient to ensure competition? Hearing before the Subcommittee on Antitrust, Competition Policy and Consumer Rights, Committee on the Judiciary United States Senate*, 109th Cong., 2nd sess., 2006. Comments attributed to various individuals are paraphrased from the text. Where direct quotes are used, reference is made to the appropriate page numbers in the parenthesis from the above-mentioned hearing.
2. Author's note. The industry's so-called voluntary initiative was in fact created at the behest of the Subcommittee with the avowed purpose of forestalling the enactment of Senate Bill 2880 which would have entrusted "the oversight of this industry to the U.S. Department of Health and Human Services, charging it with drafting rules for this industry to ensure that each GPO conformed with principles of competition, ethical standards and the goal of maintaining access to products necessary for proper patient care. If a GPO failed to follow these rules, it could lose its exemption from the safe harbor under that proposed legislation," p. 2.

1 Healthcare Industry in the United States

1. K. Davis, C. Schoen, S. Guterman, T. Shih, S. C. Schoenbaum, & I. Weinbaum, *Slowing the growth of U.S. healthcare expenditures: What are the options?* The Commonwealth Fund, January 2007. Retrieved May 14, 2008, http://www.commonwealthfund.org/usr_doc/Davis_slowinggrowthUShltcareexpenditureswhatareoptions_989.pdf?section=4039
2. M. Tanner, *The grass is not always greener: A look at national healthcare systems around the world.* Cato Institute, March 2008. Retrieved May 5, 2008, http://www.cato.org/pubs/pas/pa-613.pdf
3. United States Department of Health and Human Services, Centers for Medicare & Medicaid Services, *National Health Expenditure Data Web Tables* (n.d.). Retrieved May 1, 2008, http://www.cms.hhs.gov/NationalHealthExpendData/downloads/tables.pdf

4. United States Department of Health and Human Services, Centers for Medicare & Medicaid Services, *National Health Expenditure Fact Sheet* (n.d.). Retrieved May 1, 2008, http://www.cms.hhs.gov/NationalHealthExpendData/25_NHE_Fact_Sheet.asp

5. WHO Report cited in University of Maine, Bureau of Labor Education, *The U.S. health care system: Best in the world, or just the most expensive?* 2001, p. 2. Retrieved May 16, 2008, http://dll.umaine.edu/ble/U.S.%20HCweb.pdf

6. Ibid.

7. Ibid.

8. The Commonwealth Fund, *Why not the best? Results from the national scorecard on U.S. health system performance, 2008*, July 2008. Retrieved July 23, 2008, http://www.commonwealthfund.org/publications/publications_show.htm?doc_id=401577

9. T. Bodenheimer, High and rising health care costs. Part 2: Technologic innovation, *Annals of Internal Medicine 142* no. 11 (2005): 932–937, doi: 142: 932–937.

10. C. E. Carpenter, Health Care in the United States: Is it the best in the world? *Journal of Financial Service Professionals 59* no. 2 (March 2005): 29–31. Retrieved June 27, 2008, ABI/INFORM Global database (Document ID: 803162681).

11. United States Department of Health and Human Services, Centers for Medicare & Medicaid Services (n.d.), *National Health Expenditure Accounts 2006 Highlights*. Retrieved May 1, 2008, http://www.cms.hhs.gov/NationalHealthExpendData/02_NationalHealthAccountsHistorical.asp#TopOfPage

12. Ibid.

13. C. DeNavas-Walt, B. D. Proctor, & J. Smith, *Income, poverty, and health insurance coverage in the United States: 2006,* US Census Bureau Current Population Reports, August 2007, pp. 60–233. Retrieved May 2, 2008, http: //www.census.gov/prod/2007pubs/p60–233.pdf. p. 1.

14. The Kaiser Family Foundation and Health Research and Educational Trust, *Employer health benefits 2007 annual survey,* 2007. Retrieved May 27, 2008, http://www.kff.org/insurance/7672/upload/76723.pdf

15. The Kaiser Family Foundation. *Fast facts: Costs/Insurance* (n.d.). Retrieved June 3, 2008, Kaiser Fast Facts http://facts.kff.org/

16. DeNavas-Walt, Proctor, & Smith, *Income, poverty, and health insurance.*

17. The Commonwealth Fund, *Why not the best?*

18. Cited in U. E. Reinhardt, P. S. Hussey, & G. F. Anderson, U.S. health care spending in an international context, *Health Affairs* 23, no. 3 (2004): 10–25, doi: 10.1377/hlthaff.23.3.10.

19. Bodenheimer, High and rising health care costs, 932–937.

20. The Commonwealth Fund, *Why not the best?*

21. Ibid.

22. Ibid.

23. *"Underinsured"—those who are insured all year but have medical bills or deductibles that were high relative to their incomes. For details refer* The Commonwealth Fund, *Why not the best?*

24. The Commonwealth Fund, *Why not the best?*

25. Ibid.

26. The Kaiser Family Foundation, *Fast facts: Uninsured / Coverage* (n.d.). Retrieved June 3, 2008, Kaiser Fast Facts http://facts.kff.org/

27. T. Bodenheimer, High and rising health care costs. Part 3: The role of health care providers. *Annals of Internal Medicine* 142, no. 12 (2005): 996–1002, doi: 142: 996–1002.

28. Special Investigations Division, Committee on Government Reform, U.S. House of Representatives, *Prescription drug prices in Canada, Europe, and Japan,* April 11, 2001. Retrieved May 20, 2008, http://oversight.house.gov/Documents/20040629103247-74022.pdf

29. G. Anders, Health-Care gold mines: Middlemen strike it rich—Rewarding career: As patients, doctors feel pinch, insurer's CEO makes a billion. *Wall Street Journal,* April 18, 2006, p. A1.

30. Ibid.; V. Galloro, Tenet settles outlier lawsuit, *Modern Healthcare* 36, no. 9 (February 27, 2006): 8–9. Retrieved June 10, 2008, ABI/INFORM Global database (Document ID: 885831651); V. Fuhrmans, Medco gets subpoena tied to criminal probe: Florida officials seek data on records tied to business with managed-care firms. *Wall Street Journal* (Eastern edition) 2003, p. A21.

31. A. Bamezai, J. Zwanziger, G. A. Melnick, & J. M. Mann, Price competition and hospital cost growth in the United States (1989–1994), *Health Economics* 8, no. 3 (1999): 233–243; G. Gowrisankaran, & R. J. Town, Competition, payers, and hospital quality. *Health Services Research* 38, no. 6, part 1 (2003): 1403–1421; P. S. Romano, & R. Mutter, The evolving science of quality measurement for hospitals: Implications for studies of competition and consolidation. *International Journal of Health Care Finance and Economics* 4, no. 2 (2004): 131–157.

2 Industry Structure of Group Purchasing Organizations

1. For details, please visit HIGPA Web site at https://www.higpa.org/about/about_faqs.asp

2. R. E. Bloch, S. P. Perlman, & J. S. Brown, *An analysis of group purchasing organizations contracting practices under the antitrust laws: Myth and reality.* Presented at the Joint FTC/DOJ Hearings on Health Care and Competition Law and Policy (n.d.). Retrieved http://www.ftc.gov/ogc/healthcarehearings/docs/030926bloch.pdf

3. Knowledge Source, *Group purchasing organizations,* May 2005 (the report is based on data solely provided by GPOs).

4. C. Becker, Of two minds. *Modern Healthcare* 35, no. 33 (August 15, 2005): S1—S5. Retrieved September 28, 2007, ABI/INFORM Global database (Document ID: 885831651) (the report is based on data solely provided by GPOs); Knowledge Source, *Group purchasing organizations.*

5. Knowledge Source, *Group purchasing organizations*; Muse and Associates, *The role of group purchasing organizations in the U.S. healthcare system,* March 2000; Becker, Of two minds, S1—S5; L. L. C. Verispan, *Multi-Hospital systems and group purchasing organization market report,* 2003; H. Hovenkamp, *Competitive effects of group purchasing organizations' (GPO) purchasing and product selection practices in the health care industry,* April 2002 (prepared for the Healthcare Industry Group Purchasing Association). Retrieved June 1, 2007, http://www.higpa.org/pressroom/hovenkamp.pdf

6. Knowledge Source, *Group purchasing organizations*; It must be pointed out that information regarding GPO industry differs widely within the sources, check for example Muse and Associates, *Role of group purchasing organizations.*

7. A. Sager, & D. Socolar, *Health costs absorb one-quarter of economic growth, 2000–2005.* February 9, 2005. Retrieved May 15, 2008, http://www.globalaging.org/health/us/2005/quarter.pdf; U.S. Bureau of Economic Analysis, *Gross domestic product by industry, 2005,* April 2006. Retrieved October 2, 2007, http://www.bea.gov/newsreleases/industry/gdpindustry/2006/gdpind05.htm.

8. T. H. Brock, Hospitals, group purchasing organizations, and the antitrust laws. *Healthcare Financial Management* 53, no. 3 (March 2003): 38–42. Retrieved November 9, 2007, http://findarticles.com/p/articles/mi_m3257/is_3_57/ai_98953926; for further discussion on the oligopolistic structure of the GPO industry and the government granted protection for the industry, see chapters 3 and 4.

9. U.S. Government Accountability Office, *Use of contracting processes and strategies to award contracts for medical-surgical products* (Publication No. GAO-03—998T), July 2003. Retrieved May 12, 2008, General Accounting Office Reports Online http://www.gao.gov/new.items/d03998t.pdf; U.S. Government Accountability Office, *Pilot study suggests large buying groups do not always offer hospitals lower prices* (Publication No. GAO-02-690T), April 2002. Retrieved May 15, 2008, http://www.stopgpokickbacks.org/documents/9GAO.pdf

10. R. D. Barlow, Healthcare group purchasing milestones in history. *Healthcare Purchasing News,* November 2, 2004. Retrieved October 25, 2007, Business Source Premier Database.

11. U.S. GAO, *Use of contracting processes*; U.S. GAO, *Pilot study.*

12. Knowledge Source, *Group purchasing organizations*; Muse and Associates, *Role of group purchasing organizations.*

13. United States Department of Health and Human Services, Office of Inspector General, *Review of revenue from vendors at three group purchasing organizations and their members* (OIG Publication No. A-05-03-00074), January 2005. Retrieved August 8, 2007, http://oig.hhs.gov/oas/reports/region5/50300074.pdf

15. Bio-Medicine, HIDA calls for scrutiny of group purchasing organization distributor fee structure, September 2007. Retrieved November 12, 2007, http://www.bio-medicine.org/medicine-news-1/HIDA-Calls-for-Scrutiny-of-Group-Purchasing-Organization-Distributor-Fee-Structure-594-1/

16. L. J. Everard, The impact of group purchasing on the financial prospects of health systems: Changing value perceptions and unintended consequences, V.I.P.E.R. Group, 2003. Retrieved September 7, 2007, http://www.stopgpokickbacks.org/documents/7Everard.pdf

17. S. Rhea, Moving beyond the hospital. *Modern Healthcare* 37, no. 35 (September 3, 2007): S1—S5. Retrieved May 27, 2008, ABI/INFORM Global database (Document ID: 1334858761).

18. Ibid.

19. For details, refer to chapter 5.

20. Rhea, Moving beyond the hospital, S1—S5.

21. Ibid.

22. Overview of Global Healthcare Exchange (GHX) (n.d.). Retrieved August 10, 2008, http://premium.hoovers.com/subscribe/co/factsheet.xhtml?ID=jrksfrtcxksyyc

23. For details, please visit Amerinet Web site at www.amerinet-gpo.com.

24. MedAssets HSCA joins GHX e-commerce network, bringing site near "critical mass," *Hospital Materials Management* 28, no. 5 (May 2003). Retrieved August 6, 2008, ABI/INFORM Global database (Document ID: 334545721).

25. MedAssets offers automated charge master control, *Hospital Materials Management* 28, no. 9 (September 2003).

26. Overview of MedAssets Inc (n.d.). Retrieved August 21, 2008, http://premium.hoovers.com/subscribe/co/overview.xhtml?ID=fffrffhhhfsyshtfkf

27. Rhea, Moving beyond the hospital, S1—S5.

28. Ibid.

29. Knowledge Source, *Group purchasing organization.*

3 Market Dominance and Anticompetitive Conduct of GPOs

1. For a theoretical analysis of the dynamics of competition, industry structure, and individual company strategy, please see M. E. Porter, *Competitive strategy: Techniques for analyzing industries and competitors* (New York: Free Press, 1980), Chapter 1, p. 74.
2. Knowledge Source, *Group purchasing organizations*; Becker, Of two minds, S1—S5.
3. Hovenkamp, *Competitive effects*.
4. Healthcare Industry Group Purchasing Association Frequently Asked Questions, available at http://www.higpa.org/about/about_faqs.asp. See also P. Lastra, Hijacking at the hospital: Purchasing groups created to hold down health costs seem to be holding up patients instead, *Fort Worth Weekly*, November 23, 2005, pp. 8–13. Retrieved November 7, 2007, http://www.fwweekly.com/content. asp?article=3419
5. *Hospital group purchasing: Lowering costs at the expense of patient health and medical innovation? Hearing before the Subcommittee on Antitrust, Business Rights, and Competition of the Committee on the Judiciary United States Senate*, 107th Cong., 2nd sess., 2002; *Hospital group purchasing: Has the market become more open to competition? Hearing before the Subcommittee on Antitrust, Business Rights, and Competition of the Committee on the Judiciary United States Senate*, 108th Cong., 1st sess., 2003; *Hospital group purchasing: How to maintain innovation and cost savings. Hearing before the Subcommittee on Antitrust, Business Rights, and Competition of the Committee on the Judiciary United States Senate*, 108th Cong., 2nd sess., 2004; *Are the industry's reforms sufficient?* 109th Cong., 2nd sess., 2006; U.S. GAO, *Use of contracting processes*; U.S. GAO, *Pilot study*.
6. Becker, Of two minds, S1—S5.
7. Ibid.
8. Ibid.; C. Becker, Hanging tough. *Modern Healthcare* 34, no. 33 (August 16, 2004): S1—S5. Retrieved September 26, 2007, ABI/INFORM Global database (Document ID: 682264161).
9. Becker, Of two minds, S1—S5.
10. Health Industry Distributors (HIDA) & The Major Accounts Exchange (The MAX), Group Purchasing Organization (GPO) market report, 2006, p. 2.
11. Rhea, Moving beyond the hospital, S1—S5.
12. Knowledge Source, *Group purchasing organizations*, pp. 1–224; Becker, Of two minds, S1—S5.
13. Becker, Of two minds, S1—S5.
14. Hovenkamp, *Competitive effects*.
15. J. Andrews, Consorta-HPG deal: A sign of things to come? *Healthcare Finance News*, March 1, 2007. Retrieved December 3, 2007 http://www.healthcare financenews.com/story.cms?id=6158.
16. HealthTrust Purchasing Group, *Consorta, Inc. finalizes agreement to become sixth equity owner of HealthTrust Purchasing Group* (April 18, 2007). [Press release]. Retrieved December 3, 2007 http://www.healthtrustcorp.com/news-highlights. php#1
17. Andrews, Consorta-HPG deal: A sign of things to come?
18. Ibid.
19. J. J. Laffont, *The economics of uncertainty and information. 4th ed* (Cambridge, MA: MIT Press, 1993), pp. 180–195, cited by H. J. Singer, The budgetary impact of eliminating the GPO's safe harbor exemption from the anti-kickback statue of the social

security act. *Criterion Economics, LLC* 2006, pp. 1–29. Retrieved November 10, 2007 http://www.stopgpokickbacks.org/documents/1Singer_002 pdf

4 Government Created Protections of the GPO Industry: Financial Burden of GPO Activities on the U.S. Healthcare Industry

1. W. Bogdanich, B. Meier, & M. W. Walsh, Medicine's middlemen; Questions raised of conflicts at 2 hospital buying groups, *The New York Times*, March 4, 2002, p. A1; *Lowering costs*, 107th Cong., 2nd sess., 2002.
2. Section 1128B(b) of the Social Security Act [42 U.S.C. 1320a-7b(b)] ["the anti-kickback statute"] provides criminal penalties for individuals or entities that knowingly and willfully offer, pay, solicit, or receive remuneration in order to induce business reimbursed under the federal or state health care programs.
3. "Statement 7: Joint Purchasing Arrangements among Health Care Providers," *Statements of Antitrust Enforcement Policy in Health Care*; Federal Trade Commission and Department of Justice, August 1996, p. 54.
4. Federal Trade Commission and the Department of Justice, Improving health care: A dose of competition, July 2004. Retrieved October 24, 2007, http://www.ftc. gov/reports/healthcare/040723healthcarerpt.pdf
5. Section 1128B(b) of the Social Security Act [42 U.S.C. 1320a-7b(b)] ["the anti-kickback statute"] provides criminal penalties for individuals or entities that knowingly and willfully offer, pay, solicit, or receive remuneration in order to induce business reimbursed under the federal or state health care programs.
6. For a detailed discussion of Healthcare Group Purchasing Industry Initiative, please see chapter 10.
7. United States Department of Health and Human Services, Office of Inspector General, *Review of revenue from vendors at three additional group purchasing organizations and their members* (OIG Publication No. A-05-04-00073), May 2005. Retrieved August 8, 2007, http://oig.hhs.gov/oas/reports/region5/50400073.pdf; United States DHHS, OIG, *Review of revenue from vendors.*
8. Federal Trade Commission and Department of Justice, *Statements of Antitrust Enforcement Policy in Health Care, 1993,* cited in *Innovation and cost savings*, 108th Cong., 2nd sess., 2004 (testimony of David A. Balto).
9. "Statement 7: Joint Purchasing Arrangements among Health Care Providers," *Statements of Antitrust Enforcement Policy in Health Care*; Federal Trade Commission and Department of Justice, August 1996, p. 54.
10. Ibid.
11. Ibid.
12. Brock, Hospitals, group purchasing organizations, pp. 38–42.
13. The FTC and DOJ report states: "Health Care Statement 7 and its safety zone aim to address monopsony and oligopoly concerns with the formation of a GPO. This statement does not address all potential issues that GPOs may raise. The Agencies believe amending the statement to address some, but not all potential issues, is likely to be counterproductive. Health Care Statement 7 does not preclude Agency action challenging anticompetitive contracting practices that may occur in connection with GPOs. The Agencies will examine, on a case-by-case basis, the facts of any alleged anticompetitive contracting practice to determine whether it violates the antitrust laws." For details see FTC and DOJ, Improving health care.
14. L. J. Everard, Defining and measuring product-based cost savings in the health care supply chain, February 2005, pp. 1–20. Retrieved December 5, 2007, http://www.medicaldevices.org/public/documents/DefiningandMeasuring

Product-BasedCostSavings_000.pdf; M. A. Dula, Testing the GPO waters. *Healthcare Financial Management* 58, no. 6 (June 2004): 70–76. Retrieved October 9, 2007, http://findarticles.com/p/articles/mi_m3257/ is_6_58/ai_n6080537/pg_1?tag=artBody;col1

15. Singer, Budgetary impact. It should be noted here that financial support for this report was provided by the Medical Device Manufacturers Association. Nonetheless, the quality of economic analysis and resulting conclusions are based on sound logic and defensible.

16. U.S. GAO, *Use of contracting processes*; U.S. GAO, *Pilot study.*

17. U.S. GAO, *Use of contracting processes*, cited by Singer, Budgetary impact.

18. U.S. GAO, *Use of contracting processes.*

19. Ibid.

20. J. Lawn, The GPOs where do they go from here? January 2005. Retrieved April 17, 2001, http://food-management.com/business_feature/fm_imp_7554/ Food Management.

21. Singer, Budgetary impact.

22. United States DHHS, OIG, *Review of revenue from vendors.*

23. For more details see Premier's Web site: www.premierinc.com.

24. United States DHHS, OIG, *Review of revenue from vendors at three additional group purchasing organizations*; United States DHHS, OIG, *Review of revenue from vendors.*

25. Becker, Of two minds, S1—S5; For Frequently Asked Questions regarding Healthcare Group Purchasing Industry Initiative, please visit HIGPA Web site at http://www.healthcaregpoii.com/initiative-faq.pdf; Charter of the Healthcare Group Purchasing Industry Initiative (2005, May). Available at http://www.healthcaregpoii.com/initiative-charter.pdf

26. *Are the industry's reforms sufficient?* 109th Cong., 2nd sess., 2006 (testimony of Richard Bednar).

27. Becker, Of two minds, S1—S5; Knowledge Source, *Group purchasing organizations.*

28. U.S. GAO, *Use of contracting processes*; U.S. GAO, *Pilot study suggests large buying groups do not always offer hospitals lower prices*; United States DHHS, OIG, *Review of revenue from vendors at three additional group purchasing organizations*; United States DHHS, OIG, *Review of revenue from vendors.*

29. Bogdanich, Meier, & Walsh, Medicine's middlemen, p. A1; R. Holding, & W. Carlsen, Watchdogs fail health workers: How safer needles were kept out of hospitals. *San Francisco Chronicle,* April 15, 1998, p. A1. Retrieved October 18, 2007, http://www.sfgate.com/cgibin/article.cgi?file=/chronicle/archive/1998/04/15/ MN1902.DTL&type=special; Lastra, Hijacking at the hospital, pp. 8–13.

30. U.S. GAO, *Pilot study.*

31. United States DHHS, OIG, *Review of revenue from vendors at three additional group purchasing organizations*; United States DHHS, OIG, *Review of revenue from vendors.*

32. Everard, Defining and measuring product-based cost savings in the health care supply chain, pp. 1–20.

5 GPO Activities, Conflict of Interest, and Their Adverse Consequences for the Healthcare Providers

1. Bogdanich, Meier, & Walsh, Medicine's middlemen, p. A1; M. W. Walsh, When a buyer for hospitals has a stake in drugs it buys, *The New York Times,* March 26, 2002, p. A1; M. W. Walsh, Hospital group's link to company is criticized, *The New York Times*, April 27, 2002, p. A1; *Lowering costs*, 107th Cong., 2nd sess., 2002.

2. See chapters 2 and 3.
3. Bogdanich, Meier, & Walsh, Medicine's middlemen, p. A1; *Masimo Corp. v. Tyco Healthcare Group*, L.P., No. 02-CV-4770 (C.D. Cal.).
4. Ibid.
5. *Innovation and cost savings*, 108th Cong., 2nd sess., 2004.
6. Ibid.
7. Ibid.
8. *Lowering costs*, 107th Cong., 2nd sess., 2002 (submission for the record by Thomas J. Shaw). See also Holding & Carlsen, Watchdogs fail health workers, p. A1; Lastra, Hijacking at the hospital; *Retractable Technologies v. Becton Dickinson & Co. Inc.*, No. 01-CV-036 (E.D. Tex.).
9. P. L. Zweig & W. Zellner, Locked out of the hospital: Are medical buying consortiums squelching innovation? *BusinessWeek*, March 16, 1998.
10. Anonymous, Retractable Technologies raises GPO compliance issues on national news. *Health Industry Today* 61, no. 6 (June 1998). Retrieved November 6, 2007, from ABI/INFORM Global database (Document ID: 30032104). KaiserNetwork, Safer needles' not in use in most U.S. hospitals, "60 minutes" reports. *Kaiser Daily HIV/AIDS Report*, February 26,2001. Retrieved June 11, 2007, http://www.kaisernetwork.org/Daily_reports/rep_index.cfm?DR_ID=3024. See also Holding & Carlsen, Watchdogs fail health workers, p. A1; Lastra, Hijacking at the hospital; *Retractable Technologies v. Becton Dickinson & Co. Inc.*, No. 01-CV-036 (E.D. Tex.)
11. *Lowering costs*, 107th Cong., 2nd sess., 2002 (submission for the record by Thomas J. Shaw). See also Holding & Carlsen, Watchdogs fail health workers, p. A1; Lastra, Hijacking at the hospital; *Retractable Technologies v. Becton Dickinson & Co. Inc.*, No. 01-CV-036 (E.D. Tex.).
12. Ibid.
13. Ibid.
14. Tom Shaw had no doubt that such dinner registration fees are a form of a bribe. Moreover, he has reasons to believe that the $25,000 is only the price of an appetizer, "the entrée is in the millions." Bogdanich, Meier, & Walsh, Medicine's middlemen, p. A1.
15. *Lowering costs*, 107th Cong., 2nd sess., 2002 (submission for the record by Thomas J. Shaw).
16. Ibid.
17. *Lowering costs*, 107th Cong., 2nd sess., 2002 (submission for the record by Thomas V. Brown).
18. Bogdanich, Meier, & Walsh, Medicine's middlemen, p. A1.
19. More open to competition? 108th Cong., 1st sess., 2003 (submission for the record by Said Hilal); Applied Medical Res. Corp. v. Johnson & Johnson, Inc., No. 03-CV-1329 (C.D. Cal.), available online: http://www.rkmc.com/Recent-Medical-Device-Antitrust-Cases-March-2006.htm.
20. *Lowering costs*, 107th Cong., 2nd sess., 2002 (submission for the record by Mitchell Goldstein).
21. Walsh, Hospital group's link to company is criticized, p. A1; See also comments by the Service Employees International Union on Hospital Group Purchasing Organizations before the *Innovation and cost savings*, 108th Cong., 2nd sess., 2004.
22. Bogdanich, Meier, & Walsh, Medicine's middlemen, p. A1; Walsh, When a buyer for hospitals has a stake in drugs it buys, p. A1.

23. Bogdanich, Meier, & Walsh, Medicine's middlemen, p. A1.
24. Ibid.
25. Ibid.
26. U.S. GAO, *Pilot study*; M. W. Walsh & B. Meier, Hospitals find big buying groups may not come up with savings. *The New York Times,* April 30, 2002, p. A1.
27. Walsh & Meier, Hospitals find big buying groups, p. A1.
28. Bogdanich, Meier, & Walsh, Medicine's middlemen, p. A1; Walsh & Meier, Hospitals find big buying groups, p. A1.
29. Walsh & Meier, Hospitals find big buying groups, p. A1.
30. *Lowering costs*, 107th Cong., 2nd sess., 2002 (submission for the record by Mitchell Goldstein).
31. Ibid.
32. *Lowering costs*, 107th Cong., 2nd sess., 2002 (testimony of Mark McKenna).
33. *More open to competition?* 108th Cong., 1st sess., 2003.
34. Ibid.
35. Anonymous, GPO fans, critics agree there's improvement. *Hospital Materials Management* 28, no. 9 (September 2003). Retrieved June 19, 2007, from ABI/INFORM Global database (Document ID: 407037481).
36. P. DeJohn, Hospitals want to be heard in GPO debate, *Hospital Materials Management* 28, no. 11 (November 2003): 10. Retrieved September 4, 2007, from ABI/INFORM Global database (Document ID: 459506351).
37. Escutia, Senator—CA (D), bill SB749 "Hospital Group Purchasing Organizations," available at http://www.maplight.org/map/ca/bill/2230/default/history/action-14684.
38. *Lowering Costs*, 107th Cong., 2nd sess., 2002.
39. Data provided by the Spokesman of Retractable Technologies, Inc. on July 18, 2006.
40. *Lowering Costs*, 107th Cong., 2nd sess., 2002 (testimony of Thomas V. Brown).
41. C. Becker, The silent treatment, *Modern Healthcare* 34, no. 7 (February 16, 2004): 17. Retrieved October 4, 2007, from ABI/INFORM Global database (Document ID: 547849341).
42. Ibid.
43. For details, please refer to Novation Operating Principles available at http://www.masimo.com/pdf/home/NovationNOP.pdf
44. *More open to competition?* 108th Cong., 1st sess., 2003 (submission for the record by Robert L. Aromando).
45. *More open to competition?* 108th Cong., 1st sess., 2003.
46. Ibid.
47. Ibid (submission for the record by Robert L. Aromando).
48. A. W. Singer, Spattered and scorched, premier seeks the "high road," *Ethikos and Corporate Conduct Quarterly*, May/June 2004. Retrieved October 3, 2007, http://www.singerpubs.com/ethikos/html/premier.html
49. Anonymous, HIGPA: Administrative fees should not be considered as part of Medicare pricing, *Hospital Materials Management* 29, no. 8 (August 2004): 6. Retrieved September 17, 2007, from ABI/INFORM Global database (Document ID: 671987401).
50. Anonymous, Premier continues relationship with Agfa in two new pacts for imaging products. *Hospital Materials Management* 29, no. 1 (January 2004): 7. Retrieved October 3, 2007, from ABI/INFORM Global database (Document ID: 526245281).

51. Becker, The silent treatment, p. 17.
52. C. Becker, Premier's portfolio, *Modern Healthcare* 33, no. 39 (September 29, 2003): 20. Retrieved May 22, 2007, from ABI/INFORM Global database (Document ID: 417712481).
53. C. Becker, Going on the record, *Modern Healthcare* 34, no. 26 (June 28, 2004): 26. Retrieved August 3, 2007, from ABI/INFORM Global database (Document ID: 658848321).
54. Becker, The silent treatment, p. 17.
55. Ibid.
56. C. Becker, In search of a breakthrough, *Modern Healthcare* 32, no. 31 (August 5, 2002): 28–32. Retrieved July 18, 2007, from ABI/INFORM Global database (Document ID: 146406341).
57. Becker, The silent treatment, p. 17.
58. P. B. Gray, Stick it to 'em, FSB: Fortune Small Business 15, no. 2 (March 2005): 82–88. Retrieved September 4, 2008, from ABI/INFORM Global database (Document ID: 809783781); Retractable Technologies v. Becton Dickinson & Co. Inc., No. 01-CV-036 (E.D. Tex.), available online: http://www.rkmc.com/Recent-Medical-Device-Antitrust-Cases-March-2006.htm.
59. *Innovation and cost savings*, 108th Cong., 2nd sess., 2004.
60. VHA Health Foundation IRS Form 990, 2002, 2001; cited in Comments by the Service Employees International Union on Hospital Group Purchasing Organizations before *Innovation and cost savings*, 108th Cong., 2nd sess., 2004.
61. *Innovation and cost savings*, 108th Cong., 2nd sess., 2004. (submission for the record by Service Employees International Union).
62. Ibid.
63. C. Becker, Lucrative liaison? *Modern Healthcare* 34, no. 39 (September 27, 2004): 8–9. Retrieved October 4, 2007, from ABI/INFORM Global database (Document ID: 707621561).
64. Ibid.
65. *Innovation and cost savings*, 108th Cong., 2nd sess., 2004 (submission for the record by Service Employees International Union).
66. Becker, Going on the record, p. 26.
67. FTC and DOJ, Improving health care.
68. L. J. Everard, Health policy statement no. 7 does not sufficiently protect patients and caregivers. Presented at the Joint FTC/DOJ hearings on Health Care and Competition Law and Policy, September 26, 2003. Retrieved September 12, 2007, http://www.ftc.gov/ogc/healthcarehearings/docs/030926lynneverad.pdf; S. Hilal, Healthcare market conditions today. Presented at the Joint FTC/DOJ hearings on Health Care and Competition Law and Policy, September 26, 2003. Retrieved September 12, 2007, http://www.ftc.gov/ogc/healthcare-hearings/docs/030926hilal.pdf; E. Elhauge, Antitrust analysis of GPO exclusionary agreement comments regarding hearing on health care and competition law and policy—Statement for DOJ-FTC hearing on GPOs—September 26, 2003. Retrieved September 12, 2007, from http://www.ftc.gov/os/comments/healthcarecomments2/elhauge.pdf
69. FTC and DOJ, Improving health care.
70. *Innovation and cost savings*, 108th Cong., 2nd sess., 2004 (testimony of David A. Balto); C. Becker, No more Mr. nice guys, *Modern Healthcare* 34, no. 38 (September 20, 2004): 8. Retrieved August 14, 2007, from ABI/INFORM Global database (Document ID: 709182801).

71. *Are the industry's reforms sufficient?* 109th Cong., 2nd sess., 2006 (testimony of Richard Blumenthal).

72. United States DHHS, OIG, *Review of revenue from vendors*; M. W. Walsh, Blowing the whistle, many times. *The New York Times*, November 18, 2007, p. 1.

73. United States DHHS, OIG, *Review of revenue from vendors at three additional group purchasing organizations.*

74. Lastra, Hijacking at the hospital.

75. C. Becker, Masimo wins new round. *Modern Healthcare* 35, no. 13 (March 28, 2005): 17. Retrieved September 26, 2007, from ABI/INFORM Global database (Document ID: 823445491).

76. Big Suits, *Masimo Corp. v. Tyco Healthcare Group,* L.P., No. 02-CV-4770 (C.D. Cal.) *American Lawyer* 28, no. 6 (June 1, 2006).

77. *Are the industry's reforms sufficient?* 109th Cong., 2nd sess., 2006 (testimony of Richard Blumenthal).

78. Ibid.

79. W. Bogdanich, Group settles health sales conflict case, *The New York Times,* January 25, 2007, p. 1.

80. *Are the industry's reforms sufficient?* 109th Cong., 2nd sess., 2006 (testimony of Richard Blumenthal).

81. Bogdanich, Group settles health sales conflict case, p. 1.

82. W. Bogdanich, Hospital chiefs get paid for advice on selling, *The New York Times,* July 17, 2006, p. 1; Bogdanich, Group settles health sales conflict case, p. 1.

83. Bogdanich, Group settles health sales conflict case, p. 1.

6 Congressional Deliberations of GPO Operations

1. *Lowering costs*, 107th Cong., 2nd sess., 2002 (statement of Senator Herb Kohl).

2. Ibid.

3. Mark McKenna, President, Novation, LLC; Richard A. Norling, Chief Executive Officer Premier, Inc.; Trisha Barrett, Assistant Director, Material Services, Value Analysis Facilitator, UCSF Medical Center; Mitchell Goldstein, Neonatologist, Citrus Valley Medical Center; Joe Kiani, President and Chief Executive Officer, Masimo Corporation; Elizabeth A. Weatherman, Managing Director, Warburg Pincus, LLC.; Lynn R. Detlor, Principal, GPO Concepts, Inc.

4. *Lowering costs*, 107th Cong., 2nd sess., 2002 (testimony of Richard A. Norling).

5. Ibid.

6. Ibid.

7. Ibid.

8. Ibid., testimony of Mark McKenna.

9. Ibid., testimony of Mitchell Goldstein.

10. Ibid.

11. Ibid., testimony of Joe Kiani.

12. Ibid., testimony of Joe Kiani from United States Senate Committee on the Judiciary Web site.

13. Ibid., testimony of Elizabeth A. Weatherman.

14. Ibid.

15. Ibid., statement of Senator Herb Kohl.

16. Ibid., statement of Senator Orrin G. Hatch.

17. Ibid., testimony of Joe Kiani.

18. Ibid., statement of Senator Strom Thurmond.

19. *More open to competition?* 108th Cong., 1st sess., 2003 (statement of Senator Mike DeWine).
20. Ibid.
21. Mark McKenna, President, Novation, LLC; Richard A. Norling, Chief Executive Officer Premier, Inc Elizabeth A. Weatherman, Managing Director, Warburg Pincus, LLC; Said Hilal, Chairman and CEO, Applied Medical Resources Corporation; Thomas Brown, Executive Vice President, Biotronik Inc; Gary Heiman, President and CEO, Standard Textile; Lynn James Everard, Hospital Purchasing Consultant.
22. *More open to competition?* 108th Cong., 1st sess., 2003 (testimony of Richard A. Norling).
23. Bogdanich, Meier, & Walsh, Medicine's middlemen, p. A1.
24. *More open to competition?* 108th Cong., 1st sess., 2003 (testimony of Thomas Brown).
25. Ibid.
26. Ibid., testimony of Said Hilal.
27. Ibid.
28. Ibid., testimony of Elizabeth A. Weatherman.
29. *Innovation and cost savings*, 108th Cong., 2nd sess., 2004; Becker, No more Mr. Nice Guys, p. 8.
30. *Innovation and cost savings*, 108th Cong., 2nd sess., 2004.
31. Ibid.; Becker, No more Mr. Nice Guys, p. 8.
32. *Innovation and cost savings*, 108th Cong., 2nd sess., 2004; *Anonymous,* Senators mull tighter regulation of GPOs. *Hospital Materials Management* 29, no. 10 (October, 2004): 8. Retrieved September 2, 2007, from ABI/INFORM Global database (Document ID: 711922371).
33. *Innovation and cost savings*, 108th Cong., 2nd sess., 2004 (testimony of Joe Kiani).
34. Ibid., testimony of David A. Baldo.
35. Ibid., testimony of Robert Betz.
36. "The Proposal for Enacting the Hospital Group Purchasing Organization Reform Act," Discussion Draft, 108th Congress, 2nd sess., pp. 1–8; "S.2880—Medical Device Competition Act 2004," Discussion Draft, 108th Congress, 2nd sess., pp. 1–3; "Ensuring Competition in Hospital Purchasing Act," Discussion Draft, 109th Congress 1st sess., pp. 1–3.

7   Congressional Drive toward Regulatory Reform

1. "The Proposal for Enacting the Hospital Group Purchasing Organization Reform Act," Discussion Draft, cited in *Innovation and cost savings,* 108th Cong., 2nd sess., 2004, pp. 1–8; "S.2880—Medical Device Competition Act 2004," Discussion Draft, cited in *Innovation and cost savings,* 108th Cong., 2nd sess., pp. 1–3; "Ensuring Competition in Hospital Purchasing Act," Discussion Draft, cited in *Are the industry's reforms sufficient?* 109th Cong., 2nd sess., 2006, pp. 1–3.
2. See I. Ayres & J. Braithwaite, *Responsive regulation: Transcending the deregulation debate* (New York: Oxford University Press, 1992); J. Braithwaite, *Convergence in models of regulatory strategy. Current Issues in Criminal Justice* 2 (1990): 59–65. J. Braithwaite, *To punish or persuade: Enforcement of coal mine safety* (Albany, NY: State University of New York Press, 1985) (extending theories of self-regulation to the coal industry); J. Braithwaite, Enforced self-regulation: A new strategy for

corporate crime control, *Michigan Law Review* 80, no. 7 (1982): 1466–1507 (proposing a new concept of regulatory cooperation).

3. J. Braithwaite, Institutionalizing distrust, enculturating trust, in *Trust and governance* ed. V. Braithwaite & M. Levi, pp. 343–375 (New York: Russell Sage, 1998).

4. W. S. *Laufer, Corporate bodies and guilty minds: The failure of corporate criminal liability* (Chicago: University of Chicago Press, 2006).

5. Compare to civil false claim act cases, see J. T. *Boese, Civil false claims and qui tam actions* (Aspen Law & Business, New York: Aspen Publishers, 2006), pp. 2–6.

6. For the importance of verification, see Braithwaite, Enforced self-regulation, 1466–1507; B. Fisse & J. Braithwaite, *Corporations, crime and accountability* (New York: Cambridge University Press, 1993), p. 159.

7. "Ensuring Competition in Hospital Purchasing Act," Discussion Draft, cited in *Are the industry's reforms,* 109th Cong., 2nd sess., 2006, pp. 1–3.

8. Hovenkamp, *Competitive effects*; E. S. Schneller, The value of group purchasing in the health care supply chain. [White paper]. School of Health Administration and Policy, Arizona State University College of Business (n.d.)., pp. 1–20. Retrieved December, 5, 2007, http://wpcarey.asu.edu/hap/upload/group_purchasing_pdf. pdf; P. DeJohn, HIGPA enters new phase with year-end Betz exit. *Hospital Materials Management* 30, no. 8 (August 2005): 9–11. Retrieved September 5, 2008, from ABI/INFORM Global database (Document ID: 887232321); Bloch, Perlman, & Brown, *Analysis of group purchasing organizations.*

9. U.S. GAO, *Use of contracting processes*; Singer, Budgetary impact (financial support for this report was provided by the Medical Device Manufacturers Association).

8 The GPO Industry's Efforts in Creating a Voluntary Code of Conduct: The Hanson Report

1. Brock, Hospitals, group purchasing organizations, pp. 38–42; Bogdanich, Meier, & Walsh, Medicine's middlemen, p. A1; *More open to competition?* 108th Cong., 1st sess., 2003 (submission for the record by Said Hilal); *Are the industry's reforms,* 109th Cong., 2nd sess., 2006 (testimony of Richard Blumenthal).

2. Medical Device Link, the online information source for the medical device industry http://www.devicelink.com/mddi/archive/05/09/002.html

3. Singer, Spattered and scorched.

4. S. P. Sethi, *Setting global standards: Guidelines for creating codes of conduct in multinational corporations* (New York: John Wiley & Sons, 2003); S. P. Sethi & O. Emelianova, A failed strategy of using voluntary codes of conduct by the global mining industry, *Corporate Governance: The International Journal of Business and Society* 6, no. 3 (2006): 226–238.

5. K. O. Hanson, *Best ethical practices for the group purchasing industry* (Premier, 2002), pp. 1–23.

6. These are extracts from the report's section on "Inherent Tensions in the GPO Industry": "The tension between good medical outcomes and cost control. These two primary goals of GPOs are at times in conflict ... The tension between the unit cost of goods and services and their total cost in use after assessing their effectiveness in use, technological capabilities and data on medical outcomes ... The tension between the cost and other advantages of working with 'familiar vendors' ... The tension between being a private for-profit organization which must sustain its own financial strength and being owned by nonprofit organizations." It

should be apparent that these so-called tensions encompass most of the charges of unethical and illegal practices by GPOs. To call them "tensions" appears to be an attempt to ignore the obvious and thus move away from a recognition of the very practices for which the GPOs have been accused.

7. Hanson, *Best ethical practices*, pp. 9–10.
8. Ibid., pp. 11–12.
9. Ibid., p. 7.
10. C. Becker, Say what? *Modern Healthcare* 32, no. 43 (October 28, 2002): 8–9. Retrieved September3, 2007 from ABI/INFORM Global database (Document ID: 227995811).
11. Hanson, *Best ethical practices,* p. 13.
12. Ibid., pp. 1–23.
13. Ibid., p. 12.
14. Ibid., p. 14.
15. Ibid., p. 23.
16. *Are the industry's reforms sufficient?* 109th Cong., 2nd sess., 2006 (testimony of Richard Bednar).
17. Hanson, *Best ethical practices*, pp. 14–19. The definitions used in this report are the same as those used for the HIGPA code of conduct.
18. Other ethical policies common to all companies include adherence to all applicable laws, business relationships with companies other than vendors, outside employment by employees, the protection of confidential and proprietary information, the protection of company assets, respect for copyright, accurate accounting and financial reporting, fair competition toward competitors, industrial espionage, sexual harassment, and a commitment to diversity programs in hiring and promotion.
19. Prohibitions such as #3 and #4 should apply to immediate family members (spouse and dependents) of employees as well as the employees themselves. In some cases, exceptions may be granted if spouses of employees are employed by participating vendors and stock ownership is incidental to that employment. In these cases, disclosure and recusal by the employee from any decisions regarding that vendor may be adequate.
20. This provision excludes equities owned in mutual funds over which the individual exercises no investment control, and in completely blind trusts. New employees who come to Premier with substantial deferred compensation in the form of equity in participating vendors that cannot be liquidated without a substantial loss of value may retain that interest, but must disclose it to the company and recuse themselves from any decisions involving the participating vendor in which they hold the interest.
21. This provision and #10 apply to advisors who serve on standing committees providing advice to GPOs. GPOs occasionally use other subject matter experts on a one-time or rotating basis in focus groups or other informal settings. These clinicians provide input to standing advisory committees that vote and advise the GPO. Provided that such a subject matter expert discloses all gifts, entertainment, or compensation from a Participating Vendor and any equity held in such a vendor, they may serve as an informal advisor. However, their conflicts of interest must be disclosed every time their advice is communicated to decision-making committees or individuals.
22. GPOs may wish to consider making vendor adherence to these ethical responsibilities or to the GPO code of conduct a standard requirement in contracting. Some other industries and companies have done this.

23. Practices 24 through 33 are all recommended to Premier as "going forward" practices. Future contracts should be written consistent with these standards. If existing contracts are substantially amended, however, these standards should be incorporated.

24. Products and services that fit this category (in practices 24 through 27) are to be identified by the individual Clinical Advisory Committees. The category includes those items in which the choice of particular products or services by individual physicians or other clinicians is determined by the Clinical Advisory Committees to be strongly related to patient outcomes. This includes many, but not all, "physician preference items" and some "clinical preference items."

25. It is anticipated that there will be few exceptions to the three-year limitation and that exceptions will be approved by senior management and reported to the board of directors at the next board meeting.

26. This is one of the most significant departures from current practice being recommended. Application of this practice in one area of Premier contracting may be impractical. In branded pharmaceuticals, Premier's strategy is to provide clinicians with maximum choice of branded pharmaceuticals by attempting to place all branded pharmaceuticals on contract. These contracts are written *by manufacturer* rather than by therapeutic class. To put all branded pharmaceuticals on contract, it has been necessary to negotiate individual administrative fee arrangements with each vendor. This practice is reasonable for the present, as long as administrative fees are standardized for (1) all *generic pharmaceuticals*, (2) *branded pharmaceuticals that have generic equivalents*, and (3) all *branded pharmaceuticals considered for the Rational Choice Plan*, a Premier plan whereby one of several competing branded pharmaceuticals is offered at preferential prices.

27. The requirement for the Designated Ethics Officer and the Designated Compliance Officer to report annually should be a minimum. It is probably wise for these meetings to be more frequent, even quarterly.

28. One of the most important tasks of the Designated Compliance Officer is to create a vehicle by which employees, members, and vendors may communicate regarding violations of the GPO's ethical practices, or to request interpretations of those practices. This is accomplished in most organizations with an "ethics help line" or "ethics hot line."

29. By current policy, ethics practices are applied consistently across all Premier entities. No distinction is made between Premier and Premier Purchasing Partners, the GPO subsidiary. Other GPOs have different structures and Premier may evolve its organization in the future into more discreet operations. This section is included to address that future possibility.

30. This provision permits other business relationships—with reservations. Some relationships, such as the sale of products or services to participating vendors by a non-GPO subsidiary for standard prices, should not present a problem. Others, where doing business with a non-GPO subsidiary gives a participating vendor an advantage in contracting decisions, would be unacceptable. The goal of this provision is to create a continuing scrutiny of such relationships to assure that they do not influence contracting decisions.

9 Theoretical Underpinnings for Creating Effective Industry-wide Voluntary Codes of Conduct

1. Knowledge Source, *Group purchasing organizations*; For Frequently Asked Questions regarding Healthcare Group Purchasing Industry Initiative, please visit

HIGPA Web site at http://www.healthcaregpoii.com/initiative-faq.pdf; Healthcare Group Purchasing Industry Initiative, *Key senators and largest hospital groups express support for new initiative promoting greater GPO transparency,* July 12, 2005. [Press release]. Retrieved September 18, 2006. http://www.healthcaregpoii.com/hgpii-initiative-release-71205.pdf

2. Becker, Say what? pp. 8–9; A. Yuspeh, Strengthening ethics and compliance programs, *Vital Speeches of the Day* 71, no. 13 (April 15, 2005): 390–396. Retrieved September 8, 2008, from Academic Search Premier database.

3. Hanson, *Best ethical practices,* pp. 1–23; *Are the industry's reforms sufficient?* 109th Cong., 2nd sess., 2006 (testimony of Richard Bednar).

4. Hanson, *Best ethical practices,* pp. 1–23; For Frequently Asked Questions regarding Healthcare Group Purchasing Industry Initiative, please visit HIGPA Web site at http://www.healthcaregpoii.com/initiative-faq.pdf

5. S. P. Sethi, The effectiveness of industry-based codes in serving public interest: The case of international council on mining and metals, *Transnational Corporations* 14, no. 3 (2005): 55–99.

6. R. W. Roberts & J. M. Kurtenbach, State regulation and professional accounting education reforms: An empirical test of regulatory capture theory, *Journal of Accounting and Public Policy* 17, no. 3 (1998): 209–217; J. S. Wiley, Jr., A capture theory of antitrust federalism, *Harvard Law Review* 99, no. 4 (1986): 713–790; G. Stigler, The theory of economic regulation, *Bell Journal of Economics and Management Science* 2 (1971): 3–21; S. Peltzman, Toward a more general theory of regulation, *Journal of Law and Economics* 19, no. 2 (1976): 335–358.

7. E. C. Cioffi, A friend of the court, *Risk Management* 51, no. 8 (2004): 44; B. Mullins, Politics & economics: U.S. lobbying tab hits a record; Bush's social security plan, tort-reform issues drive Washington spending spree, *Wall Street Journal* (Eastern Edition) (February 16, 2006), p. A6.

8. S. Murty & R. R. Russell, Externality policy reform: A general equilibrium analysis. *Journal of Public Economic Theory* 7, no. 1 (February, 2005): 117–150; M. Herve, Uniform externalities: two axioms for fair allocation, *Journal of Public Economics* 43, no. 3 (December 1990): 305–327; P. H. Dybvig & C. S. Spatt, Adoption externalities as public goods, *Journal of Public Economics* 20, no. 2 (1983): 231–347.

9. Sethi & Emelianova, A failed strategy of using voluntary codes of conduct by the global mining industry, pp. 226–238; R. Melrose, Big business is usually seen as being interested only in making money. But more and more companies are realizing that it pays to put something back into the community, *The Guardian,* March 22, 2004, p. 2; A. Kolk, Trends in sustainability reporting by the fortune global 250. *Business Strategy and the Environment* 12, no. 5 (2003): 279–291.

10. S. P. Sethi, Globalization and the good corporation: A need for proactive co-existence, *Journal of Business Ethics* 43, no. 1–2 (2003): 21–31; Sethi, *Setting global standards;* S. P. Sethi, Corporate codes of conduct and the success of globalization, *Ethics & International Affairs* 16, no. 1 (2002): 89–106; Laufer, *Corporate bodies and guilty minds;* R. *Tapper, Voluntary agreements for environmental performance improvement: Perspectives on the chemical industry's responsible care programme. Business Strategy and the Environment 6, no. 1 (1997): 287–292;* R. Jenkins, Globalization, production, employment and poverty: Debates and evidence, *Journal of International Development* 16, no. 1 (2004): 1–12.

11. Sethi, The effectiveness of industry-based codes in serving public interest, 55–99; A. Kolk, A & R. Van Tulder, Setting new global rules? TNCs and codes of conduct. *Transnational Corporations* 14, no. 3 (2005): 1–28; K. K. Herrmann, Corporate

social responsibility and sustainable development: The European Union initiative as a case study, *Indiana Journal of Global Legal Studies* 11, no. 2 (2004): 204–216.

12. Sethi, *Setting global standards*; Melrose, Big business is usually seen as being interested only in making money, p. 2.

13. Sethi, The effectiveness of industry-based codes in serving public interest, 55–99; S. P. Sethi, *Multinational corporations and the impact of public advocacy on corporate strategy: Nestlé and the infant formula controversy* (Boston: Kluwer Academic, 1994); Herrmann, Corporate social responsibility and sustainable development, 204–216.

14. G. A. Akerlof, The market for "lemons": Quality uncertainty and the market mechanism, *Quarterly Journal of Economics* 84 (1970): 488–500; J. P. Johnson & M. Waldman, Leasing, lemons, and buybacks, *Rand Journal of Economics* 34, no. 2 (2003): 247–263; J.-C. Kim, The market for "lemons" reconsidered: A model of the used car market with asymmetric information, *American Economic Review* 75, no. 4 (1985): 836–843.

15. Sethi, Corporate codes of conduct and the success of globalization, 89–106; E. B. Kapstein, The corporate ethics crusade, *Foreign Affairs* 80, no. 5 (2001): 105–120.

16. D. O'Rourke, Outsourcing regulation: Analyzing nongovernmental systems of labor standards and monitoring, *Policy Studies Journal* 31, no. 1 (2003): 1–30; B. *Paton, Voluntary environmental initiatives and sustainable industry, Business Strategy and the Environment 9, no. 5 (2000): 328–338.*

10 Healthcare Group Purchasing Industry Initiative (HGPII)

1. *Are the industry's reforms sufficient?* 109th Cong., 2nd sess., 2006.

2. Knowledge Source, *Group purchasing organizations*. The nine founding members and initial signatories of HGPII are: Amerinet, Inc., Broadlane, CHCA, Consorta, Inc., GNYHA Ventures, Inc., HealthTrust Purchasing Group, MedAssets, Novation, and Premier, Inc. Of the nine GPOs covered by the HGPII, four GPOs, namely CHCA, Consorta, GNYHA, and Premier serve exclusively not-for-profit hospitals. Two others (HealthTrust and MedAssets) serve exclusively for-profit hospital alliances. The remaining three GPOs (Amerinet, Broadlane, and Novation) serve both not-for-profit and for-profit hospital alliances; For Frequently Asked Questions regarding Healthcare Group Purchasing Industry Initiative, please visit HIGPA Web site at http://www.healthcaregpoii.com/initiative-faq.pdf and Healthcare Group Purchasing Industry Initiative, *Key senators and largest hospital groups,* July 12, 2005 [Press release]. Retrieved September 18, 2006. http://www.healthcaregpoii.com/hgpii-initiative-release-71205.pdf

3. Becker, Say what? pp. 8–9; Yuspeh, Strengthening ethics and compliance programs, pp. 390–396.

4. Charter of the Healthcare Group Purchasing Industry Initiative (May 2005) available at http://www.healthcaregpoii.com/initiative-charter.pdf

5. It should be noted here that Mr. Bednar is also the current coordinator of the Defense Industry Initiative. He asserts that "DII is widely held to be a success story ... and that it continues to experience strong public and government confidence in its sincere commitment to the highest ethical and conduct standards." *Are the industry's reforms sufficient?* 109th Cong., 2nd sess., 2006 (testimony of Richard Bednar). Mr. Bednar's praise of DII notwithstanding it is doubtful that the defense

industry's ethical conduct has markedly improved either because of DII or despite it. Recent scandals involving Boeing, Halliburton, and other defense contractors would suggest otherwise.

6. Hanson, *Best ethical practices*, pp. 1–23; *Are the industry's reforms sufficient?* 109th Cong., 2nd sess., 2006 (testimony of Richard Bednar).

7. Hanson, *Best ethical practices,* pp. 1–23; For Frequently Asked Questions regarding Healthcare Group Purchasing Industry Initiative, please visit HIGPA Web site at http://www.healthcaregpoii.com/initiative-faq.pdf

8. S. P. Sethi, Imperfect markets: Business ethics as an easy virtue. *Journal of Business Ethics* 13, no. 10 (October 1994): 803–815; W. J. Baumol with S. A. B. *Blackman, Perfect markets and easy virtue* (Cambridge, MA: Blackwell, 1991).

9. J. Andreoni & M. C. McGuire, Identifying the free riders: A simple algorithm for determining who will contribute to a public good, *Journal of Public Economics* 51, no. 3 (1993): 447–455; J. R. Conlon & P. Pecorino, Policy reform and the free-rider problem. *Public Choice* 120, no. 1–2 (July 2004): 123–142.

10. O. Fabel & E. E. Lehmann, Adverse selection and the economic limits of market substitution: An application to commerce and traditional trade in used cars. *Diskussionbeiträge* Series I, no. 301 (February 21, 2000). Retrieved on March 4, 2005, http://ssrn.com/abstract=213088; C. Wilson, The nature of equilibrium in markets with adverse selection, *Bell Journal of Economics* 11, no. 1 (1980): 108–130.

11. The framework presented here is adapted from S. P. Sethi & L. Sama, Ethical behavior as a strategic choice by large corporations: The potential impact of industry structure and market place competition, *Business Ethics Quarterly* 8, no. 1 (January 1998): 85–104.

12. Becker, Of two minds, S1—S5. It must be mentioned here that out of 65 GPOs only 19 organizations responded to the survey and Modern Health Care does not audit the reported results. This survey is carried out by sending the questionnaire to the GPOs and the GPOs fill in the information and send it back. Survey figures and interpretation is based on this. But all this surveys are signed by their respective CEO or CFO's. Only 5 GPOs reported any financial data.

13. Knowledge Source, *Group purchasing organizations,* pp. 1–224.

14. Becker, The silent treatment, p. 17.

15. For Frequently Asked Questions regarding Healthcare Group Purchasing Industry Initiative, please visit HIGPA Web site at http://www.healthcaregpoii.com/initiative-faq.pdf

16. Ibid.

17. V. Pandit, Toward a transparent financial system. *The Wall Street Journal*, June 27, 2008, p. A.ll.

18. *Are the industry's reforms sufficient?* 109th Cong., 2nd sess., 2006.

19. Ibid., testimony of Richard Blumenthal.

20. *Innovation and cost savings*, 108th Cong., 2nd sess., 2004 (testimony of David A. Baldo).

21. For a discussion of Sarbanes-Oxley and the Sentencing Guidelines see, Laufer, *Corporate bodies and guilty minds*. See also, L. W. Cunningham, The Sarbanes-Oxley yawn: Heavy rhetoric, light reform (And it might just work), *Connecticut Law Review* 35 (2003): 915–947; R. Romano, The Sarbanes-Oxley Act and the making of quack corporate governance, *Yale Law Journal* 114, no. 7 (2004): 1521–1611; C. Coglianese, T. J. Healey, E. K. Keating, & M. L. Michael, *The role of government in corporate governance* (Rep. No. RPP-08) (Cambridge, MA: Center

for Business and Government, John F. Kennedy School of Government, Harvard University, 2004).

22. For Frequently Asked Questions regarding Healthcare Group Purchasing Industry Initiative, please visit HIGPA Web site at http://www.healthcaregpoii.com/initiative-faq.pdf

Epilogue: A Whistleblower Files a Law Suit against Novation

1. United States of America and the State of Texas, ex rel Cynthia I. Fitzgerald vs. Novation, LLC, VHA, Inc., University HealthSystem Consortium, and Healthcare Purchasing Partners International, LLC, "Complaint for Violation of Federal False Claims Act 31 U.S.C. § 3730 and Texas Medicaid Fraud Prevention Act" in the U.S. District Court, Northern District of Texas, Dallas Division. The complaint was originally filed on July 15, 2003 but was kept under seal until 2007, when it was amended and finally unsealed on May 23, 2007. The complaint was served on the defendants on September 18, 2007.

2. On March 6, 2008, at the request of the plaintiffs, the U.S. District Court agreed to dismiss charges, without prejudice against defendants Healthcare Purchasing Partners International, LLC, University HealthSystem Consortium, Johnson & Johnson, Global Healthcare Exchange, Cardinal Health, Inc., Allegiance Corp., Owens & Minor, Inc., Nycomed, Inc., Ben-Venue Laboratories, Dupont Nuclear, Merck and Co., Abbott Laboratories, and Bristol-Myers Squibb Co. U.S. District Court, Northern District of Texas, Dallas Division. Docket No: 3: 03-CV-1589-N.

3. 31 U.S.C. § 3729 et seq., as amended ("the Federal FCA").

4. §§ 36.001 et seq ("the Texas MFPA"), The Federal FCA and Texas MFPA each provide that any person who knowingly submits or causes to be submitted a false or fraudulent claim to the government (Federal Government and the government of the State of Texas) for payment or approval is liable for a civil penalty of up to $11,000 for each such claim submitted or paid, plus three times the amount of the damages sustained by the government. Liability attaches both when a defendant knowingly seeks payment that is unwarranted from the government and when false records or statements are knowingly created or caused to be used to conceal, avoid, or decrease an obligation to pay or transmit money to the government. The Federal FCA and Texas MFPA each allow any person having information regarding a false or fraudulent claim against the government to bring an action for herself (the "relator" or "*qui tam* plaintiff") and for the government and to share in any recovery. The complaint is filed under seal for at least 60 days (without service on the defendants during the period) to enable the government: (a) to conduct its own investigation without the defendants' knowledge and (b) to determine whether to join the action.

5. The complaint, p. 9.

6. Ibid.

7. Ibid., p. 2.

8. As used herein, the term "vendor" shall refer to manufacturers, distributors, and/or suppliers.

9. The complaint, p. 2.

10. Ibid., p. 3.

11. Ibid.

12. The complaint, p. 3.

13. Ibid.
14. Pablo Lastra, Putting the bite on hospitals, *Fort Worth Weekly,* http://www.fwweekly.com/content.asp?article=6344 (October 4).
15. The complaint, p. 10.
16. Mary W. Walsh, "Accusation of conflicts at a supplier to hospitals," *The New York Times*, Business/Financial Desk; Section C, August 1, 2002, p. 1.col. 2.
17. The complaint, p. 11.
18. Walsh, "Accusation of conflicts," p. 1.col. 2.
19. Ibid.
20. 42 U.S.C. § 1302a-7b(b).
21. 24 C.F.R. § 1001.952(j).
22. 42 U.S.C. § 1302a-7b(b)(emphasis added), cited in The complaint, p. 8.
23. In 2002, Novation's President Mark McKenna earned $928,000 ($403,000 in annual base salary; $357,000 under Novation's Retention Long-Term Incentive Program; $145,000 under Novation's Annual Incentive Plan; and $23,000 under Novation's Rewarding Excellence Incentive Plan).
24. The complaint, p. 10.
25. Walsh, "Blowing the whistle, many times."
26. The complaint, p. 14.
27. Ibid.
28. Ibid., p. 15.
29. Ibid., p. 16.
30. Ibid., p. 17.
31. Ibid.
32. Ibid., p. 18.
33. Ibid., p. 22.
34. Ibid., p. 24.
35. Ibid., p. 21.
36. Ibid., p. 26.
37. Walsh, "Blowing the whistle, many times."
38. The complaint, p. 29.
39. Ibid., pp. 29–32.
40. Ibid., p. 32.
41. Ibid., p. 33.

Bibliography

Akerlof, G. A. The market for "lemons": Quality uncertainty and the market mechanism, *Quarterly Journal of Economics* 84 (1970): 488–500.

Anders, G. Health-Care gold mines: Middlemen strike it rich—Rewarding career: As patients, doctors feel pinch, insurer's CEO makes a billion. *Wall Street Journal,* April 18, 2006, p. A1.

Andreoni, J., & M. C. McGuire. Identifying the free riders: A simple algorithm for determining who will contribute to a public good. *Journal of Public Economics* 51, no. 3 (1993): 447–455.

Andrews, J. Consorta-HPG deal: A sign of things to come? *Healthcare Finance News* (March 1, 2007). Retrieved from http://www.healthcarefinancenews.com/story. cms?id=6158

Anonymous. Retractable Technologies raises GPO compliance issues on national news. *Health Industry Today* 61, no. 6 (June 1998). Retrieved November 6, 2007, from ABI/ INFORM Global database. (Document ID: 30032104).

———. GPO fans, critics agree there's improvement. *Hospital Materials Management* 28, no. 9 (September 2003). Retrieved June 19, 2007, from ABI/INFORM Global database. (Document ID: 407037481).

———. HIGPA: Administrative fees should not be considered as part of Medicare pricing. *Hospital Materials Management* 29, no. 8 (August 2004). Retrieved September 17, 2007, from ABI/INFORM Global database. (Document ID: 671987401).

———. Premier continues relationship with Agfa in two new pacts for imaging products. *Hospital Materials Management* 29, no. 1 (January 2004). Retrieved October 3, 2007, from ABI/INFORM Global database. (Document ID: 526245281).

———. Senators mull tighter regulation of GPOs. *Hospital Materials Management* 29, no. 10 (October 2004). Retrieved September 2, 2007, from ABI/INFORM Global database. (Document ID: 711922371).

Applied Medical Res. Corp. v. Johnson & Johnson, Inc., No. 03-CV-1329 (C.D. Cal.).

Ayres, I., & J. Braithwaite. *Responsive regulation: Transcending the deregulation debate.* New York: Oxford University Press, 1992.

Bamezai, A., J. Zwanziger, G. A. Melnick, & J. M. Mann. Price competition and hospital cost growth in the United States (1989–1994). *Health Economics* 8, no. 3 (1999): 233–243.

Barlow, R. D. Healthcare group purchasing milestones in history. *Healthcare Purchasing News,* November 2, 2004. Retrieved October 25, 2007, from Business Source Premier Database.

Baumol, W. J. with S. A. B. *Blackman. Perfect markets and easy virtue.* Cambridge, MA: Blackwell, 1991.

Becker, C. Going on the record. *Modern Healthcare* 34, no. 26 (June 28, 2004). Retrieved August 3, 2007, from ABI/INFORM Global database. (Document ID: 658848321).

———. Hanging tough. *Modern Healthcare* 34, no. 33 (August 16, 2004): S1–S5. Retrieved September 26, 2007, from ABI/INFORM Global database. (Document ID: 682264161).

———. In search of a breakthrough. *Modern Healthcare* 32, no. 31 (August 5, 2002): 28–32. Retrieved July 18, 2007, from ABI/INFORM Global database. (Document ID: 146406341).

———. Lucrative liaison? *Modern Healthcare* 34, no. 39 (September 27, 2004): 8–9. Retrieved October 4, 2007, from ABI/INFORM Global database. (Document ID: 707621561).

———. Masimo wins new round. *Modern Healthcare* 35, no. 13 (March 28, 2005). Retrieved September 26, 2007, from ABI/INFORM Global database. (Document ID: 823445491).

———. No more Mr. nice guys. *Modern Healthcare* 34, no. 38 (September 20, 2004). Retrieved August 14, 2007, from ABI/INFORM Global database. (Document ID: 709182801).

———. Of two minds. *Modern Healthcare* 35, no. 33 (August 15, 2005): S1–S5. Retrieved September 28, 2007, from ABI/INFORM Global database. (Document ID: 885831651).

———. Premier's portfolio. *Modern Healthcare* 33, no. 39 (September 29, 2003). Retrieved May 22, 2007, from ABI/INFORM Global database. (Document ID: 417712481).

———. Say what? *Modern Healthcare* 32, no. 43 (October 28, 2002): 8–9. Retrieved September 3, 2007, from ABI/INFORM Global database. (Document ID: 227995811).

———. The silent treatment. *Modern Healthcare* 34, no. 7 (February 16, 2004). Retrieved October 4, 2007, from ABI/INFORM Global database. (Document ID: 547849341).

Big Suits. Masimo Corp. v. Tyco Healthcare Group, L.P., No. 02-CV-4770 (C.D. Cal.) American Lawyer 28, no.6 (June 1, 2006).

Bio-Medicine. HIDA calls for scrutiny of group purchasing organization distributor fee structure, September 2007. Retrieved November 12, 2007, from http://www.bio-medicine.org/medicine-news-1/HIDA-Calls-for-Scrutiny-of-Group-Purchasing-Organization-Distributor-Fee-Structure-594-1/

Bloch, R. E., S. P. Perlman, & J. S. Brown. *An analysis of group purchasing organizations contracting practices under the antitrust laws: Myth and reality.* Presented at the Joint FTC/DOJ Hearings on Health Care and Competition Law and Policy, n.d. Retrieved from http://www.ftc.gov/ogc/healthcarehearings/docs/030926bloch.pdf

Bodenheimer T. High and rising health care costs. Part 2: Technologic innovation. *Annals of Internal Medicine* 142, no.11 (2005): 932–937, doi: 142: 932–937.

———. High and rising health care costs. Part 3: The role of health care providers. *Annals of Internal Medicine* 142, no. 12 (2005): 996–1002, doi: 142: 996–1002.

Boese, J. T. Civil false claims and qui tam actions. Aspen Law & Business, New York: Aspen Publishers, 2006.

Bogdanich, W. Group settles health sales conflict case. *The New York Times,* January 25, 2007, p. 1.

———. Hospital chiefs get paid for advice on selling, *The New York Times,* July 17, 2006, p. 1.

Bogdanich, W., B. Meier, & M. W. Walsh. Medicine's middlemen; Questions raised of conflicts at 2 hospital buying groups. *The New York Times,* March 4, 2002, p. A1.

Braithwaite, J. *Convergence in models of regulatory strategy. Current Issues in Criminal Justice 2* (1990): 59–65.

———. Enforced self-regulation: A new strategy for corporate crime control. *Michigan Law Review* 80, no. 7 (1982): 1466–1507.

———. Institutionalizing distrust, enculturating trust. In Trust and governance, ed. V. Braithwaite & M. Levi, pp. 343–375. New York: Russell Sage, 1998.

———. *To punish or persuade: Enforcement of coal mine safety.* Albany, NY: State University of New York Press, 1985.

Brock, T. H. Hospitals, group purchasing organizations, and the antitrust laws. *Healthcare Financial Management* 53, no. 3 (March 2003): 38–42. Retrieved November 9, 2007, from http://findarticles.com/p/articles/mi_m3257/is_3_57/ai_98953926

———. Hospitals, group purchasing organizations, and the antitrust laws. *Healthcare Financial Management* 57, no. 3 (March 2003): 38–42. Retrieved September 14, 2007, from ABI/INFORM Global database. (Document ID: 320789121).

Carpenter, C. E. Health Care in the United States-Is it the best in the world? *Journal of Financial Service Professionals* 59, no. 2 (March 2005): 29–31. Retrieved June 27, 2008, from ABI/INFORM Global database. (Document ID: 803162681).

Charter of the Healthcare Group Purchasing Industry Initiative. May 2005, available at http://www.healthcaregpoii.com/initiative-charter.pdf

Cioffi, E. C. A friend of the court. *Risk Management* 51, no. 8 (2004).

Coglianese, C., T. J. Healey, E. K. Keating, & M. L. Michael. *The role of government in corporate governance* (Rep. No. RPP-08). Cambridge: Center for Business and Government, John F. Kennedy School of Government, Harvard University, 2004.

The Commonwealth Fund. *Why not the best? Results from the national scorecard on U.S. health system performance, 2008.* July 2008. Retrieved July 23, 2008, from http://www.commonwealthfund.org/publications/publications_show.htm?doc_id=401577

Conlon, J. R., & P. Pecorino. Policy reform and the free-rider problem. *Public Choice* 120, no. 1–2 (July 2004): 123–142.

Cunningham, L. W. The Sarbanes-Oxley yawn: Heavy rhetoric, light reform (And it might just work). *Connecticut Law Review* 35 (2003): 915–947.

Davis, K., C. Schoen, S. Guterman, T. Shih, S. C. Schoenbaum, & I. Weinbaum. *Slowing the growth of U.S. healthcare expenditures: What are the options?* The Commonwealth Fund, January 2007. Retrieved May 14, 2008, from http://www.commonwealthfund.org/usr_doc/Davis_slowinggrowthUShltcareexpenditureswhatareoptions_989.pdf?section=4039

DeJohn, P. HIGPA enters new phase with year-end Betz exit. *Hospital Materials Management* 30, no. 8 (August 2005): 9–11. Retrieved September 5, 2008, from ABI/INFORM Global database. (Document ID: 887232321).

———. Hospitals want to be heard in GPO debate. *Hospital Materials Management* 28, no. 11 (November 2003). Retrieved September 4, 2007, from ABI/INFORM Global database. (Document ID: 459506351).

DeNavas-Walt, C., B. D. Proctor, & J. Smith. *Income, poverty, and health insurance coverage in the United States: 2006.* US Census Bureau Current Population Reports, pp. 60–233, August 2007. Retrieved May 2, 2008, from http: //www.census.gov/prod/2007pubs/p60-233.pdf. p. 1

Dula, M. A. Testing the GPO waters. *Healthcare Financial Management* 58, no. 6 (June 2004): 70–76. Retrieved October 9, 2007, from http://findarticles.com/p/articles/mi_m3257/is_6_58/ai_n6080537/pg_1?tag=artBody;col1

Dybvig, P. H., & C. S. Spatt. Adoption externalities as public goods. *Journal of Public Economics* 20, no. 2 (1983): 231–347.

Elhauge, E. Antitrust analysis of GPO exclusionary agreement. Comments regarding hearing on health care and competition law and policy—Statement for DOJ-FTC hearing on GPOs—September 26, 2003. Retrieved September 12, 2007, from http://www.ftc.gov/os/comments/healthcarecomments2/elhauge.pdf

Escutia, Senator–CA (D), bill SB749 Hospital Group Purchasing Organizations available at http://www.maplight.org/map/ca/bill/2230/default/history/action-14684.

Everard, L. J. Defining and measuring product-based cost savings in the health care supply chain, pp. 1–20, February 2005. Retrieved December 5, 2007, from http://www.medicaldevices.org/public/documents/DefiningandMeasuringProduct-BasedCostSavings_000.pdf

———. Health policy statement no. 7 does not sufficiently protect patients and caregivers. Presented at the Joint FTC/DOJ hearings on Health Care and Competition Law and Policy, September 26, 2003. Retrieved September 12, 2007, from http://www.ftc.gov/ogc/healthcarehearings/docs/030926lynneverad.pdf

———. The impact of group purchasing on the financial prospects of health systems: Changing value perceptions and unintended consequences, V.I.P.E.R. Group, 2003. Retrieved September 7, 2007, from http://www.stopgpokickbacks.org/documents/7Everard.pdf

Fabel, O., & E. E. Lehmann. Adverse selection and the economic limits of market substitution: An application to commerce and traditional trade in used cars. *Diskussionbeiträge Series I,* no. 301 (February 21, 2000). Retrieved March 4, 2005, from http://ssrn.com/abstract=213088

Federal Trade Commission and the Department of Justice. *Improving health care: A dose of competition,* July 2004. Retrieved October 24, 2007, from http://www.ftc.gov/reports/healthcare/040723healthcarerpt.pdf

Fisse, B., & J. Braithwaite. *Corporations, crime and accountability.* New York: Cambridge University Press, 1993.

For details about Questions and Answers regarding Healthcare Group Purchasing Industry Initiative, please visit HIGPA Web site at http://www.healthcaregpoii.com/initiative-faq.pdf

For details, please refer to Novation Operating Principles available at http://www.masimo.com/pdf/home/NovationNOP.pdf

For details, please visit Amerinet Web site at www.amerinet-gpo.com.

For more details see Premier's Web site: www.premierinc.com.

Fuhrmans, V. Medco gets subpoena tied to criminal probe; Florida officials seek data on records tied to business with managed-care firms. *Wall Street Journal* (Eastern edition), 2003, p. A21.

Galloro, V. Tenet settles outlier lawsuit, *Modern Healthcare* 36, no. 9 (February 27, 2006): 8–9. Retrieved June 10, 2008, from ABI/INFORM Global database. (Document ID: 885831651).

Gowrisankaran, G., & R. J. Town. Competition, payers, and hospital quality. *Health Services Research* 38, no. 6, part 1 (2003): 1403–1421.

Gray, P. B. Stick it to 'em. *FSB: Fortune Small Business* 15, no. 2 (March 2005): 82–88. Retrieved September 4, 2008, from ABI/INFORM Global database. (Document ID: 809783781).

Hanson, K. O. *Best ethical practices for the group purchasing industry.* Premier, 2002, pp. 1–23.

Health Industry Distributors (HIDA) & The Major Accounts Exchange (The MAX). Group Purchasing Organization (GPO) market report, 2006.

Healthcare Group Purchasing Industry Initiative. *Key senators and largest hospital groups express support for new initiative promoting greater GPO transparency,* July 12, 2005. [Press release]. Retrieved from http://www.healthcaregpoii.com/hgpii-initiative-release-71205.pdf

Healthcare Industry Group Purchasing Association Frequently Asked Questions, available at http://www.higpa.org/about/about_faqs.asp.

HealthTrust Purchasing Group. *Consorta, Inc. finalizes agreement to become sixth equity owner of HealthTrust Purchasing Group,* April 18, 2007. [Press release]. Retrieved from http://www.healthtrustcorp.com/news-highlights.php#1

Herrmann, K. K. Corporate social responsibility and sustainable development: The European Union initiative as a case study. Indiana Journal of Global Legal Studies 11, no. 2 (2004): 204–216.

Herve, M. Uniform externalities: Two axioms for fair allocation. *Journal of Public Economics* 43, no. 3 (December 1990): 305–327.

Hilal, S. Healthcare market conditions today. Presented at the Joint FTC/DOJ hearings on Health Care and Competition Law and Policy, September 26, 2003. Retrieved September 12, 2007, from http://www.ftc.gov/ogc/healthcarehearings/docs/030926hilal.pdf

Holding, R., & W. Carlsen. Watchdogs fail health workers: How safer needles were kept out of hospitals. *San Francisco Chronicle,* 1998, p. A1. Retrieved October 18, 2007, from http://www.sfgate.com/cgi- bin/article.cgi?file=/chronicle/archive/1998/04/15/MN1902.DTL&type=special

Hospital group purchasing: Are the industry's reforms sufficient to ensure competition? Hearing before the Subcommittee On Antitrust, Competition Policy And Consumer Rights, Committee On The Judiciary United States Senate, 109th Cong., 2nd sess., 2006.

Hospital group purchasing: Has the market become more open to competition? Hearing before the Subcommittee on Antitrust, Business Rights, and Competition of the Committee on the Judiciary United States Senate, 108th Cong., 1st sess., 2003.

Hospital group purchasing: How to maintain innovation and cost savings. Hearing before the Subcommittee on Antitrust, Business Rights, and Competition of the Committee on the Judiciary United States Senate, 108th Cong., 2nd sess., 2004.

Hospital group purchasing: Lowering costs at the expense of patient health and medical innovation? Hearing before the Subcommittee on Antitrust, Business Rights, and Competition of the Committee on the Judiciary United States Senate, 107th Cong., 2nd sess., 2002.

Hovenkamp, H. *Competitive effects of Group Purchasing Organizations' (GPO) purchasing and product selection practices in the health care industry,* April 2002. Retrieved June 1, 2007, from http://www.higpa.org/pressroom/hovenkamp.pdf

Jenkins, R. Globalization, production, employment and poverty: Debates and evidence. *Journal of International Development* 16, no. 1 (2004): 1–12.

Johnson, J. P., & M. Waldman. Leasing, lemons, and buybacks. *The Rand Journal of Economics* 34, no. 2 (2003): 247–263.

The Kaiser Family Foundation. *Fast facts—Costs / Insurance,* n.d. Retrieved June 3, 2008, from Kaiser Fast Facts http://facts.kff.org/

———. *Fast facts—Uninsured / Coverage,* n.d. Retrieved June 3, 2008, from Kaiser Fast Facts http://facts.kff.org/

The Kaiser Family Foundation and Health Research and Educational Trust. *Employer health benefits 2007 annual survey,* 2007. Retrieved May 27, 2008, from http://www.kff.org/insurance/7672/upload/76723.pdf

KaiserNetwork. Safer needles' not in use in most U.S. hospitals, "60 minutes" reports *Kaiser Daily HIV/AIDS Report,* February 26, 2001. Retrieved June 11, 2007, from http://www.kaisernetwork.org/Daily_reports/rep_index.cfm?DR_ID=3024.

Kapstein, E. B. The corporate ethics crusade, Foreign Affairs 80, no. 5 (2001): 105–120.

Kim, J. C. The market for "lemons" reconsidered: A model of the used car market with asymmetric information, *The American Economic Review* 75, no. 4 (1985): 836–843.

Knowledge Source. *Group purchasing organizations,* May 2005.

Kolk, A. Trends in sustainability reporting by the fortune global 250. *Business Strategy and the Environment* 12, no. 5 (2003): 279–291.

Kolk, A., & R. Van Tulder. Setting new global rules? TNCs and codes of conduct. *Transnational Corporations* 14, no. 3 (2005): 1–28.

Lastra, P. Hijacking at the hospital: Purchasing groups created to hold down health costs seem to be holding up patients instead. *Fort Worth Weekly,* November 23, 2005, pp. 8–13. Retrieved November 7, 2007, from http://www.fwweekly.com/content.asp?article=3419

Laufer, W. S. *Corporate bodies and guilty minds: The failure of corporate criminal liability.* Chicago: University of Chicago Press, 2006.

Lawn, J. The GPOs where do they go from here? January 2005. Retrieved April 17, 2001, from http://food-management.com/business_feature/fm_imp_7554/

Masimo Corp. v. Tyco Healthcare Group, L.P., No. 02-CV-4770 (C.D. Cal.).

MedAssets HSCA joins GHX e-commerce network, bringing site near "critical mass". *Hospital Materials Management* 28, no. 5 (May 2003). Retrieved August 6, 2008, from ABI/INFORM Global database. (Document ID: 334545721).

MedAssets offers automated charge master control. *Hospital Materials Management* 28, no. 9 (September 2003). Retrieved August 6, 2008, from ABI/INFORM Global database. (Document ID: 407037341).

Medical Device Link, the online information source for the medical device industry http://www.devicelink.com/mddi/archive/05/09/002.html

Melrose, R. Big business is usually seen as being interested only in making money. But more and more companies are realizing that it pays to put something back into the community. *The Guardian,* March 22, 2004, p. 2.

Mullins, B. Politics & economics: U.S. lobbying tab hits a record; Bush's social security plan, tort-reform issues drive Washington spending spree. *Wall Street Journal* (Eastern Edition), February 16, 2006, p. A6.

Murty, S., & R. R. Russell. Externality policy reform: A general equilibrium analysis. *Journal of Public Economic Theory* 7, no. 1 (February 2005): 117–150.

Muse & Associates. *The role of group purchasing organizations in the U.S. healthcare system.* March 2000.

O'Rourke, D. Outsourcing regulation: Analyzing nongovernmental systems of labor standards and monitoring. Policy Studies Journal 31, no. 1 (2003): 1–30.

Overview of Global Healthcare Exchange (GHX). (n.d.). Retrieved August 10, 2008, from http://premium.hoovers.com/subscribe/co/factsheet.xhtml?ID=jrksfrtcxksyyc

Overview of MedAssets Inc. (n.d.). Retrieved August 21, 2008, from http://premium.hoovers.com/subscribe/co/overview.xhtml?ID=fffrffhhhfsyshtfkf

Pandit, V. Toward a transparent financial system. *Wall Street Journal,* June 27, 2008, p. All.

Paton, B. *Voluntary environmental initiatives and sustainable industry. Business Strategy and the Environment* 9, no. 5 (2000): 328–338.

Peltzman, S. Toward a more general theory of regulation. *The Journal of Law and Economics* 19, no. 2 (1976): 335–358.

Porter, M. E. *Competitive strategy: Techniques for analyzing industries and competitors.* New York: Free Press, 1980.

Questions and Answers regarding the Healthcare Group Purchasing Industry Initiative available at http://www.healthcaregpoii.com/initiative-faq.pdf

Reinhardt U. E., P. S. Hussey, & G. F. Anderson. U.S. health care spending in an international context. *Health Affairs* 23, no. 3 (2004): 10–25, doi: 10.1377/hlthaff.23.3.10.

Retractable Technologies v. Becton Dickinson & Co. Inc., No. 01-CV-036 (E.D. Tex.).

Rhea, S. Moving beyond the hospital. *Modern Healthcare* 37, no. 35 (September 3, 2007): S1–S5. Retrieved May 27, 2008, from ABI/INFORM Global database. (Document ID: 1334858761).

Roberts, R. W., & J. M. Kurtenbach. State regulation and professional accounting education reforms: An empirical test of regulatory capture theory. *Journal of Accounting and Public Policy* 17, no. 3 (1998): 209–217.

Romano, P. S. & R. Mutter. The evolving science of quality measurement for hospitals: Implications for studies of competition and consolidation. *International Journal of Health Care Finance and Economics* 4, no. 2 (2004): 131–157.

Romano, R. The Sarbanes-Oxley Act and the making of quack corporate governance. *Yale Law Journal* 114, no. 7 (2004): 1521–1611.

Sager, A., & D. Socolar. *Health costs absorb one-quarter of economic growth, 2000–2005,* February 9, 2005. Retrieved May 15, 2008, from http://www.globalaging.org/health/us/2005/quarter.pdf

Schneller, E. S. *The value of group purchasing in the health care supply chain* [White paper]. School of Health Administration and Policy, Arizona State University College of Business, n.d., pp. 1–20. Retrieved December 5, 2007 from http://wpcarey.asu.edu/hap/upload/group_purchasing_pdf.pdf

Sethi, S. P. Corporate codes of conduct and the success of globalization. *Ethics & International Affairs* 16, no. 1 (2002): 89–106.

———. The effectiveness of industry-based codes in serving public interest: The case of international council on mining and metals. *Transnational Corporations* 14, no. 3 (2005): 55–99.

———. Globalization and the good corporation: A need for proactive co-existence. *Journal of Business Ethics* 43, no. 1–2 (2003): 21–31.

———. Imperfect markets: Business ethics as an easy virtue. *Journal of Business Ethics* 13, no. 10 (October 1994): 803–815.

———. *Multinational corporations and the impact of public advocacy on corporate strategy: Nestlé and the infant formula controversy.* Boston: Kluwer Academic, 1994.

———. *Setting global standards: Guidelines for creating codes of conduct in multinational corporations.* New York: John Wiley & Sons, 2003.

Sethi, S. P. & L. Sama. Ethical behavior as a strategic choice by large corporations: The potential impact of industry structure and market place competition. Business Ethics Quarterly 8, no. 1 (January 1998): 85–104.

Sethi, S. P. & O. Emelianova. A failed strategy of using voluntary codes of conduct by the global mining industry. *Corporate governance: The International Journal of Business and Society* 6, no. 3 (2006): 226–238.

Singer, A. W. Spattered and scorched, premier seeks the "high road". *Ethikos and Corporate Conduct Quarterly* (May/June 2004). Retrieved October 3, 2007, from http://www.singerpubs.com/ethikos/html/premier.html.

Singer, H. J. *The budgetary impact of eliminating the GPO's safe harbor exemption from the anti-kickback statue of the social security act.* Criterion Economics, LLC, 2006, pp. 1–29. Retrieved from http://www.stopgpokickbacks.org/documents/1Singer_002. pdf

Special Investigations Division, Committee on Government Reform, U.S. House of Representatives. *Prescription drug prices in Canada, Europe, and Japan,* April 11, 2001. Retrieved May 20, 2008, from http://oversight.house.gov/ Documents/20040629103247-74022.pdf

Stigler, G. The theory of economic regulation. *Bell Journal of Economics and Management Science* 2 (1971): 3–21.

Tanner, M. *The grass is not always greener: A look at national healthcare systems around the world.* Cato Institute, March 2008. Retrieved May 5, 2008, from http://www. cato.org/pubs/pas/pa-613.pdf

Tapper, R. Voluntary agreements for environmental performance improvement: Perspectives on the chemical industry's responsible care programme. Business Strategy and the Environment 6, no. 1 (1997): 287–292.

U.S. Bureau of Economic Analysis. *Gross domestic product by industry, 2005.* April 2006. Retrieved October 2, 2007, from http://www.bea.gov/newsreleases/industry/ gdpindustry/2006/gdpind05.htm

U.S. Department of Justice and Federal Trade Commission. *Statements of Antitrust Enforcement Policy in Health Care.* August 1996, pp. 1–179. Retrieved October 24, 2007, from http://www.usdoj.gov/atr/public/guidelines/0000.pdf

U.S. Government Accountability Office. *Pilot study suggests large buying groups do not always offer hospitals lower prices* (Publication No. GAO-02-690T), April 2002. Retrieved May 15, 2008, from http://www.stopgpokickbacks.org/documents/ 9GAO.pdf

———. *Use of contracting processes and strategies to award contracts for medical-surgical products* (Publication No. GAO-03-998T), July 2003. Retrieved May 12, 2008, from General Accounting Office Reports Online http://www.gao.gov/new.items/ d03998t.pdf

United States Department of Health and Human Services, Centers for Medicare & Medicaid Services. *National Health Expenditure Accounts 2006 Highlights,* n.d. Retrieved May 1, 2008, from http://www.cms.hhs.gov/NationalHealthExpendData/ 02_NationalHealthAccountsHistorical.asp#TopOfPage

———. *National Health Expenditure Data Web Tables,* n.d. Retrieved May 1, 2008, from http://www.cms.hhs.gov/NationalHealthExpendData/downloads/tables.pdf

———. *National Health Expenditure Fact Sheet,* n.d. Retrieved May 1, 2008, from http://www.cms.hhs.gov/NationalHealthExpendData/25_NHE_Fact_Sheet.asp

United States Department of Health and Human Services, Office of Inspector General. *Review of revenue from vendors at three group purchasing organizations and their members.* (OIG Publication No. A-05-03-00074), January 2005. Retrieved August 8, 2007, from http://oig.hhs.gov/oas/reports/region5/50300074.pdf

———. *Review of revenue from vendors at three additional group purchasing organizations and their members.* (OIG Publication No. A-05-04-00073), May 2005. Retrieved August 8, 2007, from http://oig.hhs.gov/oas/reports/region5/50400073.pdf

United States of America and the State of Texas, ex rel Cynthia I. Fitzgerald vs. Novation, LLC, VHA, Inc., University HealthSystem Consortium, and Healthcare Purchasing

Partners International, LLC, "Complaint for Violation of Federal False Claims Act 31 U.S.C. § 3730 and Texas Medicaid Fraud Prevention Act" in the U.S. District Court, Northern District of Texas, Dallas Division. Docket No: 303CV1589D. May 23, 2007.

United States of America and the State of Texas, ex rel Cynthia I. Fitzgerald vs. Novation, LLC, VHA, Inc., University HealthSystem Consortium, and Healthcare Purchasing Partners International, LLC, "Complaint for Violation of Federal False Claims Act 31 U.S.C. § 3730 and Texas Medicaid Fraud Prevention Act" in U.S. District Court, Northern District of Texas, Dallas Division. Docket No: 3:03-CV-1589-N. March 6, 2008.

University of Maine, Bureau of Labor Education. *The U.S. health care system: Best in the world, or just the most expensive?* 2001, p. 2. Retrieved May 16, 2008, from http://dll.umaine.edu/ble/U.S.%20HCweb.pdf

Verispan, L. L. C. *Multi-Hospital systems and group purchasing organization market report,* 2003.

Walsh, M. W. Blowing the whistle, many times. *The New York Times*, November 18, 2007, p. 1.

———. Hospital group's link to company is criticized. *The New York Times*, April 27, 2002, p. A1.

———. When a buyer for hospitals has a stake in drugs it buys. *The New York Times*, March 26, 2002, p. A1.

Walsh, M. W. & B. Meier. Hospitals find big buying groups may not come up with savings. *The New York Times,* April 30, 2002, p. A1.

Wiley, J. S. Jr. A capture theory of antitrust federalism. *Harvard Law Review* 99, no. 4 (1986): 713–790.

Wilson, C. The nature of equilibrium in markets with adverse selection. *Bell Journal of Economics* 11, no. 1 (1980): 108–130.

Yuspeh, A. Strengthening ethics and compliance programs. *Vital Speeches of the Day* 71, no. 13 (April 15, 2005): 390–396. Retrieved September 8, 2008, from Academic Search Premier database.

Zweig, P. L. & W. Zellner. Locked out of the hospital: Are medical buying consortiums squelching innovation? *BusinessWeek,* March 16, 1998.

Index